PAST RECALL

When Love and Wisdom Transcend Time

By

NITA HUGHES

ISBN: 1-4033-7884-3 (e-book)
ISBN: 1-4033-7885-1 (Paperback)
ISBN: 1-4033-7886-X (Dust Jacket)

This book is printed on acid free paper.

1stBooks - rev. 04/07/03

ACKNOWLEDGMENTS

There are many to thank, but I would especially like to mention: Melody Leopard, who first suggested I join her in taking a writing class, P. Gail Mahoney, who provided a cottage in the heart of the Cathar country, Alexander Reed, who was so generous with his time and expertise in editing all drafts of the book, Tom Hughes, whose attention to detailed edits set the pace, Eileen Crump, an unbiased reader, whose input was helpful, Valerie Storey, writer, editor and friend, whose advice and editing was invaluable, Veronique Villeneuve, who offered historical detail of France during that period, Rocky, Annie and Brooke Butler, Rex Beach, Robyn Ormiston and Michael Hall, dear friends who kept my morale high, Melissa Price, Karen Horowitz and Liz Updike, fellow writers who knew the path and shone a light when most needed and Nancy Lynn Kleban, whose copy editing skills proved priceless. All of my family, but especially my children, Kim Brady and Kris Gerbracht, whose enthusiastic comments spurred me on, and to the Cathar souls, whose spirits made the writing of the book an imperative.

For Douglas, who lovingly gave of his encouragement and support

and

For my mother, Audrey Davis, who provided a lifetime of inspiration

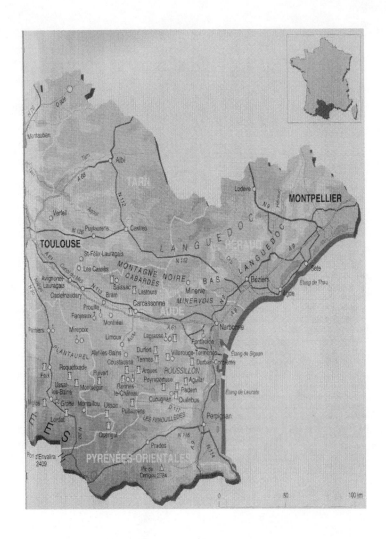

"No crime is too heinous to commit, and no heinous crime is as gleefully committed as when the perpetration thereof is sanctioned and justified by religious belief."
　　　　　　　　—French writer and philosopher, Pascal

"Only our love hath no decay."
　　　　　　　　—John Donne

ONE

Mirepoix, France – March 1242

It was midnight. The toll of the church bells was absorbed by the night. A dark shroud of malevolent clouds spread a canopy that obliterated all light. The blackness brought with it an oppressive sense of something encroaching, a something that required complete stillness.

Clotilde stood unmoving at the open shutters, her skill at remaining unseen second nature. Her focus on identifying the nature of that which menaced was even more acute. A deer had taught her well. As a child, abandoned in the forest, such skills had meant survival. Only her eyes moved, gauging the blackness, looking for motion. Her acute hearing strained as it plumbed the ominous absence of sound. Nothing—no light, no sound and no movement—betrayed the nature of the unknown horror that neared. Nothing except her heartbeat. It thundered in tempo with her deepening dread.

If stillness doesn't expose it, she thought, action might. Turning with bravado she didn't feel, she reached for a candlestick, fumbling with the tinderbox. Even as the flame leapt, bringing the room into being, anxiety remained. She looked around, seeking consolation in the familiar. A solid house, while not grand, it had expanded gracefully during the past two generations as the Armand de Mirepoix family prospered. She studied her bedchamber, feeling blessed that of all outward signs of prosperity none was more unique than that of her private

1

sleeping area. Her gaze rested on the deep blue of the velvet draperies that enshrouded her bed against the winter's cold. It wasn't the luxury, but the sanctuary it bestowed that impressed her. As her eyes moved from the pushed-aside woolen coverlet to the exposed emptiness of the bed's larger indentation, her expression darkened.

A sudden chill consumed her, its intensity prompted more from passing a sleepless night enveloped in fear than from actual cold. The solemn urgency of Jean's parting words hung in the air. "If I should not return, go quickly to Fabrisse."

They had awakened just before dawn of this endless day— startled by a loud pounding on the door. Clotilde had followed Jean down the narrow stone stairway. Unable to hear his words, she had watched his face as he turned from the messenger. A strong face, a loving face, a known and familiar face, it shocked her by its depth of horror. Jean said not a word as he grabbed his cloak and raced toward the stables. He rode away at dawn, revealing only that he must rendezvous with his brother, Bernard. The memory of his anxious backward glance before he vanished over the crest of the hill remained.

What could it be, she wondered? She winced as her abdomen gripped with fear at the thought of Jean being in danger. Walking to the bedside table, she placed the candlestick alongside a small vase brimful of spring jonquils. A sigh of relief escaped her at the awareness that her restless tossing hadn't dislodged the egg-shaped piece of marble nestled beneath the blooms. She ran her fingers over the inscribed symbol of a dove whose wings embraced her and Jean's entwined initials. Holding it to her cheek, she took comfort in its shape, the coolness of the stone and the love in Jean's eyes when he presented his gift. He was *her* rock, she thought, the reminder soothing her fear of abandonment. "God keep him safe," she murmured as she replaced her talisman.

And yet, she thought, such a prayer could not extinguish reality. Every Cathar faced extreme jeopardy. More vanished each day. Most as victims of the Inquisition, others slipped away by night to join a growing exodus seeking safety at Montsegur. She dare not indulge the folly of hoping that her village of Mirepoix could escape the encroaching horror.

Frustrated at her impotence, Clotilde yanked her nightshirt, a fraying garment scented of Jean, tightly around her. It wrapped her slight girth nearly twice around. She'd not gained back so much as a feather's weight since the loss of their unborn child a month ago, she thought.

How can a mother bear the loss of her child, she wondered, as her eyes moved to her pillow. A bit of rough woolen fabric protruded from its linen cover. She drew it out and held it to her nostrils, inhaling deeply all that remained of her mother. An image surfaced, as fresh as if it were yesterday. Her mother's wild dark hair tangled around her tear-streaked face, large, brown eyes filled with anguish as she left her child—more than an infant and yet very young—in the forest. The howls of that child, clutching the blanket as her mother ran away, rang in the deepest recess of her heart. A bit of blanket and dark hair remained Clotilde's only legacy.

A tear escaped. She glanced down as its wet course ended on her still-tender breast. If only their child was nestled there, warm against her heart, instead of this visceral ache, she thought.

"What...?" She listened intently, eyes widening as the sounds drew near. She stepped to the window, standing on tiptoe to peer out over the ledge, seeing nothing, but hearing a pounding of hooves. Horses—many horses—galloped closer, accompanied by the shouts of men. She strained, unsuccessfully, to identify the rider of the lead horse as he reared to a halt under her window. As he dismounted, she backed, like a shadow, away from the window.

Repeated blows rained against the barred door, the noise of shattering wood giving way to a shrill cry. "Is no one here to greet us on our victory?" The question was drowned in a frenzied laugh that reverberated throughout the house.

Clotilde darted her gaze about the room, seeking ways of escape. The window would plunge her three floors to the ground, the doorway into the path of the intruder. With silent calculation, she reached for the silver candlestick. She held it tightly, its weight ready to be put to use as she planted her bare feet securely and waited. The manic chuckle grew closer as heavy footsteps took the stairway in loud, staggering steps. A solid kick shoved wide the door. A demon burst through.

"Jacques?" The candlestick fell, its flame extinguished, as Clotilde fixed every sense on the wavering shadow in the doorway. Her heart pounded and her thoughts raced as she strained to identify the intruder. Surely the lisp-edged voice was that of Jacques de Montaillou. But how could this cackling fiend be someone known to her? The image of a phlegmatic young man, who'd shocked the town by killing his dog to impress his peers with his bravery, stirred in her memory. Instinctively she crossed her arms over her chest and became very still. Her eyes widened as the apparition lurched across the floor. The scent of blood—its rancid, earthy smell—filled the room.

"What's happened, Jacques? Where is Jean?" She heard the strange calm in her reasoned tones. Using them as a shield, she slowly backed away from his outstretched hand. He moved closer, so close that even with the dim light emanating from the hallway she could see the crazed horror in his eyes.

"Clotilde—my sweet reward!" He shouted as he swept her into the fierce grip of his bloodied arms and bent to force his violent kiss.

"Jacques—let her go!" Jean's voice filled the room with the commanding tone one used with the insane.

"Jean—thank God." Clotilde whispered as Jean yanked Jacques to the floor and swept Clotilde into the safety of his arms. The light of someone's candle cast shadows on Jean's profile. She watched his expression turn as dark and penetrating as a shard of obsidian as he looked upon the maniacal gaze of the bloodied form of Jacques de Montaillou. "In God's name, Jacques—what have you done?" Jean's rage whipped like a whirlwind throughout the room. His question met with an echoing chorus as several men followed on the heels of Jean's entrance.

Jacques froze, his wild look fixed as if rooted in some devilish tableau.

Clotilde's soft "nothing" faded into the shouts from the men who entered.

"Answer him!" The voice of Bernard, Jean's brother, erased all others as it boomed throughout the room. Bernard bolted forward like a bull, brandishing a knife in one hand as the other lifted Jacques from the floor by the scruff of his cloak. He dangled him at eye level with the gleaming blade as he spat out, "Now!"

Fear riveted Jacques, his howls escalating as a man moved forward and placed one arm on Bernard's. Spinning around, Bernard's look flashed fury. It quickly faded as he registered the only man whose hand could restrain his—Pierre-Roger de Mirepoix. Bernard released Jacques, bowed and backed away in favor of his liege lord. Pierre-Roger's look, eyes narrowed, jaw clenched, frightened Clotilde almost as much as Jacques' embrace. Fearlessness shone from the Lord of Mirepoix's eyes, with ferocity rumored to have stunned a raging bear.

His master's look prompted Jacques' howls to heighten in terror. His distress seemed too overpowering to allow his mouth to shape any word but "Well." He glared wildly about, repeating it in a cackling singsong—"Well. Well."

Pierre-Roger jerked Jacques forward, dragging him through the doorway. "Downstairs. Now." A path quickly formed as the men fell in line behind their leader and made their way down the stairwell.

Jean, still holding Clotilde, escorted her gently in their wake. As they approached the group settling around the table, Jean hesitated, looking from Jacques to Pierre-Roger before releasing his grip on Clotilde. His expression held misery too deep to fathom. "What happened?" she asked. "Leave us" was his only reply.

Clotilde withdrew to the back of the house, seeking the furthest corner of the kitchen area. She pulled a stool as close to the fireplace as she could without being in the glowing embers. Enfolding herself in stillness, she pressed her fists against her ears to drown out such unthinkable words as "murder" and "axe." Who was murdered, and why? Cathars could not have killed, she thought. No other religious group existed with as much reverence for all living things. A loud outburst met with a chorus crazed with glee. Sickened, Clotilde sprang upright, heart pounding with revulsion as she hurried down into the root cellar and out its door. Running soundlessly, she reached the stables.

Head down, she murmured soothing sounds as she neared Jean's horse, Coeur de Lyon. Without stirring from his bed of straw, he neighed softly as she curled alongside him. He seemed to welcome her as if she were his own foal. She burrowed beneath the straw, near enough to his broad flanks to feel their radiating warmth, her bond with animals an enduring legacy of her time in the forest.

So much was implanted then, Clotilde thought. Her rescuers attributed her miraculous survival to her fey skill with animals. She knew that such resourcefulness went beyond animals, beyond humans, beyond even her own vast inner strength. It lay deep within, a source invisible and invincible. She felt its infallible guidance as pure love and light. She gave a silent prayer for wisdom in applying such a gift.

The night continued as it had begun—with watchful waiting. In spite of Jean's return, whatever threatened, she knew, had not only remained but was gathering power. Clotilde held very still,

take its measure. An image of a monstrous wave of
...whose vastness threatened to encompass the entire world,
filled her.

Pierced with the certainty of terrible times ahead, she vowed to use everything in her power and everything outside it, to safeguard Jean and those she loved. Listening intently for any further affirmations from within, her focus was drawn away, not by any external sound, but by its absence. She sat up, her ears straining to comprehend the unthinkable—the pre-dawn angelus of the church bells, the heartbeat of the village, was silent.

TWO

Carcassonne, France – Present

I shook my head and looked away, as Carcassonne's medieval conical towers seemed to waver among the encircling clouds. Fighting the buckling of my knees, I was determined not to let the surreal impact of Carcassonne's "La Cite" unhinge my grip on reality. Having arrived less than three hours ago, I chalked my dizziness up to jet lag and headed back to my hotel.

"Remember, Dana—don't give way to any 'woo-woo.'" My friend Evie's words rang in my ears as I moved along the cobbled walkways. Thinking of her reminded me of how long I had taken before confessing my bizarre episodes, and how relieved I had felt at her reaction.

"Trust me, Dana," Evie had said, a rare serious look accompanying her solemn tones. "I know you well enough to be convinced you're incapable of losing it big time. But I also know how stressful these last few months have been. Perhaps you should rethink going to France." Her low-key disapproval soon escalated when she saw how determined I was to go. "The source isn't in the south of France," she'd added. "It's within you, Dana. Going could exacerbate such experiences."

The scene, along with my reaction, returned sharply now. A publicist for many of the leading pop-psychology gurus, Evie enthusiastically promoted them and their theories. When her pedantic tones deepened and her dark eyebrows rose in emphasis, I remember saying, "Hold everything, Evie. You're forgetting your illustrious C.G. Jung and synchronicity. You must admit that my getting an assignment, out of the blue, to go to France, *and* to photograph Cathar sites, is more than coincidence."

"I must admit that the Cathar bit threw me." Her eyes had widened as she added, "Statistically way out of the ballpark." We ended up laughing, our conversation brimming with the latest development in my compulsion with the Cathars. Evie was nearly as curious as I was over what awaited me in France. Whatever it was, I knew then and I know now—the answer is here.

Not that I'd had time as yet to confirm my conviction. Barely enough time to take a taxi from Toulouse Airport to Carcassonne, check into the hotel and examine my cameras and lenses. The security examination of my hand-carried baggage had been lengthy and nerve-wracking. Once assured all were in order, I decided to walk around Carcassonne's ancient inner city. So far, either because I was too entranced or too zonked, I hadn't taken even one photograph. Since that was my explicit purpose for being here, I headed for an empty bench, sat down and took out my camera. A familiar sense of security blossomed as I adjusted the lens, peered through the viewfinder, and snapped a series of shots of one of La Cite's ancient entryways.

Cloaked in the shadows of late afternoon, its Gothic curves seemed both to allow and to conceal a special quality of light. It was that aspect of light that, as a photographer, I'd long sought to capture. With some success, I thought, remembering the Santa Barbara showing of my black and white photos, billed as "Illumination's Sacred Legacy." I felt a shiver of anticipation at the opportunities to capture on film the soul of the twelfth and thirteenth centuries, the *structuram clariorem*, the lucid structures so venerated during that time.

Carefully storing the lenses, I recalled another of Evie's psychobabble axioms. She insisted that I used photography to escape, like Alice, but through a lens instead of a looking glass. Any port in a storm, I thought, suddenly aware that my left thumb was stroking my empty ring finger. A sharp pain filled me as images of my former fiancè, Alex, rose as fresh and raw today as four months ago. His charming persuasiveness had failed him as he stared at the intimate email I had held in my hand—a damning communiqué that exposed his infidelity, if not the name of his lover. The agonizing twinge intensified, warning me away from grief still too fresh to plumb. I hurried into the lobby of the hotel and headed for the café.

As I passed the mirrored wall at the entry, I startled at my red-suited reflection. Although a last minute buy, and quite unlike me, the suit looked great, accenting my dark hair and eyes. But I decided it would take at least a double espresso to brighten its wearer.

The waiter guided me through the empty restaurant and seated me in the outside patio where a few late-lunchers lingered over coffee. Some glanced my way, but none matched the description of my new cohort, Eric Taylor. "Espresso, please," I ordered, causing the waiter to lower his pen with a faint moue of disappointment. I quickly added, "I'm waiting for a colleague to arrive."

As he walked away I fell into a bit of a reverie, trying to imagine what the writer half of my assignment would be like. All I knew was that he was British and had a successful writing background. Whether old and stuffy, or young and brash, I hadn't a clue. As long as he was open-minded, I decided, as the waiter returned with my coffee. Demitasse and strong, a few tentative sips of the heavenly brew convinced me that I'd landed in a very different South than that of Georgia. I stared across the room and out over the hedge that separated the patio from the cobbled walkway. A *frisson* of pleasure filled me as I read the poster on the stone wall across the way. "Pays de Cathare," it announced— the Land of the Cathars.

The depth of my emotion confirmed that which I had so strongly denied with Evie—that my passion for the Cathars exceeded anything normal. A year ago it was easy to dismiss my sudden compulsion to read everything about the little-known group of heretics decimated in the Inquisition. I loved to read and regularly became consumed with learning something new. What wasn't so easy to admit, let alone explain, were my increasing bouts of feeling that I had known them.

I shook my head, returning to reality as I brushed away a bit of lint from my new suit. As I glanced down at my camera bag a heavy sigh escaped at the thought of just how important it was that I do well by this assignment. Actually, it wasn't the assignment itself, but the Cathars that compelled my success. My inexplicable fear at somehow letting them down, was so sharp that it prompted a silent prayer, "Dear God, please…" Unexpected words followed, "Don't let me be a flash in the pan."

My hands shook as I lowered my clattering cup to its saucer. I thought I had lain to rest that legacy from my father—my adored, clever, handsome, seldom-pleased father. He'd sneered as he uttered his epithet, not caring how indelibly it would remain on my soul, its branding made more acute by its having come near the end of his life.

The hated memory had a will of its own, I thought, as images returned. I remembered rushing into the house to break the news of my first professional assignment as a photographer. My father had sneered, saying, "Enjoy it while it lasts, Dana." He then dismissed my mother's well practiced "Don't, William" look, saying, "We all remember when Dana won the singing contest and decided to become a singer. That was followed by her passion for animals as she headed for the University to become a veterinarian." It was the meanness that made his words so painful. "That lasted exactly one year before she committed to becoming a photographer." He pinned me with his infallible look. "Face it, Dana. You're just a 'flash in the pan.'"

My mother's covert efforts to explain that he, not I, was the "flash in the pan" had fallen on deaf ears. Within a year, my father was dead, the victim of a heart attack during a trip to Seattle to search for a new job.

I shook my head, refusing to let such memories color my growing confidence that I was in the right place at the right time. So deep was my conviction that I stared out at the fanciful towers, daring them to wobble. Reassuringly motionless, I recalled some mention of their having inspired the design for Disneyland's Sleeping Beauty Castle, as well as providing backdrops for films.

Confidence rekindled, I turned to reality, bristling as I looked down at my watch. Where is this colleague of mine? I unsnapped my briefcase, retrieved the email he'd sent and confirmed that I hadn't misread our meeting-place. What could have happened, I wondered, my stomach churning with worry, combined with too much caffeine. As I renewed my scan of the few men in the café, the waiter rushed over. I declined any more coffee, deciding I'd give it ten more minutes before I returned to my room.

As the minutes elapsed, I gave a brisk shake of my head and muttered, "What could be keeping this Eric Taylor character?" Just then a hand briskly appeared from behind me, accompanied by a voice liquid with a James Bond-British overlay.

"At your service, Dana Palmer, but bloody late due to the mingling of my Twingo with a Saab." I fought to steady myself as I leaped from my chair.

"Those things happen," I responded while trying to recover, aware that my hand remained in his. Breaking free, I stepped back to look up into deep-set, hazel eyes. Their directness seemed to go with the suave, casual composure of the smiling man who stood in front of me. Neither young nor old, they sparkled with faint amusement as they stared into my sleep-deprived, brown ones.

"I won't even ask how your flight was." His gaze lingered on my dazed look. "Purgatory, it seems. Do sit down." He held out my chair before folding his six-foot frame smoothly into the chair opposite mine and motioning for the waiter. *"Deux whiskey, s'il vous plait."* He nodded conspiratorially in my direction. "A little pick-me-up is just what the doctor ordered. You *will* join me?"

"No thanks." I replied. Eric nodded and turned to discuss his order.

As he deliberated over the waiter's description of many brands, I took the chance to study him. He looked unruffled, his light blue shirt and tan pants dry-cleaner fresh, a cashmere sweater casually draped over his wide shoulders. He seemed simply too, too—too what—too contrived to trust, I decided. As he turned back, his eyes, accented by a seductive sweep of sandy blond hair, stood out in contrast with the lightness of his manner. Close up they appeared heavy lidded, a bit reddened and underscored by lines that were deeply etched, their depths hinting at perhaps a few drinks too many. Deliver me from the stereotypical writer-as-lush colleague, I thought, as he placed his order and looked at his watch.

"Five-fifty I make it." His firm nod was followed by, "As an experienced traveler, I consider it my duty to help reset your body clock. You *must* stay awake until at least eight o'clock. That should give us time to get acquainted, maybe even check out the lay of the land." Paralyzed by his energy, I hesitated before replying.

"Perhaps you're right." I glanced out at the softening light. "I would like to take a few photos of Carcassonne at dusk." Adding a more gracious lilt to my voice, I smiled as I turned back to him, "I take it you've been here awhile, Mr. Taylor."

"'Eric,' please. Twenty four hours, enough time enough to add to my research." He waved toward the street. "There's a great bookstore just around the corner. I bought every book in English on the Cathars. In fact, it was my searches further afield that caused my delay. They recommended another bookstore and, while trying to navigate and study their directions, I rear-ended

11

another car." He gave a shrug and a lopsided grin as he drew out a gold case, tapped out a cigarette, and extended it. As my mouth poised to protest, he halted. "May I?"

"Might as well." I said, finding it difficult to tear my focus away from his half-opened lips. I turned to motion toward the smoke-filled bar. "Seems there is no such a thing as a non-smoking area in France."

"Right. He returned the cigarette to his case. Even so, I'll spare you," he said as the waiter placed his whiskey in front of him. Downing a long swallow, his mouth broke into a grin wide enough to reach his eyes, forcing me to consider reclassifying their etched furrows as laugh lines. "I promise no tardiness in future. This assignment is much too important to me."

"To me as well." I rushed to cover my deep sigh with a logical explanation. "I've longed to escape from photographing stately Southern mansions. This assignment is…."

"Is apt to either make our careers, or brand us as…" Lifting his glass, he swirled the remaining amber liquid, his mouth skewed in a frown as he replaced it untouched. "Dare I say—*heretics*?" His look was that of a cobra with a mongoose.

I could feel my neck stiffen as I fought to keep my jaw unclenched. Its resistance warned me that I might be overreacting. Eric's stare, steady and implacable, decided me to probe his thoughts on Cathars as heretics. "The word, 'heretic,' as applied to the Cathars, raises my hackles. Wouldn't you agree?"

"Seems you're caught up in the Cathar mystique." His smile failed to soften the gentle chiding in his words.

"Enough to have done my research, Mr. Taylor. And to have discovered that the Cathars were good Christians who honored the original tenets of the Christian faith, those practiced by Christ. If anything, it was the Catholics who were the heretics." My voice rose, overriding my intent to remain neutral. "How one Christian group could have used such a label to massacre another is, is…" The look in his eyes forced me to an abrupt stop. Could he be intending to approach our series from the perspective that the world is well rid of such heretics?

"Hold on there now, Ms. Palmer, while I remind you of our assignment description." He reached down and drew out a leather folder, along with a pair of reading glasses, from his briefcase. "We are," he cleared his throat, looking professorial as he ran his finger across the page, "to produce an objective series, with emphasis on the scholarly approach in explaining the resurgence of interest in the Cathars."

"All well and good, but..." I took a slow, deep breath. "Sorry. I trust a solid night of sleep will restore my objectivity."

He downed the dregs of his whiskey and motioned for the check. I turned away, caught by the sun glazing russet tones across the rock-walled buildings lining the Place Saint Louis. "While you're settling the bill I'll head on out and take a few light readings." I said as I stood up. "I want to take a few shots before dark."

Eric studied me, his reply amiable. "I'll catch you up when I'm through here."

I stepped out into a cobbled lane of cluttered shop-fronts, their façades supported by moss-covered, ancient walls. The bustle of commerce announced unequivocally that, for the merchants anyway, the definition of "Cathar" was "business." Tourists were besieged on all sides by offerings of Cathar breads, Cathar museums, Cathar crosses, postcards, statuettes and other theme-park-tacky souvenirs.

Commercialism aside, nothing could erase my joy in being here, I decided, relieved at breaking away from Eric. Something about him reminded me of Alex. It wasn't that the two were physically alike, I thought, trying to pinpoint just what it was. I decided it was Eric's glib, playful patter and his smooth way of handling himself with a subtle undercurrent of seductiveness. I was gun-shy of any such charming sensitivity, convinced such excess either disguised a lack of any real emotions or walled off those too deep to expose. Neither bode well for relationship.

That having been acknowledged, I felt my tiredness lift. Catching sight of an impressive church up ahead, I headed for it. A perfect subject, I decided as I unfolded my tripod, took light readings and inserted high-speed film. Lost in photographing the exterior, I turned at the sound of my name.

"Dana. I knew I'd find you at the church," Eric called out.

"Photos of thirteenth century churches seem appropriate," I replied.

He glanced at the church's main entry. "Righto, so let's go have a look."

"Be right with you." I stored my gear before entering the Eglise Ste-Nazaire.

I stepped into the soaring vastness of a space that should have felt hallowed—but didn't. As Eric wandered up front, I glanced around. The church's massive interior was cold and dark, weirdly haunted in a nearby corner by a beggar holding a basket of coins in one hand and a large sandwich in the other. My eyes quickly moved away from him to the Romanesque nave, the oldest remaining part of Saint-Nazaire Basilica. Massive pillars directed my gaze upward to their twelfth century decorations, away from the cavernous spaces that incorporated centuries of rebuilding.

Deep sorrow hung suspended in the still air. To shield such emotions, I studied the sober arches as if through a camera, focusing on their power and endurance. As I moved my gaze to the stained-glass window's scenes from the Old and New Testaments, I looked again in disbelief. Instead of radiating luminosity and color, their panes cast an opaque mien upon tombs whose recumbent effigies gave a funerary feel—less holy than accursed. I shivered as I looked around to locate Eric.

He stood at the edge of a group gathered up front. Catching my gaze, he motioned for me to join him. As I approached, an English-speaking tour guide was directing everyone's attention to the floor. "That which you are looking at is not the final resting place of Simon de Montfort, but a memorial only."

The name's resonating force prompted painful memories. De Montfort was to the Cathars of thirteenth century France what Hitler was to the Jews of World War Two—"The Butcher." I broke my stare from the slab to whisper to Eric, "I want to get more exterior shots before dark."

"The tour ends in thirty minutes; I'll find you then." His words dimly registered as I hurried toward the exit. Grateful for fresh air, I moved aimlessly along the cobbled courtyard, relieved that the mobs of tourists had thinned. I soon found myself at the entrance to the Chateau Comtal, the castle of Raymond-Roger Trencaval, Viscount of Albi, Bezier and Carcassonne—and legendary hero. I drew a deep breath, suffused by a flood of anger and sadness. Anger at the brutalities of Simon de Montfort, and sadness at Viscount Trencaval's bravery in sacrificing his young life for the people of Carcassonne.

I glanced at the schedule of castle tours posted on the admission booth as the final tour of the day disgorged a large group. At their rowdy exit, I found myself feeling distinctly, even proprietarily, irritated at such a carnival atmosphere. Maybe I'll feel less testy after a good night's sleep, I thought.

I lowered my camera from views obscured by notices of concerts and cassoulet, and placed it back into its case. If I can't erase the Cathars' extinction, I thought, at least let my photos rescue them from the trite death of commercialism.

Following the far side of the castle walls, I discovered that their curvature soon led away from the central courtyard. Reaching a remote area, I stopped and stared. The castle wall, old and recessed, ended in a desolate corner that appeared, with some imagination, to have once contained a narrow entrance. Exactly the imagery I want, I thought, eager to photograph the dying light as it struck a solitary slit of window in the upper-right of the impenetrable corner.

Mid-focus, an image suddenly appeared in my viewfinder as a strangely dressed man moved toward the corner. Dismayed at having the solitude intruded upon, I nevertheless snapped a hasty shot. Any annoyance died as the figure turned, leaving me gaping in shock at his medieval garb. I suddenly remembered the hotel clerk's description of this evening's spectacular. "*Son et Lumiere,*" he'd explained, a sound and light show reenacting the horrors of Simon de Montfort's defeat of the young lord Trencaval in the year 1209. I lowered my camera and rushed forward to ask if he would pose as an image of the past. But he turned and, with a furtive move in the direction of the corner, vanished.

Baffled, I followed, only to find myself facing an impregnable corner. But when I looked down, I could make out a faint outline of stone steps that must, long ago, have provided entry. Barely recognizable as steps, the rubble ended in solid stone walls. Puzzled, but determined, I placed my camera case carefully alongside the mound. As I opened my camera's aperture to maximum, I regretted having left a more powerful flash back in my room. Undaunted, I balanced on the top of the rubble, ignored my inappropriate climbing gear and reached for the narrow window. My left hand clung to the cold stone as I aimed the lens into the slit.

"What on God's earth are you doing?" Eric's shout caught me mid-shot. I prayed not to break the expensive lens, or my neck, as I lost my footing and landed, camera held high, splayed like a rag doll, onto the rubble below. Angry, indignant and possibly injured, I turned slowly as he approached.

"Are you all right?" Eric's expression moved from concern to amusement as I struggled unassisted to a stand. "Creative or crazy, my dear colleague, I'm not sure what brought you to this God-forsaken site."

I slapped at the film of brown dust covering my new red suit. "Yes, I'm all right, no thanks to you. What brought me here was my search for some place undefiled by ads for cassoulet." And undisturbed by rash intruders, I thought as I stared beyond him. "Did you see anyone dressed in a knight's costume?"

He looked back down his route. His "no" as he turned was accompanied by a puzzled grin.

I shook my head. "How peculiar. Not five minutes ago a man dressed in medieval clothing walked up, headed for this corner, and vanished." I shook my head, puzzled by the emptiness of the cobbled street. "You must have seen him."

"Sorry to disappoint you. But I saw no one—in costume or out." Eric turned, eyebrow slightly raised and grin widened. "Maybe your chap was what you photographers call a 'trick of the light.'"

"No way, I captured him on film." I looked over at the clearly solid corner. "Just as I hit the flash, he vanished into..."

Eric followed my stare. "Into that wee little slit, of course."

After a second's defensiveness, I unclenched my teeth, his teasing laughter prompting me to see it through his eyes. "I guess jetlag really has scrambled my senses," I said as I removed my completed roll of film. "Even so, he *was* there. And this roll of film will prove it."

As I turned to go, I gave a little wince, favoring my bruised shin. Instantly, Eric shouldered my camera case and guided me with the indulgent care of a nurse. "I don't suppose I can interest you in trying some cassoulet for dinner?" Eric asked as we reached the hotel. "It's half past eight and you've not eaten."

I yawned, feeling the depth of my exhaustion. "Thanks, but room service, a little soup and a lot of sleep, is what I need."

He seemed relieved. "Sounds just the ticket. Give me a call when you wake up and want a bite of breakfast." He motioned across the lobby in the direction of the bar. "As for me, I intend to partake of the local atmosphere." His broad wink and hasty "*bonne nuit*" as he turned away, puzzled me. But I was too tired to examine anything or anyone any further. I walked over to Reception to retrieve my key.

"*Bonsoir*, Mademoiselle Palmer. I have here something for you," the concierge said, taking awhile to riffle through stacks of paper before turning with a shrug and heading for a door marked "Private." It seemed endless before he returned and handed me my key and a phone message. My eyebrow rose in surprise as I saw that it was from Evie. Excited, I asked when the call arrived. Straining for the proper English, the concierge replied, "A little before eight hours, Mademoiselle."

"Very well. Thank you." I smiled and turned toward the stairwell—suddenly doubling back. "Excuse me, I have some film I'd like developed. Can you help me?" I looked down, panicked to discover my camera bag was missing. The concierge's response was matter-of-fact.

"But of course, Mademoiselle. One hour to develop."

Anxiously scanning the area around the reception desk, I suddenly remembered that Eric had carried my camera. I gave a hasty explanation to the concierge and hurried toward the bar.

Before entering, I halted to allow my eyes to adjust to the gloom—and the noise. Incongruously, a disc jockey's raucous music reverberated, strobe lights beating in accompaniment. As my vision focused, I could make out Eric sitting toward the back of the room. He seemed deep in discussion. My eyes widened at the incongruity of the man who was with him—the last person I'd expect in a bar whose atmosphere seemed like the entry to Hell. Even a non-Catholic like myself could recognize a priest. Perhaps more than a priest, I thought as I caught sight of another priest hovering obsequiously nearby. Or simply more entertainers in costume, I thought as I stared, patently unnoticed, so intent were they in their dialogue.

Relief filled me as I saw that Eric's hands gripped my camera case. And yet, in the same instant, something in his manner restrained my walking over to reclaim it. Logic said he'd have to get his key at the desk. I'd leave a note asking him to give the film to the concierge for developing and safeguard my camera until morning.

Exiting discreetly, I walked back to the concierge and explained, as I left the note that Mr. Taylor would be dropping off the film. He nodded and bid me good night as I walked over to the hotel's ancient stone stairwell.

Its dim light cast shadows on the worn stone steps as I circled cautiously upward. At one of the landings, a suit of armor, lance held high in iron glove as if in warning, reared imposingly. I felt a sudden chill, consumed by an inexplicable sense that the mystery of the Cathars might prove less elusive than that of Eric Taylor.

THREE

Carcassonne, France – Present

As I entered my room and closed the door on the events and emotions of a dramatic day, I felt instant relief—and strong temptation. The bed's white coverlet with its masses of European down pillows beckoned seductively.

Instead, I kicked off my shoes, changed out of my suit and slipped into my favorite outfit—a tee shirt and tights. Carefully unpacking my minimal wardrobe of neutral, mix-and-match basics, I frowned as I hung them away and looked back at the empty case, suddenly aware of what I didn't bring. No silver-framed photo of Alex and no little love notes tucked among my undies. "Love notes? Lie notes," I said as I gave the empty case a solid shove into the closet.

Make-up removed, I frowned as bits of gravel, a souvenir of my fall, tumbled out of my dark hair. I brushed it and drew it into the clasp of a barrette. After doing a twenty-minute yoga routine, I began to feel centered enough to return the phone call. I should catch Evie at home, I thought as I dialed—if she didn't have an early morning appointment. The phone rang five times before going to the recording machine. "Evie, it's Dana," I said, glancing at my watch. "Either call me within the hour or eight hours later. I'm about to go to bed." I hung up and dialed the café.

Twenty minutes later, a waiter arrived pushing a cart carrying lentil soup, bread, butter, a glass of wine and a pot of chamomile tea. The soup's aroma awakened my taste buds, surprising me at the discovery of how hungry I was. After sopping up the last bit of broth, I took my wine and went in to run a bath that met my definition of luxury—lavender bath salts, scented candles and a deep bathtub. I lit the candles, sank under the bubbles, head propped against my travel bath pillow, and sipped appreciatively at the wine as I thought of Evie's typically dramatic message, "Call me. Good news." And of the events that had led me here.

The good news for me seemed to have always included her friendship. She was my rock during those nightmarish times when I seesawed between anger and grief over Alex's betrayal. It's strange, I thought, that I withheld sharing my obsession with the Cathars.

Evie and I had always confessed secrets. From grade-school days to Ritz Carlton champagne lunches, something wasn't real until it was shared. It took an especially dramatic session, after a lengthy outpouring of tears over Alex and lots of red wine, to finally reveal it. I remember how my hands had sweated as I began, nervous at having hid my obsession. Breathless after a nonstop account of my compulsive interest in the Cathars, I had slowly raised my eyes, baffled at her strange expression. Before I could fathom its meaning, Evie poured more wine and chuckled.

"You, my little *shiksa* friend, who has no traditional religious bent, suddenly captivated by an esoteric religious group called Cathars—*that is* a surprise." She refilled my glass, ignoring my "no thanks." "But a lot more interesting, I must say, than most of your sudden passions."

"You don't find *this* unusual?" I'd pointed to stacks of books on Cathars.

"Not for you, Dana." She'd laughed as she said it. "You've always immersed yourself in anything that captures your fancy. Remember the circus bit that followed your missionary in Africa passion? You dragged me to the circus mess tent and volunteered us to wash dishes so you could learn to become a trapeze artist." She downed her glass of wine and added, "About the only thing that came of that was my first crush, Henry Honig, the lion tamer's assistant. I was crazy about him. But he only had eyes for you!"

I had let her persuade me, smiling now at how much I'd wanted to believe that the Cathars were just another one of my off-the-wall enthusiasms. But I knew it wasn't the same. And so did she—when I finally leveled with her about what she'd come to call the "woo-woo" parts.

"It feels like a haunting," I confessed as I described certain episodes: A photograph of a chateau that had filled me with such repulsion that I'd slammed the book closed, only to learn that it was the home of Simon de Montfort. And my knowing, as I read about the burning of the Cathars at Montsegur, that it wasn't heat they felt, but chilling cold. Evie had listened, her psychiatrist-persona concluding, "strange, but not certifiable." Until the day she and I met for lunch in Atlanta. I'd gone into the city to photograph yet another venerable southern manse and to meet Evie, who had flown in to attend an art exhibit.

It was a memorable day from start to finish. My agent, Mike Reno, had called early that morning. "The editor of *International Horizons* magazine wants you for an assignment in France…" My heart had begun to slam against my ribcage at his next words, "…to shoot a story on the Cathars. Ever heard of 'em?" I was mute, in total shock, unsure at that point of what was real. Only Mike's raised voice saying, "Look, Dana. It doesn't matter whether you've heard of them. Do you want to take it or not?" finally startled me into a "Yes."

I remained in a daze as I drove to meet Evie at the Ritz-Carlton for lunch. Ten minutes early, I felt grateful for a few minutes to collect myself as I settled onto the banquette in the restaurant.

Evie, as always, had made an entrance. I envied such grandstanding. She'd breezed through the door with the confidence of a Valkyrie, larger than life as she flung her head back, blond tendrils spilling from the clasp that tried to hold her mass of naturally curly hair in place. Her intensely myopic stare searched the room. A husky "Dana" boomed throughout the dining room as she swirled her trailing paisley shawl across her statuesque frame and strode imperiously, ignoring the subtle stares, to our table. After a warm embrace, she sat down beside me, ordered "a great Montrechet" and said, "Out with it. Your look begs for release."

She'd listened raptly as I ended with, "That does it. I'm convinced that I'm being drawn to France."

Her psychologist-mien had replaced her diva-glitter smile. "Interesting phenomenon." She deliberated a moment before adding, "I assume you're familiar with Jung's collective unconscious?"

"Only in a general sense," I'd replied as I waited.

21

"Your episodes have similar elements of connecting with a soul memory of a highly charged period of history. Given its intensity, it could have left an imprint."

"But why me?" I remember asking more than once. "If reincarnation exists, it might make some sort of sense. Even so, why me, why now, and, more importantly, toward what end?"

To her credit, Evie hadn't dismissed such remarks. "I don't have any answers about reincarnation, but I do know how shocked you are by today's news of your assignment." She'd given me a searching stare. "As to why you—who knows. But it doesn't mean that you're predestined to go."

"Not go?" I still felt the same shock I had felt then, "That's simply not an option." I'd raised my voice. "Anyway—I know I'm being guided."

"Well then. I trust you'll continue to be." Recognizing our positions as irreconcilable, her solemnity faded. "Lighten up, Dana. Remember your circus bit. Whatever happens, it can't be harder than swinging through the air without a net."

I grinned at the memory of our rehashing all the craziness we'd shared since fourth grade. With the wine's assist, I'd actually been able to laugh at her joking reference to "this whole Cathar thing" by the time dessert arrived. Feeling lighter, I agreed to an exploration of the posh shopping center alongside the hotel.

While I headed for a travel store to pick up an electrical converter for France, Evie disappeared into a bookstore. We agreed to meet in the mall's central courtyard in fifteen minutes.

She arrived late, thrusting a package at me. "Open it while I go find a phone and let my client know that I've arrived and am staying at the Ritz Carlton." As she walked away, I examined the lovely, coffee-table book, *Beautiful France*. I turned the pages, stopping at photos of a village called Mirepoix. I let out a long sigh as I stared at the picturesque village square's ancient buildings crisscrossed with wooden beams. Just then Evie returned.

Except, as I looked up, it wasn't Evie. Suddenly the courtyard of the mall, Evie and her briefcase, became an ancient cobbled street, with Evie dressed in strange clothing and carrying a woven basket. Just as quickly, the image flickered, returning somewhat unsubstantially, to a chic woman in a modern shopping center.

Evie's words had sounded fuzzy. "Dana—you look like you've seen a ghost."

I remember jumping up, saying, "Let's walk." What an effort it had been to force myself to focus on the shops we passed as I fought to reclaim the here and now. At some point I had begun, haltingly, to describe my experience.

"Disassociation," she had pronounced as she looked at me long and hard. "You know, mentally removing yourself when under strain." She squeezed my hand. "Breaking up with Alex could have been traumatic enough to cause you to schiz out." I'd held my breath, my heart racing at her words. "Relax, Dana. I still hold to what I said earlier. Your psychological make-up just isn't the kind to opt for disassociation, at least not big time." Evie couldn't quite camouflage her concern. "But after this episode, I trust you'll cancel your trip to France and get on with real life."

Obviously she knew I wouldn't take such advice, I thought as I recalled her chiding capitulation, "Dana, you're a typical Aquarian, spearheading the unknown and let the devil take the hindmost." Still smiling at the memory of her words, the ringing of the phone burst my soap-bubble reverie. Grabbing a towel, I picked up the phone to hear her voice booming into the present.

"God, Dana—talk about synchronicity!" Evie rushed past my 'hello.' "You remember my telling you I'd put my place in Biarritz up for sale?" I didn't, but I waited for her to finish. "My agent called to say we have a buyer. I have to fly over, sign docs and remove my things." She laughed. "Some coincidence!"

"You're coming to France?" I stammered.

"Yes, and soon. I only hope the sale goes as fast. I remember the French notaire system as a bit of a nightmare. I'm sure to be there at least a week, maybe longer." She paused. "Good news, right?"

"Great news. When do you arrive?"

"I fly into Toulouse next Wednesday at four."

I reached for my schedule. "I'll be in Foix, but I'll make it."

"No need. A friend will meet me and put me up at his home in Toulouse."

"*Friend?* You've been holding out on me. Who is he?"

Her booming laugh filled the room. "He's someone I met in Paris a couple years ago when my parents died in that plane crash." Evie's animated tones vanished. "When I went to Paris to deal with it all, the airline arranged for the families to attend a conference on grief." Evie sighed, her voice lifting a bit. "Benjamin was attending an archeology conference at the same hotel. We had a few drinks and exchanged cards. I mentioned wanting to buy a second home in France and he introduced me to the owner of my Biarritz place. Now that I'm selling it, I called him for advice and he offered me a place to stay."

"Only you, Evie." I laughed. "Whatever the synchronicity, I'm glad."

"Me too. I should be in Toulouse long enough so that we can get together. Work it out with Benjamin tomorrow."

"Will do. Give me his phone number."

"No need." She lowered her voice. "Are you sitting down?"

"Yes—but from the way you sound, I should have a stiff drink in my hand." I drew back the receiver at Evie's explosive laugh.

"Get this! I'd written Benjamin Carter off as someone so long buried in bones that he could never hold any surprises. Or so I thought, until I told him about your assignment." She paused, giving a long "hmm" before continuing. "Come to think of it, that was when he invited me to stay. He claims he's not just *an expert,* but *the* expert on—get this—the Cathars!" Her excitement escalated at my "No!"

"Wait, Dana, there's more. That's why I needed to catch you before you left Carcassonne. He's giving a talk in Carcassonne tomorrow night. An invitation will arrive at your hotel—for you and your colleague."

I laughed. "You're supposed to lessen, not increase, strangeness, Evie."

"Yeah, well. We'll discuss that later. In the meantime, you can meet Benjamin and arrange for the four of us to get together."

"*Arranging* shouldn't be a problem." My emphasis was greeted by a huge guffaw that slowly faded as her voice returned.

"One caveat, Dana. Not my first night in. I've been on a book tour with a client with a total of ten hours sleep all week. I'll be a wreck."

"I'll try for a day later. But I have so much to tell you…"

"Save your first impressions until I see you. Someone is at the door." Evie's greeting was muted, her visitor's voice abruptly silent as I strained to make clear a faint familiarity. Evie returned. "I'll have to draw this to a close, Dana. My client's here. See you soon. Ciao."

I hung up and shook my head at Evie's having a never-before-heard-of friend arriving in Carcassonne to lecture on Cathars. Uncanny, I thought as I slid under the deliciously cool sheets and turned off the light, a faint question nagging—"Too uncanny?"

After hours of wakefulness I turned on the light and tried to quench a vague sense of unease by reading. I decided to finish the book I was reading on the plane, a history of the Inquisition. It was a nightmarish account until the final chapter dealing with modern-day Catholicism. As I read of the accomplishments of today's Church, I felt saddened at the Pope's frailty and nonplused by a recent expose of pedophilia among priests. I was at the brink of sleep, lulled by the segment's pedantic tones, when I came across a disturbing chapter. It contained a translation of the oath taken at the election of a new pontiff, phrases that included a vow never to lend support to any interference, opposition or any form of intervention. Their autonomy planted a cautionary seed. As I neared the end, my heart sank to read that, apart from the Mafia and the CIA, no other organization acted so secretly, and with such a large cadre of enforcement personnel to accomplish its aims, than the Catholic Church. Enshrouded in secret, the specter of clandestine activities remained, it seemed. But to what end?

Nita Hughes

FOUR

Mirepoix, France-March, 1242

Someone approached. Clotilde, tightly curled alongside Coeur de Lyon, came instantly alert. The horse rose to the ready, giving a soft neigh as Clotilde poised to run. She halted at Jean's whisper of her name. Alarm filled her at the pain etched in his face. "Have they gone?" she asked.

"Yes, my love, they've gone." The anguish in his voice softened as he began to tenderly remove straw from her hair. Enfolding her tightly in his woolen cloak, he guided her outside. She drew closer, blissful at his nearness. An enveloping mist drifted down over the limestone hills as the sun's rays met the chill in the air. She loved the feeling of being enshrouded in its cocoon. Nothing stirred, the only sound the crunch of their footsteps as they crossed the cobbled forecourt. Jean stopped at the entry to scan the horizon. "All clear. Come inside where we can talk."

He settled her onto the rough-hewn bench drawn up to a long table, sweeping aside burnt out candles as Clotilde waited. The anger in Jean's expression returned, as if sparked by the energy in the room. He paced as he spoke. "You've heard of the arrival of the two inquisitors, Guillaume Arnaud and Jean Seila."

"Yes, rumors are everywhere. They say many Cathars have and will die at their hands." Her eyes clouded with fear. "Are we to be next?"

Jean slammed one balled up fist into the other hand's palm. "No!" His expression flamed finality mixed with a strange blend of sorrow and frustration. Whatever his inward vision, he froze in silence and stared into space. She studied him for some clue. Built like the sturdiest of oaks, his solid dependability had provided her with father, brother, husband and friend. Strength of purpose was in all Jean did, his duty an honor, and questioning of loyalties unthinkable. Only once before had she seen that look in his eyes— conflicted, unable to act, anguish beyond his ability to resolve.

Clotilde felt her throat constrict with a desire to move toward him, to take his pain on as her own. Clearly such a move was unthinkable. The lines in his brow matched the muscles straining in his forearm as he tightened his clenched fist. Unable to bear his unspoken distress, she followed his gaze as he scanned the room. She looked afresh at that which his eyes settled upon: the lovingly crafted table, his own handiwork and big enough for thirty, the tapestry on the wall behind it, created by her hands, as was the flower arrangement below. A sudden sinking in her stomach brought an awareness that their home, so solid, so safe, so filled with love, was not only tainted by last night's bloody specter of Jacques. A deeper vulnerability caused her heart to sink as Jean turned to her, his voice hollow.

"Both inquisitors, Arnaud and Seila, lodged in the house of Raymond d'Alfar at Avignonet. He extended his hospitality on behalf of the Count of Toulouse." Jean turned from Clotilde's fixed gaze and stared into the fireplace flames, his fierce focus unbearably long. And yet she waited.

Clotilde released a long breath as Jean slowly came back from the depths his thoughts had plumbed. His voice delivered a numb, matter-of-fact account as he continued. "It was a treacherous hospitality. Early yesterday morning, Bernard sent a messenger to inform me of a plot to ambush the Pope's men. We met and rode directly to the rumored meeting place, hoping to intercept Pierre-Roger and his men in time to stop the assassination of the inquisitors." Jean fell silent as he walked over to the shuttered window. Opening it to the brisk breezes of a cool spring morning, he drew a deep breath and stared out into the distance. His voice returned, verging on a wail. "We were too late. Pierre-Roger was alone. He'd sent a troop of knights and soldiers, including Jacques de Montaillou, on to Avignonet. They returned just as we arrived. Blood-stained and demonic, they gloated over their success in killing the inquisitors." Jean walked over and slumped onto the

28

bench, burying his head in his hands. "With axes." He slowly turned to her, his words bleak. "Their murders will surely be avenged."

Her response was as gentle as her touch on his arm. "You did all you could, my love." She hesitated, afraid to know and yet asking, "What will it mean?"

"The fates of many rest on the answer to that question." Jean jumped up and placed a finger to his lips as a sound of hoof-beats neared. A horse and rider drew to a halt outside. A familiar shout halted Jean's reach for a sword. "Bernard returns. He rode with Pierre-Roger to make certain the route to Foix was safe." Jean rushed to the door. "Perhaps he shall have some answer for us."

Clotilde felt a surge of optimism return. Jean's trust in his older brother's support was unshakable. As Bernard's massive form, taller even than Jean's, filled the doorway, she thought he looked capable of supporting the entire building and all in it. Until she looked into his eyes and saw the exhaustion in their stare.

"Bernard, come." Clotilde offered her hand, the reality of his sleepless night dawning. "Sit, you must be tired." Made uneasy by his remaining frozen in a silent stance, so unlike his usual boisterous bravado, she began to move away. I'll bring him some spiced mead, she thought, and leave him with his brother. But impetuously, she halted her exit to rush one question forward. "Bernard, dear brother, what think you of the consequences of last night's slaughter—for us—for all Cathars?"

Her question lay heavy in the silence as Bernard took a long moment to respond. His deep voice echoed the defeat in his eyes as he said, "Stay, Clotilde. As to your question, I fear there is nothing more to hide." Like a puppet whose strings were cut, he sank heavily onto the bench, staring as his sword clanked noisily against the stone floor. "Pierre-Roger spoke of nothing else but the consequences of killing the inquisitors. Although he saw such carnage through, he is sorely anxious. As the garrison commander of Montsegur, his own fate, as well as that of all Cathars, rests with the Count of Toulouse's response." Bernard studied his brother Jean's reaction as he added, "Albeit the deed was done at the Count's dictates."

Jean spread his hands wide in a gesture of resignation, his voice matching their emptiness. "Such responsibility can never be admitted. It must seem to have been provoked by others. The power to act remains in the Count's hands..." He stared at his own. "God willing, those hands are not tied tightly by one even more powerful."

Clotilde winced as the hope in Jean's voice faded. She stared at his still open hands, offering her words as if to fill them. "Surely the Count remains one of the most powerful men in all of France."

"But the Pope is more powerful." At Jean's emphatic reply, Clotilde stiffened her stance, squaring her slim shoulders. Jean's sigh communicated more than words his inability to offer any support to her confidence. He turned to Bernard and lowered his voice. "When word of tonight's slaughter reaches the Pope…"

Bernard nodded. "As soon it will. Pierre-Roger intends to travel on from Foix to Toulouse to seek support from the Count." Bernard's pause sought Jean's agreement. "It would be monstrous should the Count fail to support the loyal servant that fulfilled his master's plot."

Jean gave a fatalistic shrug. "Whatever Raymond VII did and does, he knows full well that the Pope's reaction will be swift and merciless. And the Cathars will pay the price."

"But that's not fair!" Clotilde's head turned with a jerk, her face red with anger. "Or believable. No Cathar would lift a hand to kill, or sanction such…"

Bernard's icy tones cut through. "True, but it's through the sacrifice of the Cathars that vengeance will be claimed, exactly as in 1208 when this vicious persecution began." His contempt hung in the air like an ax unsheathed.

Clotilde sought rebuttal as she looked from Bernard to Jean. Both men stared deep into the distance. In the silence, Clotilde pondered Bernard's reference to the past. Perhaps it alone can provide a clue as to what may lie ahead, she thought as she spoke. "How did such cruelty begin?"

Jean drew her over to the bench beside him. Gently stroking a lock of pale hair from her eyes, he answered.

"Before you were born, my love, the Count of Toulouse's father, Raymond VI, strongly supported the Cathars." Jean drew a long breath, as though in relief at a question he could answer. "So strongly that the Pope sent his representative to excommunicate the Count and his entire household. Whether encouraged by the Count or not, an enraged servant took it upon himself to assassinate the Pope's legate." Jean paused as Bernard leapt up, eyes flaming.

"I was twelve then and remember it well." Bernard said. "The Pope rallied crusading knights from the north in a new crusade—a

Holy War against the Cathar heretics and any who supported them."

"'Holy war' be damned!" Jean shoved the bench back as he jumped to stand alongside his brother, his glare as bitter as his words. "Those knights were impoverished by the long crusade in Jerusalem. It was a simple matter to entice them by forgiving their debts in exchange for fighting the new 'heretics.'" The veins in Jean's neck streaked his reddening features with bulging blueness as he and Bernard locked stares.

Bernard slammed his fist on the tabletop. "Bloody mercenaries they were, plundering as they killed."

"God help them." Clotilde's desolate words settled over the room.

Jean's wrath eased at her tone as he added, "And shed mercy on us."

As passionate as she was for humanity, Clotilde wasn't easily deflected from reason. Her brow furrowed as she spoke. "But surely Raymond VII dare not repeat his father's mistake." Clotilde's look begged Jean to refute her conclusion. "It would be folly should he come to the Cathars aid."

Jean stared into space, his response measured. "That Raymond VII will attempt to support the Cathars is..." He drew a long breath as he looked from Clotilde to Bernard. "An outcome we must all fervently pray for."

Clotilde stood, turning first one way and then the other in agitation. "Pray yes—but take action." Jean took her hands as he said,

"My fierce love, as to action, for now please be quick to prepare a meal for Bernard while I see to his horse."

"Of course." Clotilde looked at Bernard as she turned to go. "Forgive me, dear Bernard. I shall return shortly with food."

As Clotilde entered the kitchen area, she walked over toward the warm glow of the fireplace. Preparing a large pot of porridge, she moved the metal arm holding the pot deeper over the coals. As she stirred a little more mash into the water, she thought of her first lesson in preparing meals. Images of her young self grabbing any proffered food and hiding it, or devouring it on the spot, stirred a rush of amazement and tenderness for that hungry child.

Were it not for the Cathars, she surely would have died of hunger. Fabrisse, one of the Cathar's most revered priestesses, rescued the young child abandoned in the forest. "A wild one, you were," Fabrisse said in describing her shock at finding a babe in a cave in the woods. "Scarcely walking," she'd said, "and as still as a fawn you were, hiding deep in that cave. Why, if Esclarmonde and I hadn't gone in to get out of a storm on our way to Coustaussa, I fear for what would have become of you." Fabrisse and her socia had taken their wild charge on to Coustaussa Castle and, when less animal and more human, back to the school for Parfaites in Montreal. Eight months later—the child still called "little wild one"—Fabrisse declared a school for Cathar priestesses to be no place to raise a babe. She soon found a proper home with a devout Cathar, Marie de Grissolles.

Clotilde had gratefully adopted all she saw demonstrated by the de Grissolles family, including their allegiance to the Cathar faith. Her new mother, Marie, was so happy to have a companion for her daughter, Blanche, that she let the ten-year old choose the foundling's name. A christening and a birthday were jointly observed where Blanche, naming her "Clotilde," announced her new little sister's age to be four years. Such loving ministrations slowly eased Clotilde's fear of abandonment.

As she grew, her sharp powers of observation revealed that, whether providing healing herbs for ailments, sharing information, or teaching others a trade, Cathars gave generously of themselves in service to others. Pure love shone from them. It was fitting, she concluded, that they were called *"bonshommes"* and *"bondammes"*—the good men and good women.

Adding a handful of chopped apple to the bubbling porridge, Clotilde left the fireplace to take down the pewter mugs. She stared into space as a contrasting image of the village priest, Father Le Clerque, came to mind. Avaricious, lecherous, and besotted most of his days, it was no wonder the villagers turned from their Catholic priests to the Cathars.

But for how much longer, Clotilde wondered? She knew that anyone found supporting a Cathar would, at best, be imprisoned, at worst, tortured and killed. Many Cathars had gone underground, living in caves from hand to mouth. For as fearful as they were of being discovered, they were more concerned about putting the townspeople in jeopardy. Growing numbers were making their way to the impregnable sanctuary of Montsegur. How soon would it be their turn, she wondered? The persecution was relentless, she knew, shivering at Bernard's chilling tale of the assault on Bezier.

Tears had run down her cheeks at the horror in his tale. Inhumanity surely reached its cruelest level that day in 1209, she thought. Twenty thousand people, young and old, newborn and clergy—all were massacred. Thousands sought God's protection by taking sanctuary with their priests in Bezier's cathedral. The Crusade's leader, Arnaud Amaury, when told that most were Catholics, coolly commanded: "Slay them all. God will recognize his own."

The *"langue d'Oc,"* her beautiful language, the language of Occitania, had many words for poetry, for love, for all the noble virtues, but none for dishonor and hatred such as that which saw Bezier's destruction. Clotilde stared off into the distance, stunned by such barbarity. "Where will it end?" burst from her, her question floating unanswered on the air.

Along with her words came a strange aroma as the smell of burnt porridge filled her nostrils. She ran over and yanked the metal arm forward in hopes of saving Bernard's meal. A cry rang out as she winced in pain, a red blister spreading across her palm. She stared mutely at her hand, a stanza from an Inquisitor's poem filling her thoughts. "'Tis fit that you should burn. The fire is lit, the pitch is hot, and ready is the stake."

Nita Hughes

FIVE

Carcassonne, France- May-Present

Groggy from a night of fitful sleep, I headed straight for the dining room and a strong espresso. Eric waved from across the room, standing to move aside his cup of coffee, an ashtray brimful of half-smoked cigarettes and what looked like every Carcassonne brochure in print. My glance settled on my camera bag. I scooped it up, affirmed all was in place except for the film he'd left for development, and sat down.

I noticed his effort to curb his transparent enthusiasm as he sat beside me. But, unwilling to comment until I'd had my coffee, I waited until the waiter turned away before saying, "Good Morning."

Eric responded with what I felt was a bit too much *bonhomie*, "Well, Sleeping Beauty, your castle awaits your royal inspection." With that, he shoved the entire sheaf of brochures under my nose. "I booked us a castle tour for noon, a private one, complete with an English speaking tour guide." I was not yet wide-awake enough to do anything but stare down at the brochures. His excess of self-satisfaction was accompanied by an annoyingly off-the-mark comment. "You look bright eyed. Sleep must have been just the ticket."

"Not exactly," I said, pausing to take a long swallow of the coffee the waiter had set down. Restored, I decided to spring *my* surprise announcement. "But the evening wasn't a complete waste." Eric looked puzzled as I reached into my briefcase, drew out an envelope and held it close with one hand as I took my coffee in the other. I took a couple of slow sips of the potent brew before extending the envelope. "The concierge handed me this as I stopped by his desk." Eric opened it, mouthing the French phrases slowly.

His head bolted upright, his expression disbelieving. "However did you manage an invitation to a lecture on the Cathars?" His eyebrows rose as I told him of Evie's call. "You're one powerful female, Ms Palmer." A look blended of curiosity and respect accompanied his smile as he said, "Hungry too, I bet."

"I'm craving…" I glanced across at a lean young man dunking a pastry into his espresso. "One of those croissants." It appeared and was promptly devoured, leaving me feeling amiable enough that the enthusiasm in my voice was genuine as I glanced at the brochures and said, "The castle tour sounds perfect."

"Perfect," as it turned out, wasn't exactly the best descriptor, but it did provide some great photo opportunities and, as a private tour, allowed for more in-depth questioning. Helene, our young French guide, proud of her recent graduation from a course in languages and tourism, provided a steady stream of information. "The Trencaval family was one of the most noble in all of France. Of them all, the young Lord was the most loved by his people." Her confident account was increasingly directed at a wide-eyed and receptive Eric. That suited me just fine.

I was intent on setting up my shots, measuring the angle and light, excited at capturing the castle's brooding mood. Not a detail was overlooked as I sought the most compelling angle for every photo. Each frame, carefully staged, seemed to come alive as I captured mystery through the viewfinder. A strange message—both intimate and distanced—the shadows withholding and the light calling for remembrance, surfaced the memory of the strange man in my photo last night. I felt compelled to strive even more to illuminate a something in the shadows.

Soon I had gone through several rolls of film, shot unobtrusively as a backdrop to Eric's non-stop questions and Helene's polished replies. Every now and then I would seek clarification. "Is that the area where they ate, slept, etc? What would have been in the great hall? Why such expansive height and those double window openings in this particular room?"

Helene's response to my questions lacked the embellishment she'd added to Eric's. "The hall was for large gatherings of other lords and ladies, troubadours and visiting dignitaries. Its current height is due to the ceiling above having fallen in."

Succinct as she was, her explanation sufficed for my needs. I continued working intently, emotions shielded by resolute professionalism. Remaining behind the camera, I sought to shield a growing fear that I could hardly breathe while in the arena of Raymond-Roger's short life and brutal death.

"Dana, you really are absorbed." Eric gave me a perplexed look, repeating a comment of such import that it bridged my distancing. "Helene just said she would show us the dungeon. Even though it's not on the tour."

"Not actually the dungeon, monsieur," Helene corrected him. "But the area of the castle where it once was, where the young Lord was imprisoned and died." My palms began to sweat as she spoke. I could sense the young lord calling to me with an urgency that somehow I must heed, or should have heeded, or... I clung to Eric's pragmatic voice as an anchor to reality.

Eric had pulled out a booklet and began to read. "It says that Raymond-Roger Trencaval died on November 10th, 1209. Of dysentery according to some, assassinated according to others."

Helene raised an eyebrow as she began her obviously well rehearsed commentary. "The official word from the Catholic Church was that Viscount Trencaval died from dysentery—after he recanted and converted to the Holy Roman faith." She paused. "Carcassonne had been given over to Simon de Montfort, and thus..." A soft *alors* accompanied her Gallic shrug. I felt irritated by its blasé dismissal, while Eric rushed to interject the conclusion.

"Thus, Raymond-Roger, after offering himself in exchange for the safety of the people of Carcassonne, had to repent and, although in the prime of life, die." Eric turned to me. "What's your take on it, Dana?"

My chest gave a sharp twinge, its overwhelming sadness threatening to explode. I turned away to busy myself in replacing one lens with another. "Politics, pure politics, then as now." My response was steadier than my hand, which busied itself with the lens, leaving them to pick up the conversational gambit.

"Politics!" Eric's contemptuous retort was aimed at Helene. "Politics and religion, strange bedfellows, wouldn't you agree, mademoiselle? My research suggests that both the King and the Pope were angling for power and property more than converts."

I peered up from my task. Their intense tableau revealed Eric as fervent orator and Helene as entranced audience. She seemed to hang on Eric's every word, although my sense was that what Eric interpreted as wholehearted agreement, was partly her focus on accurate translation. I smiled, all the while thinking how easily men were ensnared through hubris. Eric's fervor grew. "Wouldn't you agree, mademoiselle Helene, that the South of France at that time was not only richer but more tolerant, sophisticated and powerful than the provincial North?"

"*Certainement, Monsieur.* Occitania was a country rich in creativity, music and troubadours, a time of love carried to a high art." Helene's animated tones lowered. She brushed a lock of dark hair away from her eyes as they glanced swiftly down and back up to lock with Eric's. "Forgive my passion, monsieur." Her words, and Eric's "but of course," echoed with a subtle universal accent, revealing each as angling toward an even older exchange.

I felt a surge of bitterness at an image of Alex. He'd undoubtedly engaged in a similar seduction with whomever his lover was. Helene must have noticed my frown. She resumed her strict tour-guide diction. "Let us proceed to the dungeon."

We moved through the section that once housed the lodgings of the Trencavals. As we passed several large tour groups buzzing away in French and German, I tried to bury my emotions—whether the old ones of Alex, the new of the young Lord, or perhaps those of Eric—under the theatre of it all. Helene rounded the curve of a large tower, stepping cautiously into the far recesses it concealed.

"If you will look into this opening, you will see the remains of the area that led into the dungeon." Helene's voice was emphatic as she reached into her briefcase and handed us both a postcard. "To aid you to imagine the twenty four year old Raymond-Roger, I show to you this photograph as he appeared on his Viscount's seal." I stared at the handsome young man on horseback. A choke escaped.

"Yes, it is sad." Helene glanced briefly my way before returning her attention to Eric. "So young. So noble." Eric ignored her in his haste to scramble up over the pile of loose rocks and peer into the opening. Helene's tones of sympathy turned to impatience as she pointed to the narrow aperture. "Well then, let us look, and you may perhaps picture this young count."

Perhaps picture this young count? The hairs on my arm began to rise as her words faded and Eric drew me up beside him to stare into the dark area of rubble. The young man who died there, the face staring from Raymond-Roger's official seal, was the man I had photographed last night.

* * *

The knowledge haunted me all through the day. Try as I may, each time I would look through my lens, I would superimpose the features of the young man dying in the dungeon. Each corner I turned brought strange and troubling reminders: an avenue with his name, a fountain inscribed with the date of his death, books emblazoned with his image, an enigmatic doorway, locked to my touch. A subtle plaque announced it as the "Centre d'recherche Catharisme," the center for the study of Cathars, the venue for our evening's event.

I did my utmost to erase a lingering melancholia as I prepared to meet Eric in the bar for a drink before going to Benjamin Carter's presentation. Successfully, it seemed.

"You look more relaxed than the virago I spotted in town today. There can't be a corner of Carcassonne you've not photographed ten times over," Eric said as he drew my chair out. "I wish I could write as fast as you shoot."

"That's the nature of my work." I hesitated, aware that I'd buried myself behind the lens all day for more than just the perfect shot. "A photographer takes hundreds of shots in the hopes that a few are perfect."

"From what I've seen of your work, I expect more than just a few to be perfect." He looked away as the waiter came to take our drink order, returning his gaze to me as the waiter turned away. "When do you see the results?"

Thinking fast, I replied, "I should have those you left with the concierge back by tomorrow. After I preview them, I'll let you have a look."

"Whatever you say, although you will have added another hundred by then." Eric smiled as he glanced down beside my chair. "I don't see any photographer's paraphernalia for me to safeguard tonight—unless your handbag holds a tiny camera."

"It does, actually. I'm hoping to take some discreet shots of Benjamin." I gave a slight shrug and grinned. "Assuming he's the shy-scientist sort."

The waiter returned with our drinks as we took in the mellow blush of sunset spreading over Carcassonne, a cool breeze stirring through the open terrace. In silence we sipped, as I gave thanks for the wine's softening influence.

Restored, we headed out for the short walk that led to the formidable door I'd encountered earlier. I smiled as its gleaming plaque, so intimidating earlier, gave way as we entered a surprisingly large foyer.

"If my radar is true, Benjamin Carter is headed for us," Eric whispered.

I looked across to see a man of about thirty-five approaching. Tall, dark haired and smiling, he moved through a throng of well-wishers, extending his handshake as he went. An aura of confidence and entitlement surrounded him. His externals were perfect, impeccable suit, expensive shoes, designer tie and a priceless watch on the hand he thrust forward as he reached us. As he looked me up and down, his strange gaze made me wonder whether I'd committed some unknowing gaffe.

"Good. You're on time," he said as he wrenched his stare away. "I'm Benjamin Carter. From Evie's description, you must be Dana Palmer and Eric Taylor." He extended his well-manicured hand to Eric, turning with European-style, cheek brushing kisses, for me. His cologne was as subtle as his welcoming kiss, enveloping but not touching. The resumption of his intent stare as he backed away made me nervous. His eyes, black and impenetrable, remained fixed on me.

"We're so grateful for this unexpected opportunity." I heard myself babble the words, unhinged by his stare.

"At Evie's mention of your interest in the Cathars, I knew you'd find my presentation informative." Benjamin's assured manner was fast erasing any image of a shy and reticent professor. He turned as someone walked up to him.

"Professor Carter. Here are your revised notes." The man's French dialect was musical, but his look anticipated discord as he held out a sheaf of papers.

"Notes, you idiot, on cards. These pages will scatter everywhere." Benjamin shoved the loose pages into the man's hands as he looked at his watch. "You have five minutes to do it right."

I felt embarrassed as the poor fellow turned to leave, and angry with Benjamin. I wondered if my look betrayed that I understood Benjamin's harsh reprimand. Seemingly not—a smile covered his irritation, but his attention was marginal as he motioned toward the fast-filling tables in the dining room. "Locate your name cards on one of the tables. Dinner will precede my presentation."

"We're looking forward to it," Eric said as he motioned toward the podium where an overhead projector beamed its welcome in French. "Although I must confess that my knowledge of French is basic menu level."

"Of course." Condescension was suggested more by Benjamin's barely perceptible rise of his nose than his words. "I've left English translations of my speech at your table. We'll compare notes later." He glanced at his watch. "I must get back to the speaker's table."

As Benjamin departed, I leaned in toward Eric and whispered, "Definitely 'GQ'—but with an overlay of pure politician."

Eric added, "'Pure' politician meant as an oxymoron, I take it."

I stifled a laugh as I reached for my tiny camera and took a few shots of Benjamin just as he reached the podium and turned with a frown.

Eric whispered. "Not a jolly chap, I'd say."

"I'll try to reserve judgement." I said as I stashed my camera in my purse. "Let's find our table and enjoy our dinner." If not what we are about to hear, I thought as an ominous precognitive ripple made itself felt.

I glanced about until I spotted our names on the third table in from the front, far right. As we approached, introductions were made. Our tablemates consisted of a professor of history and his wife, minimal English, and a dentist and her husband, French speaking only. I did my best to smile and make what small talk with them I could. Our real concerns were addressed in asides to one another. My focus was drawn to the audience and why they were so involved with the study of the Cathars. Before I could arrive at any conclusions, the waiter appeared with our first course.

My ears caught a French phrase from the professor of history, which, although sotto voce, translated as impassioned and unflattering. "Upstart. Another evening of revelations that denigrate Cathars and elevate Carter." I camouflaged my understanding with an aside to Eric about the interesting appetizer.

"Delicious, from the looks of it," I murmured to Eric as I nodded toward the speaker's table.

"And the salad looks good too." Eric grinned as he forked up a mouthful of warm goat cheese. The aroma reminded me that I'd not stopped for lunch, my thoughts too churned to focus on food. Unable to ignore my stomach's return to life, I devoured the salad

41

and went straight for the *grille de salmon*, finishing every bite with room for apple tart smothered in *crème fraiche*. By the time the tinkling sound of knife on glass announced that proceedings were about to begin, I was ready.

Benjamin began his speech. The English translations didn't do justice to the emphasis Benjamin placed on himself as *the* Cathar expert, one whose brilliance would once again be indisputable. He enumerated all the discoveries he had made, the many digs which he'd recognized as significant, and so on, slide after slide of what looked to be a mundane collection of bits of tools and the like, but were described as second only to Solomon's treasures. Finally it ended. Benjamin concluded with a bow, seeming to take no notice of the restrained applause. We remained in our seats as our tablemates bid us *adieu* and the audience thinned out. I felt disappointed in light of what I'd anticipated learning, not to mention my initial impression of Benjamin Carter. The evening dampened my belief in synchronicity and a conviction that "all things work together for good."

"What did you think of his talk?" Eric kept his voice low.

"It pretty much followed our English translation..." I lowered my voice as I leaned in to Eric. "Except for the addition of hubris, emphasizing that Benjamin Carter knows more about the Cathars than anyone, has unearthed more Cathar relics than his colleagues, and will soon announce his latest bombshell discovery."

"I figured the 'bombshell' bit out," Eric whispered. "But given such an announcement, I was surprised at how tepid the applause seemed."

"Having overhead our table mates, I rather expected such neutrality." His frown made me question my comment, until I caught his slight nod and turned to discover our speaker approaching.

Eric held out his hand, glancing down at his English translation. "Congratulations, Benjamin. Although I only read the translation of your speech, I thought it most provocative and was intrigued by your 'bombshell' comment."

"Yes, yes." He seemed preoccupied. "It took me a while to deal with the photographers and reporters backstage. About time the local paper had some real news to announce." Benjamin smiled and nodded to the few persons remaining before turning back to us. "You weren't too daunted, I trust."

"Not at all," I said, omitting any knowledge of French. "Your notes in English proved invaluable." I turned to Eric. "I concur with Eric as to the audience's interest in your reference to announcing a dramatic new discovery. Any chance we can get a sneak preview?"

"A preview?" His manner became rigidly professional, his words revealing his scholarly reproof. "Any disclosure prior to the announcement would be out of the question, Mademoiselle Palmer."

Benjamin turned from me to Eric, his tone suddenly "hail fellow well met." "Let's discuss it over a drink, old man. Where are you staying?"

"Hotel des Remparts Ancienne." Eric looked at me, his smile accompanying my nod as he said, "By all means, please join us for a nightcap."

"Very well, I shall." Benjamin looked down at his watch. "Let's be off. I have exactly one hour before I must return to Toulouse."

As we walked back to the hotel, I couldn't help but wonder why we were the beneficiaries of his valuable hour. Maybe I'd make some sense of it over drinks, I thought, as we headed for a dark corner of the bar. Benjamin scanned the room, empty except for a couple of voluble German tourists. I figured such privacy would please Benjamin. But his expression held the letdown of a prom queen after the ball. .

Benjamin turned his attention toward me as the waiter left with our drink order. "As for your earlier question, I trust you understand that professional strictures make me unable to discuss any important discovery until after I've announced it, which shall be next week at the World Forum of Anthropologists and Archaeologists." His dark eyes remained unmoving. Deep as a well at midnight, they seemed to be draining light from mine. "However, since Evie arrives next week, I invite you to stay at my home and attend my presentation." He slowly turned to Eric. "If it's a coup for your series you're after, Albi, next Saturday, is the place to be."

"How gracious of you to invite us." Eric's imitation of Benjamin's hauteur had me biting my cheek as he continued. "We'd be honored, old chap. But, as to our arrival in Toulouse, we do have a full schedule ahead." I smiled as Eric glanced at *his* watch. "I'll have to get back to you. Next Wednesday at three."

The waiter arrived with our drinks. Just in time, I thought, rushing to camouflage my grin with, "Eric's right, Cathar country calls. We have much to explore to do justice to our series." I raised my glass. "To our series."

Benjamin gave a token touch with his glass, avoiding drinking as he responded. "You'll not find much for your series in the sentimental tales of castle caretakers." His voice held a peculiar blend of derision and curiosity. "What exactly is the focus of your series, Taylor?"

Eric drained the dregs from his glass before replying. *"Our* intent is to understand why such a strong resurgence of interest in the Cathars seven hundred years later. That entails not just castle tours, but examining tales of Cathar treasure."

"Treasure!" Benjamin let out an explosive burst of contempt. "A lot of romantic hogwash is what it is. But a good way to make money out of these ruins. A ragtag bunch of religious zealots is what they were, standing in the way of the King and the Pope's plans. Their death left little to posterity except…" Benjamin moved his hand to encompass the room, "this Disneyland in armor."

Eric winked, as he looked my way. "So Dana, seems there's little for us to discover." He turned back to Benjamin. "A pity, old chap. We looked forward to meeting the castle caretakers. Their museums seem rich in background data."

A subtle snort dismissed such a rash idea, as Benjamin set us straight. "As to discoveries, you'll quickly find all roads lead to me. When you weary of Cathar fantasy and arrive in Toulouse, I'll take you on a tour of my lab." He lifted his glass, downing it in one long swallow as he motioned for the check. "Such a visit, along with my Albi announcement, will add substance to your series." He glanced at his watch as the waiter approached. "I must be on my way."

Eric took the check the waiter extended. "You're our guest. I insist."

"Thank you. I shall expect to reciprocate soon." Benjamin stood and held out his card. "Call me with your arrival plans."

When I was certain he was out of earshot, I turned to Eric. "Why so eager to have us, I wonder? Especially since he hates Cathars and ridicules our approach."

"'Eager' isn't the word—'insistent,' I'd say." Eric reached into his jacket pocket and spread out our itinerary alongside a map. "Let's review our schedule. I suspect we'll find precious little time available to enjoy Mr. Carter's company. Tomorrow we head for the Abbey Fontfroide, with maybe a Cathar castle or two on the way to our hotel." He looked around, pulling a tragic face. "Farewell to Carcassonne and Viscount Trencaval." He watched as I examined our map.

I sighed as I began to trace our route down through the department of Aude into the Corbieres. "It shouldn't take us more than an hour or so to drive there." My finger halted as it approached a large circle of emptiness surrounding our destination, Chateau de Lumiere. "Hmm. Wonder what our accommodations will be like."

"A *gite,* it says." Eric frowned.

"That could be anything from basic bed and breakfast to..." I shrugged as he gave a sigh and resumed his survey of our hotel's full bar and modern conveniences.

His expression was transparent in its appeal. "Maybe we should remain here for another day."

"You're not serious?" I asked. "We've got a lot of territory to cover, and I've filmed every corner of La Cite. So—off we go." I lifted my glass. "To our success in the *Pays de Cathare.*"

"I'm not sure how many more signs saying 'The Land of the Cathars' I can stomach," Eric said as his wry grin widened. "Benjamin may be right in terms of their demise being the best thing for the economy of this area."

I ignored the bait. "So it's agreed, we leave Carcassonne in the morning." I pulled the map over between us, pointing out our route. "But not Trencaval territory, not for another couple of days anyway." I traced our route to the bottom of the Department of Aude, nearly into Spain. "Even the castle of Queribus, so far south, had strong ties with the Trencavals, so strong that it served as a sanctuary for Cathars as well as many *faidit* lords."

"I read about them last night—defeated lords exiled from their castles." Eric looked quizzical as he continued. "Seems you should be writing this article. You've picked up a lot of knowledge about this area."

I hesitated, my thoughts running with, Why not? Who more qualified than someone who has read, seen, felt, lived, breathed and dreamt Cathars? Better me than someone who might not honor them, I thought trying to gauge his strange stare. Its steadiness pierced my reverie, prompting a strained laugh as I responded, "All part of the job. I try to put myself in the picture, excuse the pun." His silence escalated my nervous prattle. "You see, this area represents more than just its setting." I couldn't curb my fervor. "In Cathar times, its lords embraced, not only art, music and poetry, but never had there been a society so openly inclusive of other cultures and religions, including the Cathars."

"Hold on there. Proselytizing goes beyond our pact to remain objective." His grin stretched a bit too wide, I thought as he reached over to pat my hand. "Coffee?"

"No thanks." Not coffee, and not condescension, I thought as I stood up. "I want a solid night's sleep, and I've yet to pack. Until tomorrow." My swift turn prompted a look of puzzlement on Eric's face and hid the absence of a smile on mine.

Stopping for my room key, I was annoyed to learn that the concierge was off for the night and there was no sign of my developed film. Even as I entered my room, and as inviting as my bed remained, sleep didn't come easily. My thoughts struggled with balancing the normal concerns of a professional on assignment with the Languedoc's increasingly powerful undercurrents. Wondering what approach Eric intended, I fell into fitful dreams filled with images of a deck of cards, their colorful characters clearly from the past. They seemed familiar, and yet as enigmatic as a Tarot deck in the message they tried to convey. I awoke with a start, alarmed as one of them flew up in my face— the Fool—the Joker? No! The Wild Card, I thought as I tried to make out the grinning face.

SIX

Mirepoix, France-June 1242

Clotilde pulled the coverlet up over her shoulders. Its easy movement betrayed the absence of Jean. She flung back the blanket and sat upright. Staring into the sharp light of morning, she remembered that Jean rose early to ride out and escort their special guest.

Rumors were rippling throughout the countryside. Clotilde saw evidence of the esteem with which Cathars from the surrounding villages held their visitor. The town had redoubled as many Cathars arrived in Mirepoix to await the renowned Parfaite, Fabrisse d'Arles. She had left Foix yesterday, sending word that she would break journey at Mirepoix and stay with Clotilde and Jean.

The crowds assembled in their courtyard sounded like a beehive, Clotilde thought, as murmuring sounds of heightened excitement and anxiety penetrated her closed shutters. So much depended on Fabrisse, Clotilde thought. With close family ties to both the Count of Toulouse and the Count of Foix, Fabrisse's advice would erase conjecture and bring what all Cathars sought— clarity as to their most crucial concern: should they remain, or flee to the safe haven of Montsegur?

Clotilde stared around her room. She loved her home, she thought, as a chilling awareness engulfed her. Not only did the crowd below, but she and Jean as well, resisted leaving their homes. She'd heard of many that had left to take refuge in the

47

labyrinth of caves in the Ariege region or traveled on toward remote villages in Spain. But those in Mirepoix had long clung to hope, believing that their Lord, Pierre Roger de Mirepoix—a favorite of the Count of Toulouse—would assure their safety.

Such complacency had been replaced by anxiety at news of the slaughter of the two inquisitors. Clotilde reviewed their choices, unconvinced of the wisdom of departing. Any lingering doubts would be assuaged if Fabrisse assured them that Montsegur, sitting on the top of its five hundred-foot pog, would provide safety.

"Thus far it had—but for how much longer?" Clotilde's murmured question prompted a fluttering in her stomach as she lowered her legs over the high bed. As she stood upright, a ray of sun targeted her, illuminating an insight—that the key lay not in Montsegur's strength, but in that of the Count of Toulouse.

The sound of hoofbeats filled the air. Clotilde threw open the shutters and peered down into the courtyard area. Many Cathar neighbors stared up at the opened window, their eagerness for Fabrisse's arrival transparent in their faces. Her welcome smile wavered as she recalled Jean's comment and drew back.

She withdrew into the privacy of her room, an image of Jean returning, along with his somber tones as he'd reached to douse the candles. He'd seemed mesmerized by the fire, giving voice to his thought with as much reluctance as taking a tong to a rotted tooth. "Capturing Fabrisse would be a real coup for the royal armies."

His words had poisoned her rest. She suspected her moans had alerted Jean to her fearful wakefulness. Feeling his arm draw her near, she burrowed deep within the shelter of his shoulder. "Rest assured, my love, no harm will befall Fabrisse." His hands had moved to all the familiar places, stroking, soothing and murmuring soft words to ease. "I shall guide her safely into Mirepoix."

Clotilde let out a long sigh at the memory of last night's sudden passion. She closed her eyes, recalling the extraordinary intensity of their first coupling since the loss of their child. An element of wild urgency had engulfed them. Its fierceness had eclipsed fear as it exploded all emotions into one ecstatic sensory burst. Such release opened them to a night of sharing their fears over what lie ahead. Jean had surprised her with his willingness to admit to the graveness of the situation. And yet he had rushed his reassurance that they would prevail through whatever the future held. "Light will vanquish dark," he'd said, his words lulling her into an exhausted sleep.

"Jean," she spoke his name as an incantation that all would go well, taking comfort in his strength. From the moment they met, she'd felt safe. His stance seemed securely wedded to the earth, his eyes direct, movements swift and honor impeccable. Nothing could deflect his commitments. Fabrisse would be safe.

Clotilde turned away from the window. Excitement at her guest's arrival quickened her movements. *Their* arrival, she remembered suddenly, the thought warming her as much as the simple tunic she drew over her too thin limbs.

How could she have forgotten that, not one, but two important friends would arrive today? Jean's early departure wasn't to intercept Fabrisse's party—which would come later in the day—but to escort their first guest, her dear sister, Blanche de Grissole-Auries. A messenger had arrived late last night with notice that his mistress would arrive early the following morning. Clotilde's excitement was mixed with confusion as she'd asked Jean how he could escort both Blanche and Fabrisse.

"Coeur de Lyon has carried me on much longer day's journeys," he'd replied. "I need only guide Blanche and Fabrisse their last few kilometers into Mirepoix. Never fear, I'll be back with Blanche with ample time to escort Fabrisse."

Anticipation at seeing Blanche engulfed her. Sister, mother, friend—Blanche had filled all these roles after their mother died. Mother Marie's last words still rang in her ears. "You and Blanche...must...stay together."

It had been so long since last they'd been together. As she held her baby, stillborn in the sixth month, Clotilde had yearned for long, sisterly talk. But Jean had cautioned her that little opportunity for private discussions, even of such topics as herbs or spiritual studies, would prove likely. "*Not* discuss spiritual matters," she replied, stunned. If Fabrisse—the head of the largest group of Cathar women Parfaites—had no time for spiritual discussion, surely the worst of times had arrived.

Apprehension clouded her joy as she tucked her long auburn curls tightly under her wimple and made her way down to the kitchen. The long wooden table, bearing only the remains of last night's candles, told her Jean had left without eating. Clotilde ran through the entry, nearly colliding with three elderly women who were sunning themselves by the door as they indulged in excited gossip. About to ask after her maidservant, Bernadette, she heard her voice and saw her approach.

"Madame. I stopped to see if my lazy lout of a brother caught all the fish that we'd need." She grinned with pleasure. "He has caught enough to feed the village!"

"Very good." Clotilde's tone beamed appreciation.

Bernadette lowered her voice as they stepped around the three women and entered the house. "Madame, I swear every soul in the village is in our courtyard awaiting Fabrisse, except…" Her voice faded. "Except for Pierre, the old bell ringer. He's vanished, Madame. Rumor has it he joined others in the forest."

" Many are making such a choice." Clotilde took Bernadette's heavy basket, smiling to deflect her own sorrow. "We must trust in God's guidance and prepare a special meal for our guests. These are lovely vegetables you've gathered."

"Broad beans, turnips, cabbage—more than enough to accompany our fish." Warming to Clotilde's smile, Bernadette added, "I spread the linens to air. Our guest's bedding will smell of sunlight and lavender."

"You have prepared well." Clotilde reached toward the hook near the kitchen door. Taking down a heavy woolen shawl and a basket for herbs, she paused. "I shan't be long. I'm hoping to find some basil and celery seed—and anything else you think we may need."

"Perhaps some fresh vervain for a restful brew for our guests. Meanwhile, I'll start the oven warming for the bread-baking." Bernadette ran into the kitchen, returning with a jagged half loaf of bread and a bright red apple. "Here, take this. You'll need a bit of nourishment climbing up to the meadow."

Clotilde smiled and tucked Bernadette's offering in her apron pocket. "Our guests will be pleased, as am I, with your loving contributions." Bernadette's cheeks flamed with pride as Clotilde headed out the door. She skillfully bypassed the crowds at the rear of her house.

The town square of Mirepoix seemed strangely abandoned; all had flocked to await Fabrisse's arrival. Clotilde's glance lingered on the square's two-storied buildings, topped with half-timbered houses extending over shops below. Their rosy brick façadess were accented in the highest corners with intricate carvings of beasts and birds. A prosperous town, Mirepoix nestled secure at the foot of the Pyrenean mountains, the River Hers shimmering gently in the sunlight.

Knowing how vulnerable Mirepoix was, Clotilde fixed this vision in her memory. So many Cathars had settled in the area to be near the several large houses dedicated to the training of men as Cathar Parfaits, and women as Cathar Parfaites. Even the Lord of the town, Pierre Roger de Mirepoix, although not a Cathar believer, had family members who were. Hurrying through one of the exits in the solid town walls, Clotilde headed for the mountain slopes, reviewing the herbs likely to be growing this time of year. She smiled as she recalled Blanche teaching her their uses.

She chanted at each step, "Blanche is coming. Blanche is coming." So much had happened since last they'd been together. Stopping to catch her breath, Clotilde sat beneath a shady tree and let images of that dramatic time rush in.

It began when Blanche announced the arrival of her cousin, Jean-Armand de Mirepoix. His visit to the village of Grissolles had been unexpected. A virulent fever had forced him to seek refuge before riding on. His destination was Toulouse, where he would undergo—after years of study—the ritual of becoming a Cathar Parfait. His stay extended to six weeks.

Clotilde sighed. Memories rushed in of Jean's fever-racked body, as he lay within tiny sleeping quarters. Her hands still held the memory of their gentle strokes against his heated forehead. Her eyes sent healing energy to him as she prepared cool cloths. Her ears stayed alert for each breath, as she lay wide-awake on the floor alongside his bed. Her heart repeated a prayer for his survival. As he recovered some strength, she marveled at the sound of his voice, the gentle wisdom in his warm gray-blue eyes that followed her every movement. The memory sent a shiver through her.

She would never forget the heartache she'd felt as he described his mission. Knowing that his decision to become a Parfait would mean a life of celibacy, of walking in pairs with his fellow 'socio,' bound to the faith forever, filled her with sorrow. His commitment to sharing God's light with others would put him forever away from her touch. She listened, feeling her desolation deepen as he described how excited he was to soon take the consolomentum and become a Cathar Parfait. "I have renounced all passion except for love of God."

His emphatic words had stunned her, but no less than her reply. "Then perhaps we shall join as sister and brother in the faith." When she spoke the words she'd felt a calm certainty that, whatever his choice, she would never leave him.

"God willing," he'd replied. Days slipped into weeks as the magnetic pull of a different kind of love proved irresistible. She recalled their fierce mix of joy and shame as an all-consuming passion united them. "Forever," she'd whispered.

"Forever," he'd repeated—his tone suddenly solemn. "Long have I given my life to my father and his estate. Now, in my fortieth year, with the estate bequeathed to my capable elder brother, I am free to serve the One Father of us all." His voice had filled with bewilderment. "To renounce physical love for love of God."

Night and day they had grappled with love of God versus love of one another. Finally, after days of fasting and prayer, Jean had delivered his conclusion in a voice firm with conviction. "My beloved Clotilde, we both seek to grow spiritually and someday become Parfait and Parfaite. But for now, as Believers, we shall wed, and if God wills, in time evolve beyond the physical. Meanwhile, God has surely joined us and blesses the destiny of our union. Wherever our destiny leads us, know that I love you and always will, beyond body and time—now and forever."

A deep sigh escaped as she recalled the mix of joy and sadness she'd felt the moment he was recovered enough for them to ride off together. The echo of Mother Marie's deathbed message and the look on Blanche's face at Clotilde's departure, made her feel as wrenched as Solomon's baby. Her parting words felt as hollow as they must have sounded to Blanche. "Dear Blanche, our love knows no separation."

A bird alighted on a bough in front of her, singing with repeated trills of what she chose to interpret as reassurance. She stood and stretched, happiness rekindled in anticipation of seeing Blanche—Madame Aruie. Shortly after she and Jean rode away, Blanche had married the widower, Arnaud Aruie.

Her glance seemed brighter as she spotted delicate stalks of wild asparagus hiding beneath the overgrown grasses. She placed them in her basket, pleased at the fresh delicacy of one more vegetable. Although fish was acceptable, Fabrisse consumed no animal flesh, eggs, nor milk.

Climbing up to a flat section of high meadow, she discovered a large bush of vervain with low growing comfrey sheltering beneath. Encouraged by her success, she was so focused on celery and basil that she nearly missed a fat cluster of mushrooms sheltering beneath some rotted tree limbs. "Such a bounty for our weary visitors," she said as she set her basket in the shade of a tree and walked to an overlook to scan the approach to Mirepoix. A veil of dust appeared in the distance, expanding as it neared. As it dispersed she made out Jean's horse guiding that of Blanche's and one other rider.

Her lean legs flew, bronze hair blowing all undone as she ran with the unfettered energy of her twenty-two years. Before the riders had tied up their horses at the stables, Clotilde leaped at them, too breathless for any greeting except a wild embrace that sought to capture both Blanche and Jean in her outstretched arms.

"Did I raise you to pounce, then, instead of curtsey?" The tears of joy that filled Blanche's eyes belied her words as she held Clotilde at a distance. "How thin you are. Never mind, my barley stew will fatten you up. You've grown so tall."

"It's the pride I feel in having you visit." Clotilde curtsied just long enough to exhibit a residue of manners before flinging herself back into an enfolding embrace.

"Come now, my love, restrain yourself." Jean said. "There will be time, after all, for the two of you to share your hearts." Jean's look was tender, his tone indulgent as he smiled at them. "Blanche tells me we shall have her under our roof for several days. Her manservant will unload her goods. Let us go inside." Jean offered his arm.

Clotilde settled Blanche onto the bench alongside the table while Bernadette offered a steaming tankard of warm mead to accompany the bread and soup she'd prepared. Blanche sipped her drink, leaving her food untouched.

A worried look covered her face as she turned to Clotilde. "It is so good to be together again." A glistening film formed as she looked away to address Jean. "How long I shall stay depends on Fabrisse's return from Montsegur. I'm prepared to honor her counsel and that of my dear husband, Arnaud, in respect to joining him at Montsegur." She pointed to the quantity of goods her manservant had placed inside the entryway. "As you can see." She turned from her belongings and stared at Jean, her voice firm. "What think you of the situation in Montsegur?"

Jean hesitated, as a look from Clotilde cautioned gentleness from one she loved toward another she loved. He cleared his throat. "I think Fabrisse's arrival will provide the guidance we need."

Clotilde rushed to close that avenue of conversation. "Meanwhile, you must be hungry from your travels, dear

Blanche." She extended a bowl. "Do try this lovely soup Bernadette has prepared."

Blanche remained silent as she sipped, politely but desultorily, at her soup. After a few moments, she pushed it away and, with even greater intensity, returned her focus to Jean. "Indulge me, please. Surely a siege will prove fruitless. Montsegur is impregnable." She studied Jean closely, his face unreadable, his silence endless. "Why do they persecute us so?" Her voice grew in volume as she turned to Clotilde. "Those sheltering within Montsegur couldn't possibly pose any threat to the Pope, don't you agree?"

Clotilde moved to her side and took her hand. "Dear Blanche, I know your fears for your husband. Have faith in his safety. You shall soon be together." Feeling Blanche's stiffness grow, Clotilde pressed on. "Remember that which you taught me. It is God's will working through all."

Blanche's attempt to control her mouth's slight tremble couldn't disguise the fact that her shoulders had hunched forward as if to shield her. "I trust he shan't abandon us."

Clotilde studied Blanche, appalled at what she only now let into her awareness. Blanche's once cornflower blue eyes had faded, their sparkle lost, the hand that grasped hers was corrugated by a sinewy straining of veins, its arm betraying flesh drawn inexorably by gravity. Gone was the smile that dominated her memories of the rotund, ruddy-faced sister that lived in her heart. In its place was a look of bitterness and fear. Clotilde pressed her hand and drew her gently upwards. "Forgive me, dear sister. In my excitement I failed to notice your tiredness. Let me show you to your sleeping quarters." Clotilde turned to Bernadette. "Please bring an infusion of vervain for our guest."

Blanche went upstairs willingly and lay down. Even before the tray appeared, she was asleep. Clotilde stepped quietly from the room, motioning Bernadette to silence. As Bernadette hurried off to her kitchen, Clotilde fell into Jean's outstretched arms.

"I know, my love. Our Blanche is sorely worried." Jean's voice fell. "As well she should be."

His words alarmed her, but no less than his look. Clotilde stepped back and stared at him. Her opaqueness with Blanche still fresh in her mind, she willed herself to notice just how much Jean had aged these past months. Although nearly twenty years her senior, his youthful vigor was equal to those half his age. When had his face turned ashen and lined? His once thick honey-blond hair, now streaked with gray, hung dank and lifeless.

She stood tall, willing her strength to infuse him as she spoke. "Surely the Pope will relent the raping, stoning and throwing of good Christians onto the fire. God cannot let such barbarism prevail."

Jean's silent stare curdled her conviction. "But if it should continue..." she spoke softly. "How long can Montsegur endure?"

Jean drew her over to the table. "Sit, my love. To understand we must look to the Counts of Toulouse, Carcassonne and Foix. Everything depends on their willingness for active resistance. United they could come to the aid of the Cathars sheltering within the fortress of Montsegur."

Clotilde felt her spirits rise. "Of course. What word have you?"

"Mixed. Fabrisse's account of the reaction from the Count of Foix should lend clarity." Jean stood, squaring his shoulders as he walked toward the doorway. "I must make ready to ride out and escort Fabrisse's retinue."

"But you've not eaten," she said. Before she could turn with a loaf of bread and a handful of figs, he was gone.

Burying her emotions in an obsessive frenzy of bread making failed to erase the air of depression that lingered. Only when she was pummeling the bread dough on its second rising did she remember that, in her rush to greet Blanche, she'd left her herbs on the mountainside. She put the completed loaves into the oven, asked Bernadette to monitor them, cautioned quiet so Blanche could sleep, and left.

Clotilde retraced her morning route, moving swiftly up the mountain to the overlook where she saw her abandoned basket. As she headed back she came to a small clearing that allowed for peering out in the direction of Foix. Straining her eyes, she saw a growing cloud of dust from a group of horses riding toward Mirepoix. "Fabrisse." She mouthed the name reverently as she quickened her return. Halfway down the mountainside, she stopped, shocked at the sudden cessation of hoof beats. Looking down, she noticed the horses and riders halt. Clotilde puzzled at an order to stop when so near their destination. Drawing back into the shelter of trees, she watched, trying unsuccessfully to identify Jean among them. One of the riders made a sudden motion to urge the others on. Two remained—the rider who urged them on and one other.

55

Clotilde let out a gasp as they rode toward her. At a steady canter, they headed for a rise leading into the forest where she stood. Clotilde gave a start as she recognized Jean's horse, Coeur de Lyon. She peered intently, shocked as Jean grasped the bridle of the other rider and turned both horses away from the route to Mirepoix. From the other rider's stance on horseback, straight and firm, gray hair escaping its coif, she knew it must be Fabrisse. But it simply couldn't be. She knew that Cathar Parfaits and Parfaites always traveled in pairs, just as Christ's disciples did. Nothing could cause such an unthinkable breach of custom.

She stifled an urge to rush down to them as their approach—a furtive turning, seeking, watching—halted her. They're going toward the fairy mound, she thought in alarm as she waffled between hurrying back to town or remaining to see if they were really heading for a place so feared by all. She herself would never have ventured near the strange outcrop had it not been for a wayward goat leading her there. Once having experienced the calm of its sanctuary, she'd lost her fear, delighting in her discovery of a little cave hidden just beyond the oval outcropping. A deep-seated sense of safety drew her to return to it as a place to meditate. Her childhood legacy resurfaced now, as quiet as a deer, she made her way toward her sanctuary. Feeling a mixture of fear and foolishness, she hid as they approached.

Fabrisse's faint voice reached her ears. She could only make out a few of the words. The solemn intensity of Jean's tones frightened her.

"I promise...keep hidden." Jean's strange vow frightened her. He uttered it with a fierce fervor beyond any that mere words could convey.

Fabrisse's reply stunned her. "*Must* keep hidden—until world's end."

SEVEN

Aude, France, May-Present

I felt grateful that Eric was so absorbed in his driving as we drove away from Carcassonne. My desire to capture the Cathars via my photographs had been thrown an unexpected curve. My hands still shook from the simple act of accepting a packet of developed film.

Earlier Eric had gone to bring the car around and load our luggage while I checked us out of the hotel. The concierge, presenting a large packet, apologized for not getting my film to me sooner. Impatient to have a look, I rifled through, searching for the photos of the mysterious man who had headed into the nonexistent corner.

I gasped, thrown into a tailspin when, indisputably, there was a man—or at least the eerie shadow of a man's face. Soft focus, as if filmed through a spider web, the features of Raymond-Roger Trencaval stared back from another world, his expression anxious. The shot I'd taken through the window slit was blurred, the photo only faintly having captured the outline of a man lying crouched within.

My mind raced, uncertain as to showing them to Eric. I glanced at him, his jaw rigid as he navigated carefully through the traffic streaming toward the toll road. No, I decided. At this point I can't trust his reaction, let alone deal with my own shock at conjuring the dead so graphically.

His abrupt yank on the steering wheel shook me out of my reverie. I gave a stifled yelp, leaning away from what felt like a certain collision.

"Look, Dana, you navigate, I drive," Eric said, as he caught my look. His hand moved to rub the back of his neck.

"OK. Then I say we bypass the toll road and try the country roads." When he didn't react, I added, "Look—you're not in a hurry to get to Chateau de Lumiere and I can't enjoy the landscape at a hundred miles an hour."

"Fine by me. So navigate, we're nearly on top of it."

I glanced up to see the fast-moving super-highway ahead. The *autoroute de deux mers,* which ran the breadth of Southern France, from sea to sea, would soon suck us into its flow. I checked our map for an alternate route and designated town.

"Look for a sign saying D3-Lagrasse," I yelled just as we approached the busy roundabout. Both of us strained to make out a D3 sign. It suddenly appeared, reassuringly highlighted by the word "Lagrasse." A sudden swing looped us onto a country road, serenely empty of all but local traffic.

"Damned if I didn't think we'd be doomed to this bloody mess all day." Eric let out a breath as he glanced my way, a glint of his boyish gleam in place. He turned to read a sign we just passed. *"Cave Cooperative-vente et dugustation."*

"The hotel clerk was right," I said as I looked to see if I could spot the *cave* advertised. "According to him, our route through the Corbieres is lined with *caves*—collectives of the local growers' wines. He says the Corbieres' wines are among the best in France." I stared down the road. "That suggests good restaurants nearby."

Eric looked doubtful. "Ten kilometers away from Carcassonne and we could be headed for the other side of the moon."

He was right. The terrain was fast changing from the green hills and softness of the Department of Tarn to the elemental rawness of the Department of Aude and the region called the Corbieres. I stared out at the massive hills rising in the distance. Their streaked ribs of white rock looked like the bleak skeletal remains of dinosaurs standing guard over endless fields of grapevines. I felt a stirring of familiarity, a visceral "Yes, here!" emotion of coming home.

"Look up ahead, Eric." We were approaching a village of ancient, rosy pink stone houses, all tumbling along tidy cobbled lanes lying snug in the bright light of approaching noon. Women carrying shopping baskets with crusty loaves protruding strolled by. Old men were playing a game of *boules*. Others watched from the tree-shaded lawns of the town square. All stopped to stare as we passed. I smiled as a young girl opened blue shutters and spread a coverlet in the sun.

"It's perfect," I said as Eric drove into a petrol station.

"Now it is." Eric cut the ignition and opened the door. "I was getting nervous about finding a gas station in these parts."

"Oh," I said, expanding it to an 'Ooh' as I caught sight of the flowering bushes alongside the station. I rushed over and lifted a bough up to my nose. "Lilacs!"

"Lilacs?" Eric's deep guffaw filled the air as he replaced the gas pump in its holder and walked over to where I stood. "I thought you'd found the bloody Cathar treasure." He laughed as I took another deep inhalation.

"I grew up in the Midwest where we had heaps of lilacs in our garden. After we moved to southern California, I…well… I've missed them." I shrugged, feeling happy as I returned to the car.

Eric laughed. "You, my dear colleague, I am beginning to suspect, are more than a bit barmy." He turned as the owner approached with a spray of blossoms and presented them to me. I thanked him as I buried my nose in their scent.

"One for the road, aye." Eric said as we drove toward the outskirts of the village. "Some people drink and some sniff coke—but not you. You sniff lilacs." His broad grin negated his proclamation: "You are hereby put on notice I refuse to stop for every blessed lilac bush." I took another whiff in response, feeling at ease enough to consider the possibility of our becoming friends.

Lagrasse suddenly appeared around the bend, a sign proclaiming, "One of the Most Beautiful Villages in France." Enfolded in a lush valley on the bank of the Orbiere River, a striking abbey facing it on the other side—all affirmed the honor. "Wow! You think we might have a quick look at the abbey?" I asked.

Eric ignored me, his focus on skirting a dog spread comfortably in the middle of the road and not about to relinquish his territory. "Take your pick, this abbey or Fontfroide," he said as he avoided the dog. "One abbey a day is my limit."

I relented, only after deciding that our *gite* wasn't so far afield as to preclude a return to Lagrasse. "Right, Abbey Fontfroide it should be."

"That's my girl." He said, departing Lagrasse a bit too fast if the expression on a villager's face was any indication. Oblivious, Eric said, "Let's have lunch before we reach the Abbey."

Something in his voice puzzled me. "You won't get any argument from me. Coffee and a croissant won't hold me much longer," I said. "I'll look for a café."

Twenty minutes passed. One empty little village with no sign of any restaurants, and baleful glances from Eric, had me leafing through our guidebook. "There's a hotel with a restaurant not too far ahead. Turn left at the next junction and go about six kilometers until you see a sign saying 'Chateau LaRoque.'"

"'Chateau' hmm? Like the *cave de vins,* it's probably not open on Sunday."

"It says, 'A peaceful haven with comfortable rooms, a friendly atmosphere in the restaurant and a relaxing bar situated in the 12th Century wing.'"

The muscles around his mouth noticeably eased. "Open *from?*" he asked as he slowed the car at the turnoff ahead.

"Open from Easter until Oct. Thirty-First. Every day, eight AM until midnight."

"Well then." He gunned the motor of our little car—raising a bit of dust at the turn—surprised after a few miles to see the restaurant. Fifteen minutes and one whiskey later, he began to let down. "Not bad."

I nodded, seduced by the chateau's charming country décor. After a heavy lunch of lamb and asparagus tart, washed down with a wonderful red wine, Eric mellowed. His amiable volubility vanished abruptly, though, as he turned to fetch the waiter and came face to face with a portrait across the room.

"That chap, dressed in medieval outfit, reminds me of the one you claimed spoiled your shot in Carcassonne." He frowned. "Whatever happened to that photo?"

I swallowed hard as I opted for the truth. "The concierge gave me the photos when I checked out this morning." I took the packet out of my camera bag. "I didn't know what to make of them." My hand shook as I extended the photos. "I wanted a closer scrutiny before showing them to you."

He turned to the two I'd left on top, oblivious to the nervous shredding of my napkin. Or so I thought, until he placed his hand on mine. I stared, fixated on the golden sheen of the hairs on the back of his hand, the gentle blend of firm with light that accompanied his touch. I hesitated in looking up, wary of his reaction.

"Well, well," he said. "Such photographic skills should assure us of having an award winning series on our hands." His tone was light, but his look was solemn as he stared at the image. "Seems someone besides International Horizon's Magazine wants the Cathars brought back to life."

I should have felt relieved at his response—and I did. But relief was obscured by a dawning awareness that this assignment meant more than any journalistic accolades. What lay ahead filled me with apprehension at being equal to it.

Eric noticed my sudden slump. "An espresso is what you need." He asked the waiter to bring one espresso and one brandy.

"The experience has thrown me, I admit." My words rang hollowly, my feelings buried as the waiter returned with our drinks.

"You needn't explain. We all handle stress in whatever way works." Eric lifted his glass, savoring its fumes. "My way is plenty of brandy in the brew." He fell silent, finished his drink and asked the waiter for the check. As he scrutinized the tally, I made a mental note to probe for background on my enigmatic colleague.

"Into the breach, well fortified to tackle the abbey." Eric said as he opened the car door with a wink and shoved the guidebook at me. "Read what's in store. I must confess a reluctance to return to my former life."

"Your *former* life..." The book slid off my lap as we drove away. "What do you mean by that?"

"I spent my early years training for the priesthood." His voice was neutral, his eyes fixed on the roadway. "I'd nearly reached the finish line when I couldn't ignore a strong sense of 'buyer's remorse.'"

"What made you turn away?" I listened carefully, aware of how quickly he'd descended into a leaden mood as he continued.

"I was disillusioned, you might say." His tone was bitter. "In the same way the longing to learn is often squelched at school, my search for God's love was stifled in the seminary."

The silence seemed to go on forever as he stared fixedly ahead. "Should we bypass the Abbey Fontfroide?" I asked, my question tentative.

"Not at all." He gave an infinitesimal shrug. "Read on." He turned his attention back to the road as I opened the guidebook to the section on the Abbey.

I knew the Abbey Fontfroide had played an important role in the history of the Cathars, but not one that filled me with anticipation, I thought, as I silently read the description. Almost poetically lush with hyperbole, it claimed Fontfroide as the most beautiful of all classic French abbeys. I read aloud, adding, "Not only was it 'the most beautiful,' but it was rich as Croesus. The abbey had twenty five barns to hold its tribute." I looked over at Eric. "No wonder they didn't want to abandon such sybaritic excess and exterminate heretics." I scanned silently the following paragraphs until I came upon an interesting fact. "Did you know that..." I stopped in mid-sentence. "Maybe you do—as a priest and all—that the abbey was Benedictine before it became Cistercian."

"My studies as a priest didn't include much about abbeys in France," Eric said. "You'd better read what it says."

"The Abbey de Fontfroide was established on property owned by the Counts of Narbonne. It began in 1093 as part of the Benedictine Order but by 1143 had aligned itself with the Cistercian Order and..."

"St Benedict too strict, I suppose." Eric interjected. "Sorry, go on."

I gave him a solemn look and read on. "In 1203 Pope Innocent III named two of the abbey's monks as legates with the mission of eliminating the Cathar heresy. Within the heart of the Cathar country, Fontfroide became a citadel of the Catholic Orthodox Church." I murmured a damning aside. "The center-post for immolation."

"Not good press for my erstwhile chosen career, I must say." Eric said, smiling to hide overtones of bitterness. "But not news to me. It's part of why I decided that orthodox religion had little to emulate and much to censure."

I caught the cynicism in his voice, wondering how such deep disillusionment shaped a career in writing. "So you went into journalism?" I asked.

"And therein lies a tale, but..." He nodded past me, glancing out the window at a sign saying, '*Abbaye Frontfroid, 3 kilometres.*' "One best saved for later."

Hmm, I thought, seems my partner's mysteries were beginning to equal my own. I put my questions aside as entered the long drive leading to the abbey. I had to admit it was beautiful. Warm rose and ochre shades of sandstone were perfectly offset by masses of tall cypress trees and a reverent stillness in the air. We parked by the entry and followed a mixed group of French and English tourists. Accepting a brochure in English, we skirted the large tour group to see the abbey on our own. It didn't take us long to read the brochure, leaving us at leisure to examine each area.

I found the Abbey strangely unmoving, chalking it up to its postcard sterility having erased all energies other than that of tourists. I took a brief look at its twelfth century Gothic Church before leaving Eric to the study of its faded effigies. I returned to the cloister gardens, opened the guidebook and revisited the part about Pierre de Castlenau. His assassination in 1208, reputedly at the instigation of Raymond the VI, Count of Toulouse, prompted the Pope to call for an official crusade against the Cathars. I closed the book, aware that it wasn't the last time horrors were to be visited on the Cathars due to the hubris of the lords of Toulouse and the zeal of the Abbaye de Fontfroide's Brothers. Feeling my remove fading, I shot a series of photographs, my emotions gratefully shielded behind the lens.

Satisfied with the garden shots, I headed back to the entrance, making my way to the ruins that I'd noticed just inside the entry. Barely discernable remains of a much earlier church were eclipsed by the Abbey's elegant architecture. The guidebook said the ruins of this earlier church dated back to the Romans and the Visigoths. A different energy, I thought as I captured it on film. At the end of the roll I put my camera away, sat down on a weathered outcrop, and waited for Eric.

"I guessed I'd find you here. Not impressed, I'd say."

"Yes and no, mostly I'm ready to get to our gite." I studied him. "And you?"

"Yes and no. But in a different way." He looked over at our car. "And not strongly enough to elaborate upon at this point. Let's press on."

We doubled-back, heading for the village of Durban, signs indicating castle ruins to the right and left of us. Eric turned after we passed one. "We're in the heart of the Cathar country, all right. Anything interesting in Durban?"

"Durban has a castle, but..." I stared down at my unopened guidebook.

"You stopped." Eric glanced out the window. "Did you see something?"

"Not exactly." A prickly sensation ran along my arms at knowing, without reading, about Durban's castle.

"Well then, is it Durban that bores you?"

"Just the opposite. I was thinking that we should take it slow. This area's covered with castles."

He stared into the distance. "Right you are. Look—ruins—up there."

"You have eagle eyes, *mon chauffeur.* "

"We make a good team, navigator. Do tell, were those ruins a castle or a shepherd's hut?"

I looked back before answering. "Hard to say, so little remains. My guess is castle, since it's on the highest hilltop."

Eric brightened at his success, keeping one eye on the road and one on the hills. He was the first to spot Durban's castle ruins rising in the distance. We deliberated when a sign indicated our destination was away from Durban.

"Durban's close enough to come back to." Eric's reassurance touched me, as did his genial indication of not only every pile of suspicious rocks, but also lilac bushes along the way. An easy rapport had begun as we neared Chateau de Lumiere.

Certainly the arrival at our *gite* boded well for such harmony. It was situated in a cluster of brightly colored cottages set within the courtyard of a stately old chateau at the far corner of a miniscule village. A woman rushed over as we parked.

"Monsieur Taylor and Mademoiselle Palmer?" The woman rushed on in surprisingly good English. "I am Camille, Madame Villar's assistant. Madame wishes me to say how sorry she is to be unable to greet you. She went to visit family over the Easter holidays and her return was delayed by the tempest." She halted. "Ooh la la, it was, how you call it, so terrible a storm! But Madame should return tomorrow. Now, please follow me. Your rooms are ready."

Eric looked pleasantly surprised as we approached our rooms. Formerly grape pickers' dwellings, the two-storied structure was horseshoe shaped, surrounding a large inner courtyard dotted with gracefully positioned tables and chairs tucked beside beds of daisies and daffodils. Each little attached bungalow was painted in vivid Mediterranean hues. Rose-covered doorways, natural terra cotta tiled floors and massive fireplaces prompted sighs as we toured each other's quarters.

Eric gave a trial bounce on the big bed while I admired the deep bathtub. "Oh my God, it even has heated towel racks!" I said.

He pointed to the bedside table. "Forget towel racks. Look—modern telephones!" As we walked down from the upper level to the kitchen-living room area, I spotted a large wicker basket covered with a checked cloth. I lifted it carefully. "Wow. This care package is surely out of *Elegant Gourmet*."

Eric examined each item: coffee, tea, chocolates, wine and all the makings of dinner for our first night. "Get a look at that," he said as he turned me toward the fireplace. I gasped at the huge bouquet of roses and lilacs.

He went to his quarters to unpack while I assembled dinner a *deaux* on the terrace. In no time I was raising my glass to Eric's. "To our hostess, to Madeline. What an incredibly creative woman." He nodded, lost in savoring the wine as I admired the sunset's slanting rays highlighting our table. Satiated with vegetable tart, *paté de fois gras* and wine, I looked at Eric and said, "Not half bad."

He grinned as he washed down a bit of baguette spread with *paté de foie gras.* "Carcassonne would have to go some to top this, I admit."

I stared at the light hitting lush lavender blooms bursting from bright ceramic pots. "It's all too perfect, a bit over the top in generosity, I'd say."

Eric divided the remaining wine between our two glasses. "It may have more to do with practicality. I didn't notice any restaurants for miles. Anyway, we'll have a chance to thank our hostess soon. I found a note inviting us to dinner."

"Hmm." I looked over at the main house. "Perhaps you're right," I said, studying his look of deep contentment as he gazed at our cottage doors, their top halves open to the cooling breeze.

"Whatever her reasons," he said, "if this is any example of the Cathar universe, I may never leave."

I smiled to disguise my nervousness. "When do I get to read how you're shaping that universe?"

His smile broadened. "Right you are. You were brave enough to unveil your photos. The least I can do is reciprocate. What say we do a swap, I'll bring over the draft of the opening segment of the series in exchange for the rest of your photos."

"Of course I'm willing, although they aren't culled through as yet. But I'd love to read what you've written." I gave a slight shiver.

"Hey, you're cold. It's cool after the sun goes down." He stood and drew back my chair. "Let's head in. I'll get a fire started and drop chapter one off for you."

A short time later he returned, one arm extending a plastic folder neatly enclosing a sheaf of papers, the other offering a basket of twigs.

I placed his manuscript on the table while he got the fire going. "That should hold it," he said, grinning at the fire's robust crackling.

I gingerly handed him my photos of Carcassonne. "Take care to put them back in the same order." I softened my protectiveness. "There are some notes as well."

"Not to worry. I've learned how to handle photos, edges only and with a great deal of open-mindedness." His look didn't match the lightness of his words as he halted at the doorway. "Mind you try to do the same. *Bonne nuit*, Dana."

I sat by the fire long after he'd gone, staring at the two photos I'd held back, the man's expression haunting me. I sighed as a flood of feelings broke through. What does it mean, I wondered? I laid them aside, hoping to shake my melancholy by turning my attention to Eric's folder. I hesitated, the sight of the pages stirring thoughts of Eric, which blended into thoughts of Alex. Reluctant to exhume the pain of Alex, my focus returned to Eric. I took the folder and walked upstairs.

From the opening paragraph I felt stunned, my indignation increasing as I read on, looking for something more than what read like a strong indictment against the Cathars. I couldn't believe his biased slant, especially from someone who cautioned me to objectivity. Unable to continue, I put the manuscript on my bedside table. Wide awake, I got up and tried to outpace my sense of betrayal—of the Cathars and of me. Taking a slow breath, I returned to rereading the opening, hoping to find my response overly skewed by my own bias.

"The resurgence of interest in Catharism is prompted by a belief that its followers were Christian and therefore ill-used by Catholicism. An in-depth study of the facts will examine such reasoning, showing that the heresy of Catharism provoked an understandable response to a religious sect that flaunted all that was most holy. Marriage, the Sacrament, purgatory, praying for the dead—even the symbol of Christ, the simple cross of his martyrdom, were rejected by a creed that hypnotized the south of France in Medieval times."

I couldn't go on. I put the pages down after another three pages, angry with myself for lowering my guard, and furious with Eric for presenting his poison pen after such a relaxing evening.

Any likelihood of relaxing vanished into restless hours spent trying to fathom how I could ever work with Eric Taylor. I tossed through a night of fitful dreams of bonfires, their flames fed by pages of manuscripts.

Nita Hughes

EIGHT

Mirepoix, France- June 1242

Clotilde remained crouched in the farthest recesses of the cave, her every sense acutely heightened. The wordless silence, broken only by strange sounds, puzzled her. A sudden soft neighing of one of the horses caused her to draw back in alarm, dislodging stones whose rattling noise seemed endless. Fearing she'd betrayed her presence, she froze, hearing only the perplexing sounds. She strained to identify them. Digging, or moving something? She discarded any idea of peering out from her hiding place. One last word reached her ears. "Safe," trailing away seconds before the horses' clomping stride resumed.

As the hoofbeats faded, she crawled out of her hiding place and ran down the hill, darting through thickets of gorse in the shortest line toward Mirepoix. Breathless and burdock-covered, she finally arrived at her house.

"What happened?" Bernadette's voice shook. "Were you being chased?"

"No..." Clotilde slowed her panting, "...wanted to be here...when they arrived." She stopped her futile plucking to remove burrs and strained to listen. "They're coming." She yanked off her torn apron and dashed for her bedchamber.

A splash of water, a clean tunic and five minutes later she returned, face flushed, to greet Jean and Fabrisse as they entered. Clotilde's strained smile swiftly faded at the sight of Fabrisse's thin, haggard look.

"My dear, what a joy to be with you." Fabrisse clasped Clotilde in a warm embrace. An overweening premonition of loss deepened as their embrace intensified. Clotilde shuddered. She'd long believed Fabrisse invincible. Her sudden recall of Fabrisse's actions in the forest turned such certainty upside-down.

Jean hadn't moved his focus on Clotilde's strange look. His smile flashed compassion and caution. "What refreshing repast have you readied, my love?"

"Cool barley water to revive you both." Clotilde motioned to Bernadette who hurried away and returned with a bountifully laden tray. Clotilde led Fabrisse over to the table. "Do try a little bread, some almonds and fig jam."

Fabrisse smiled as she looked from Bernadette to Clotilde. "Thank you both, but nothing for me, dear ones. I'm fasting through this day and wish only to consume myself with prayer and meditation." She settled onto the bench and let her eyes move over the expanse of table, sunlight reflecting its gleam of beeswax. Clotilde followed her gaze to the fresh spring flowers placed throughout the room. Fabrisse's smile widened as she stood and held out open arms as Blanche approached.

"Welcome, Fabrisse." Blanche broke their embrace with reluctance. "Clotilde has prepared the perfect space for your meditations. I've just enjoyed a most restful afternoon there." Clotilde studied Blanche, thinking she did look rested, her smile more like the remembered Blanche. Clotilde marveled that Blanche could contain her emotions in light of Fabrisse's obvious decline.

"My dear Blanche. How happy I was to hear that you were arriving today." Fabrisse's face radiated love as she moved her attention from Blanche to include all. "I ask your forgiveness for absenting myself until dinner time." She turned abruptly, a look of distress overcoming her. "How could I have forgotten those that have gathered to await my arrival? Please excuse me while I go to honor their long vigil and ask their patience a little longer."

"I'll take you to them." Jean gently took Fabrisse's arm.

Clotilde and Bernadette were arranging a tray of water with an infusion of vervain when they returned. Fabrisse's voice held a warm satisfaction as she walked in with Jean. "How generous my brethren are." Fabrisse looked at Jean for agreement. "So many— and all of them insisted that I rest tonight."

"Yes," Jean agreed as he turned to Clotilde. "Content at her having arrived safely, they assured her that one more night would be nothing."

Clotilde reached for Fabrisse's hand. "Come. Let me show you to your bedchamber." Fabrisse went docilely, smiling as they entered the room. "We've placed you and Blanche in the same sleeping chamber with an area of privacy for each." Clotilde motioned toward the draperies that enshrouded a bed placed along the far wall, its counterpart on the opposite end of the room. "Each bed has a washbasin," Clotilde said as she placed the tray alongside it.

Fabrisse sat down on the thick sheepskin coverlet placed atop the bed, stroking its rich softness. "Thank you. This shall do splendidly."

"Do remain at rest throughout the night should you wish." Clotilde said.

"A few hours of rest and prayer will be enough to refresh me." The heaviness of Fabrisse's words distressed Clotilde as she studied her. Gone was the well-fleshed face, replaced by a thin and haggard visage with deep lines etching her forehead. Clotilde bid her goodnight, shielding despair that any amount of rest could restore the Fabrisse she remembered. Clotilde's return was slow, the image of Fabrisse lingering.

Bernadette beamed as Clotilde entered the kitchen. "I've seen to it that Madame Fabrisse's party has received food and water. The villagers are putting up the womenfolk and the men are bedded down in the stables." She ladled her crusty load of bread onto a long wooden table, the room filled with yeasty aromas. "The first ten loaves were devoured." Bernadette's smile glistened with shy pride, her doe-brown curls escaping from the circlet worn by young women, as trails of perspiration ran down her scarlet cheeks.

"Very good, Bernadette. Have my husband and Madame Blanche eaten?"

"The master said he would join you at the evening meal." She motioned outside. "He's at the stables and Madame Blanche went out to take the air."

Clotilde neared the door, suddenly stopping and turning back. "Bernadette, thank you for seeing to Fabrisse's entourage—for everything." She looked over at the bread loaves. "I'm sorry to have been so remiss in replenishing our herbs."

71

Bernadette smiled through a moustache of flour. "My pleasure, Madame. It was no problem. I substituted fennel for the celery seed."

"Clever lass." Clotilde's response widened Bernadette's smile as Clotilde left to make her way to the stables. Horses and wagons filled the area.

"Clotilde!" Blanche's voice caused her to turn. "I've been gathering herbs nearby," Blanche said as she held out a basket filled with sheaves of green and golden grasses. "Some for medicinal use and some for nutrition."

A rush of guilt surfaced as Clotilde remembered the abandoned herbs. Echoes of Jean and Fabrisse's mysterious words at the fairy mound flooded her with confusion. With each passing moment of Jean's silence, her anxiety grew.

As she noticed Blanche's stare, Clotilde responded, "Thank you, Blanche. I'd like to discuss herbs with you, but..."Her voice cracked.

Blanche frowned. "Let's walk," she said, moving Clotilde well away from the activity surrounding the stables before asking, "What grieves you?"

Clotilde glanced back at her home. "Everything. Losing my baby was unbearable. I doubt I shall ever overcome it." She brushed away tears. "I feel besieged by sorrow. Fabrisse is so thin, Jean is so weary—and our fellow Cathars..." She pressed her fist over her eyes. "Are like hunted animals." Well out of range of sight or sound, she asked, "When will such madness end?"

Blanche drew Clotilde within the shade of a tree. "Not in our lifetime, I fear." Blanche's look mirrored the hollowness of her reply, making Clotilde regret voicing her own feelings. As Blanche turned, tears spilled down her cheeks.

Clotilde held Blanche close, shocked that Blanche, her lifetime comforter, was so in need of comfort. "You'll soon be with Arnaud, safe from such madness."

Blanche stared into the distance. "I fear Darkness will extinguish the Light."

As much as Blanche knew Clotilde's every mood, Clotilde knew Blanche's. But not this one. Despair coated Blanche's tones and hardened her stance.

Clotilde's heart filled with compassion as Blanche wiped her tears away and stood. Blanche brushed at her skirts and turned to Clotilde, a semblance of strength returned to her voice. "My dear sister, do permit me a little doubt, a little confusion, and my faith to sometimes be a little shaken." Relief flooded Clotilde as Blanche's features resumed a loving expression. "Let us return now." Blanche lifted her basket of herbs. "A warm infusion of vervain and chamomile will vanquish such gloom."

As they neared the stables, the sight of Jean sent a chill through Clotilde. He ceased the brisk combing of his steed's flanks. "Bernadette asked for Blanche."

Blanche turned to leave. "I shall go and help with the meal." Clotilde waited until the door closed behind Blanche.

"Jean…" Clotilde said, nervous at expressing what she longed to say. Not here and not now, she decided, as she turned away. "I'd best go join them."

Jean's grip spun her around as he guided her into an empty stall. "What is it?"

"That is my question of you, my love." She looked steadfastly into his red rimmed eyes. "What is going on?"

Jean clutched for support at the stable wall. She waited, feeling her world shake as she continued. "We mustn't keep secrets from one another."

Jean's face etched in anguish as he pulled her into his arms. "It is God's secret, not mine, my love. Trust in my love for you and ask naught of me now."

Turning her head away, she spoke, her voice strangulated as she forced the words out. "I wonder if we are not being punished for our love."

Jean tilted her face up to his. "Punished—why would you believe such?"

She spoke slowly. "Ever since our babe's death, I fear we are paying for…" Clotilde halted, the pain, so long choked back, threatened to explode.

"Do continue, my love." Jean's tone prompted a rush of courage. She kept her face aside as she spoke. "I recall your saying that our love is carnal, taking us away from Spirit. Surely God cannot look with favor on such love."

Jean responded with great tenderness. "Love is that which underlies our physical bodies' unity—the unity it remembers from Spirit and yearns for. That we attempt to recall it through copulation is the counterfeit of the real." She heard a faint echo of shame in his voice ease. "As such it can either deceive us deeper into physicality, or awaken us to true union in Spirit. In that fashion it serves ultimately to join us to God." He took her by the shoulders, his look burning into hers. "But until it does, God does not punish us for our love. Do you understand?"

Clotilde surrendered to the warmth of his embrace. "Whatever the truth, I could never bear to lose you." The painful memory of his strange actions on the mountainside returned. She looked up, her gaze filled with questions.

Jean's response was firm. "I cannot say more, my love—not now, perhaps not ever. Listen to your heart for it knows a truth beyond words." His warm embrace loosened with a gentle admonition. "Go now."

She went, losing herself in preparations for the evening meal. As it was nearly ready—Jean having come in to wash up—Fabrisse walked into the kitchen. "My dears, I am fully refreshed now. I must not strain the patience of my fellow Cathars any longer." Her step firm, she headed out the door, Jean and Clotilde following.

As they approached, the crowd rushed their adoratio's, bowing in honor to Fabrisse as she moved amongst them. Her voice was strong as she stepped onto a wooden pallet, her raised form visible to all. "My fellow Cathars, I bring you a message from the Count of Foix. He is deeply concerned at what may lie ahead." A wave of dismay burst like thunder from the crowd, its strength quelled as she lifted her hand and raised her voice for her next words. "The Count, however, wants you to know of his great confidence in the safety of Montsegur." Fabrisse let her gaze move over the crowd as a question broke out, echoed emphatically by all.

"We must know that it is secure enough to safeguard our children."

Clotilde felt both eager for and wary of the reply. "Not only does the Count of Foix express his confidence, but Deacon Clamens and Bishop Marty await you there. They would never expose any one of their flock—surely not children—to Montsegur if they did not have faith that it will provide sanctuary for all."

As Fabrisse described the peaceful Cathar community in Montsegur, a cry went up, "We must go and support them." A groundswell of agreement filled the air as "thank yous" reverberated and the relieved crowd began to disperse.

When all had departed, Jean, Clotilde, Bernard and Fabrisse returned to the house where Bernadette and Blanche were laying out the evening meal. All ate in silence, but for one of them it was an uncommonly pensive silence. Jean leaned in to Clotilde and whispered, "What is wrong with Bernard?" Clotilde shook her head, willing Bernard's sullen truculence to remain contained, as she focused on Fabrisse.

Fabrisse sipped water only, but, in contrast to the others, she radiated joy as she spoke. "My dear friends, you are the blessed family of my soul." Her words carried such solemnity that they roused the old yellow dog from his sleep by the fire. His ears rose erect, his hunting animal stare fixed on Fabrisse.

Clotilde's gaze was equally unmoving as she studied Fabrisse. Her expression should have filled her with peace. Instead it renewed her feelings of foreboding at a destiny that would leave them forever bereft. Fabrisse seemed aware of Clotilde's emotions. "You, dear Clotilde," She turned to include Jean. "And Jean—are so kind to provide for me and my entourage."

"You bring us great honor." Jean's words conveyed a deeper message, as he added, "*Any* service we might provide, is yours."

Clotilde felt discomfited by their exchange, her nervousness evident as she spoke. "I could only wish that your purpose were lighter, dear Fabrisse."

"It is a serious time, my child. I..." Fabrisse's reply was interrupted as Blanche leaped to her feet.

"If death is what you mean by 'serious,' then say so." Blanche looked from Fabrisse to the others, her expression iced in wrath.

Fabrisse stood and held out her hand to Blanche. "Life is serious, not death, my child. Death is the welcomed doorway to God. You must vanquish fear of death by knowing that my soul will never be lost to you." Everyone was raptly fixed on her words. All except Bernard who broke his strange silence.

"I am not ready for death at the hands of the Catholic Church." He glared at Fabrisse. "I say the greater sin is to stand idly by and accept such a fate."

Clotilde watched Jean. His look mirrored hers—shocked disbelief at the virulence in Bernard's voice. Fabrisse remained calm as she responded. "The Church sees our Cathar teachings as a threat which leads the masses away from the Catholic priests. As to standing by—"

"The Catholic priests!" Bernard slammed his fist on the tabletop. Blanche moved near and placed her hand on his.

"Bernard is right." Blanche added her anger to Bernard's. "Everyone knows the Catholic priests are nothing but libertines and drunkards. It's the bonshommes who offer love and service to all—not the priests."

"To *all*." Fabrisse's emphasis resonated as she stared at Blanche and Bernard. "That is the problem." Slowly she turned to the others. "My uncle, the Count of Foix, understands the Catholic Church's larger motive—to absorb for themselves the great wealth and power of the Languedoc. The Church aims to bring this great wealth under the Pope and the King's control by accusing our Counts and Lords of harboring heretics." She lowered her voice. "Thereby subsuming all titles and lands."

Bernard's contemptuous snort again filled the air. Jean moved swiftly to his side, his steely glare leaving his enraged brother mute but unbowed. Clotilde tried to soften the atmosphere with a plea to Fabrisse. "It's difficult to understand why all religions and peoples cannot live peaceably together. How Christ-like can it be to destroy Jews, Gypsies or Cathars—all fellow souls?" A glimmer of understanding dawned. "In eliminating all who differ, they strengthen their own power and wealth."

Fabrisse's voice held vast sadness as she spoke. "You are beginning to see beneath the issue of a peaceful, unified society to that which prevents it—the desire for worldly power. Greed blinds even religion to the reality that all are one." Fabrisse smiled. "And yet Light shall prevail."

"When?" Anger seethed in Bernard's sharp retort.

Fabrisse looked with compassion at Bernard, her words heavy with certainty. "Perhaps not in our lifetime, but a time will come when Light will vanquish Dark."

Blanche's voice chilled the room. "Meanwhile, is death our only reward?"

"Death is of the body only," Fabrisse replied. "Our souls shall return their Light when most needed." Fabrisse's words held such conviction that Clotilde trusted them to heal Blanche's anguish as she reached out her hand and gently touched Blanche's cheek. Fabrisse continued.

"Faith shall see us through this madness, dear sister. This physical world is an illusion of Satan, designed, through fear, to cloud belief and detach us from Spirit."

Clotilde waited, hoping Fabrisse would continue. She had always found the Cathar doctrine of dualism, with Good and Evil, Light and Dark locked in perpetual conflict, a difficult one. Especially perplexing was Satan's dominion over the physical world. Clotilde broke the silence. "Can it be that Evil will prevail?"

Fabrisse chose her words with care. "A good question, my child. Faith is the answer. Faith that God will always prevail though the path be dark." Clotilde felt assured, not so much by the words as by the love and trust radiating from Fabrisse.

A contrite look filled Blanche's face as she turned to Fabrisse. "I've felt so frightened, for myself and for Arnaud." A tear ran down her cheek. "For all I love. I cannot bear they should burn." A gasp rang out at such raw truth filling the air.

Fabrisse clasped Blanche's hand to her heart. "Accept your fear, my dear Blanche, but turn from its illusion. Such fear is far more destructive than any flames."

Whether from Fabrisse's words or from holding her hand on Fabrisse's heart, Blanche's voice held deep calm as she asked, "Can you forgive me?"

"Can we forgive one another?" Fabrisse looked around the table. "That is the question for our prayers." She smiled at Blanche. "You are tired, my friend. Do prepare our bedchamber, for I tire also." Blanche nodded and walked away.

Bernadette had silently moved throughout the meal, filling pewter tankards with cider, removing wooden bowls and replenishing the bread. She now brought in a steaming infusion of vervain and placed it in front of Fabrisse. "Something soothing to take up to your bedchamber. It will take the chill off the night air."

Fabrisse thanked her, but before leaving she went over to stand beside Jean and murmur a message for his ears alone. Clotilde strained at Jean's reply. "Of that you may depend." Clotilde, face tight, walked up to him, her question insistent.

"What have you agreed to?"

"I must leave tomorrow, as soon as Fabrisse is safely on her way."

"Leave?" Clotilde felt her heart begin to race.

Jean's words roused Bernard from the sullen silence he had resumed. He leapt up and assumed a stance of alert readiness beside his brother. "I shall go with you."

"No, my brother." Jean's gaze locked with Bernard's. "I must go alone."

"So! It seems I am no longer needed." Bernard's voice was as cold as ice.

Jean reached his hand to Bernard, deflected as Bernard withdrew, arms clasped firmly across his chest, eyes glowering.

Jean bridged the gap to clasp him on the shoulder. "My mission does not require your strength and action." Jean looked around. "You are needed here."

"Humph—pure pap! You think your brother not good enough." Bernard glared at Jean. "Never has been. The draft horse and the race horse, as our dear father always said." With an abrupt about-face, Bernard walked out the door. Jean made a move to follow, but Fabrisse halted him.

"Leave him, dear Jean. Bernard is overcome with the tension of this time." She lowered her voice, but somehow intensified its power. "Dear Jean and Clotilde. Such outbursts will increase. Remain steadfast. Let nothing and no one come between you. Not now—not ever." Her message would remain indelible.

NINE

Aude, France-May, Present

A shaft of sunlight spotlighted my bed, stirring me to consciousness of the sound of birds and the scent of lilies of the valley. I smiled, for one brief moment content, until I noticed Eric's manuscript. I flung the pillows aside and got out of bed.

Skirting the table with its offending pages, I staggered into the bathroom and poured bubble bath into the tub. Foam grew into mountains of white, while my thoughts shaped various scenarios to explain Eric's motives. The warm water eased my body, but not my confusion. By the time Eric called out his cheerful "Coffee's on," I'd decided to play it cool. Avoiding temptation, I left his manuscript inside.

I opened the door to more bright sunlight, the scent of roses, a table set with juice, jam, bread, and aromatic coffee. Furious that the set director could get it so wrong, I glared, not at the fickle sunshine but at the lines it etched around Eric's eyes as he poured coffee. Conflicted at a surge of empathy, I scowled in rebuttal.

Handing a cup across to me, his look took in my rigidly upright, resisting sitting down, let alone having coffee, stance. "Bad night, eh?"

"Bad night!" My anger eclipsed any decision to play it cool. "How could you? You with your constant 'let's remain objective' crap, writing such etched-in-acid, biased bullshit." I pushed the cup aside and rushed back indoors.

"Hold everything." He followed me though the door, closing it against my shouts. "I'll go—but first hear me out." He looked at me with a mix of exasperation and determination as he proceeded, eyes never leaving mine, intense as those of a lion tamer's. "From your reaction, I take it you didn't finish it."

"Finish it—I was afraid if I did I'd have fed the fire with it!"

He picked up his manuscript where I'd left it, turned to the last page and began to read. "This type of logic was proven to be rank invective of a sort never seen before or since in its inaccuracies and distortions. The Catholic Church needed to destroy these so-called heretics. For many crucial reasons—not the least of which was greed. But there existed a more significant motive than greed, revelations long hidden but critical to the Church's very foundation. Was this the secret Cathar treasure, so damning that it had to be found and destroyed?" He paged down and, with a few etceteras he handed over the last page, his finger pointing to the concluding paragraph, which he read over my shoulder. "This series will present both sides, recreating the drama of one of the most critical periods in the history of religion. The setting, the players, their actions and motives, will be brought to life in an attempt to shed light on the resurgence of interest in the Cathars. Its answer will shock, sadden, enrage, and perhaps renew, the critical spark in humanity that this holocaust so brutally extinguished."

I felt sheepish but defensive as he finished. "That's all well and good, but people reading it may do as I did and put it down in disgust before they get to that."

His look surprised me, seeming to register fully the substance of my remark and ignore its sting. Eric picked up page one and started to read. "Hmm. You might have something at that. With a bit of explanation, I could add a caveat at the opening. Something like: "The following is the official rationale for a bloodbath that saw one group of Christians annihilated by another. This series will provide a broader perspective, examining why a group long exterminated, has suddenly been resurrected." He pulled out a pencil, scribbled a few lines and looked at me. "Given your reaction, I'll need some such prologue to prevent being drawn and quartered."

"I'm sorry. For want of a few more pages..." I looked away.

"Come now." He reached out his hand. "A truce. Our coffee's getting cold."

Breakfast tasted wonderful. Our conversation flowed, hesitantly at first, but eventually as rich and flavorful as the coffee. "What's a good Catholic like me doing picking on the church, you might ask." He stared at a little finch swaying on the rose vine nearby and eyeing our breadcrumbs, hesitating as he continued. "It's not any pent-up childhood issues, or resistance to authority, or unbridled sexuality that turned me away." He chuckled. "Although the latter was a challenge." His look turned serious. "No. In fact I admire many aspects of today's Catholic Church, and can appreciate its value to its practitioners, but..."

I waited as the silence grew.

"I'm trying to put it into words without sounding either too trite or too heavy." He stared off into the distance at the hilltop ruins of a castle. I followed his gaze, remaining silent as I studied him. Beyond the subtle ravages of his physical self or even the charm that cloaked it, I sensed something more. The something was ephemeral but somehow familiar as it floated in the space between us. Familiar how—familiar what? Fleeting familiar, I decided as he resumed speaking.

"All my life I'm been searching for God." He halted, seeming to find it daunting to convey the depths of his search. "I've been drawn to read everything—history, philosophy, other religions, politics—trying to understand the actual experience of God. I came up empty. Even after training for the priesthood and spending years in prayer." He shook his head. "Worse than empty. I found religion and war inextricably connected—both bound up with power and persecution."

"So you became an agnostic."

"Far from it." The irony in his words reminded me of those abandoned lovers use. "I've moved closer to the Sufi's philosophy of God as Love and Light." Eric hesitated. "Or that of the Zen Buddhists."

"Or the Cathars?" My words floated lightly.

"Or the Cathars. Their lives of love and service captivated me." He gave a disparaging shrug. "So Christ-like. Too Christ-like, perhaps. It reminded me of someone who said that if Christ appeared now, he would be killed." His expression shifted to an attempt at lightness. "Nothing like a fierce set-to to open the lines of communication. So tell me—what's drawn *you* to this assignment?"

Whether it was the setting—the sense that everything was off the record and somehow out of time—or his patient look of openness, a look that promised receptivity without judgement, I found myself talking. Revealing not only a complete account of the 'woo-woo' I'd fought to hide, but also my heartbreak over Alex.

"With Alex I thought I'd found the special love I'd always searched for." Eric waited for me to go on. "When Alex was promoted, he bought a new house near Atlanta and asked me to join him. A bad move—he was gone all the time. I sat alone waiting for his phone call. He stopped talking wedding plans and..." I didn't realize that I'd turned away until Eric handed me a tissue.

"You felt sad. I understand."

"Very. For starters, I missed California." I stuffed my emotions under a matter of fact account. "The South felt so foreign—especially since we didn't live in Atlanta, but in a little rural suburb." I gave a wry grin as I tried to notch the atmosphere a tad lighter. "So small that cappuccinos were unknown."

"Poor baby." Eric grinned as he poured us both another cup of coffee. "No cappuccinos."

My nervous laughter threatened to segue into tears. "You got the picture, even if it does make me sound like a prima donna."

"Go on."

"Our house was large and empty. I sat alone, night after night, mourning the exciting job I'd left and resenting my few assignments to photograph antebellum homes. When Alex did come home, he seemed distant or angry. I confronted him, suspecting, but not wanting to believe, that there could be another woman." I blinked away tears. "He denied it, but not even Alex— Mr. Charm himself—could persuade me I was imagining it when an email arrived whose message left nowhere for him to hide—or for me to hope. I couldn't bear it. I left."

Eric's silent stare flustered me. "As a man, you probably find it obvious—if not laughable." I couldn't look up. "My friend, Evie, would agree. She tried to convince me that Alex had undoubtedly been deceitful with many. The Good Riddance ploy—but it hurt so much." I tightened my arms around my chest, folding myself within silence, wishing myself a million miles away, unable to believe the depth of feelings I'd just aired with a stranger. Worse, on a colleague whose confidence in my professionalism I'd doubtless eroded. I attempted to make light of it. "A real basket case, I'm sure you're thinking, enough to have pushed me over the edge into…" I hesitated. "If not a kinder world, at least out of this one."

"I don't buy that." His words startled me. "Matter of fact, I don't buy your retreating anywhere, anyway, anytime—from anything or anyone. I think you're one powerful female who's afraid of where that power might lead." He tilted my chin up. "I think you're here to finish something—or, at least, find out what the something is."

Feeling a jumble of emotions, I said, "If you're right, then I guess we'd better get out and visit a few castles." Eric nodded and in no time we were on our way.

As we drove deeper into the countryside, turning onto a one-lane road, we remained silent, wrapped in a tacit agreement to leave the morning's drama behind. Rounding a turn, evidence of a more riotous drama shocked us out of our reveries.

"That must be the 'tempest' that prevented Madeline's being on hand to greet us," I said, as we paralleled a riverbed lined with uprooted trees.

Eric seemed stunned as I mentioned the housekeeper saying a 13th century bridge had been destroyed by the storm. But, soon after we'd left the storm's evidence behind, he turned his focus to the hilltops. I yelped when a lone car approached at a sharp curve in the road. He swerved, allowing just enough room to pass before he shouted, "Look over there." I looked out and saw a hilltop with a fantasy fairy tale castle.

"Which one is it?" Eric asked. I opened our map of Cathar castles.

"Aguilar. Shall I read?"

"Later, when we reach it."

The castle caught me in its magnetic pull. Rising from the mountain as if organically part of the hilltop, stately poplars added to its vertical reach toward heaven. Awed at the unbelievable construction, I fell silent.

Eric broke my hypnotic stare as he swept our car into a sharp turn, only to screech to a halt at a barrier indicating that the route to the castle was barred. Undaunted, we retraced our route, stopping to ask a gas station attendant if there was another way. *"Non—Alors, Le Tempest."* He shook his head and pointed in the direction of the castle road. I inserted a long distance lens and took several shots.

With one last look we headed for the next castle on our itinerary, Queribus. Our route took us through the tiny village of

Padern. Scantily populated, our guidebook indicated it had castle ruins and a church that dated back to the Romans.

"Since we couldn't reach Aguilar, maybe we should stop at Padern."

Eric seemed not to hear me. "My God, Dana—look at that!" Eric pulled the car to the side of the road, reached for his notebook and began taking notes of the impossible image in the distance, while I captured the amazing structure on film.

"Queribus." My voice reflected incredulity. The mountain thrust its bold magnificence skyward, seeming to grow outcroppings of buildings, lifting one vast stone tower so high that its broad ramparts shimmered in the clouds.

"Now I understand why Queribus was the last castle to be conquered." Eric said. "I read about it last night. From the top you can see as far as Peyrepertuse Castle on one side, to the Mediterranean Sea on the other."

I continued shooting, awed by its message of enduring resilience. If one shot of one castle could convey the power of that time, this one will, I thought as I held my hand steady to capture the ray of sunlight striking the tower, as if highlighting the Divine Light it sought. Stunned, I put my camera down and turned to Eric.

"Beats me how they got building materials up to such a site, let alone water and foodstuffs," Eric said, mirroring my own amazement.

"*Formidable,*' as the French say," I said, as we drove on.

Eric gasped as we rounded a curve that brought the castle closer. "Anyone who thinks the medieval times were archaic should try to recreate this subdivision in the sky." Our car labored up the tortuous, winding incline that halted one-third of the way up the mountain.

We parked near a tourist kiosk, bought our pass and began our ascent on foot. Getting to Queribus was more formidable than imagined. Half way up the tortuous climb I halted, out of breath. "My calves don't know what hit them."

"Lucky for them that we won't get to Montsegur for a few more days. It's even higher." He seemed scarcely winded as he handed me a bottle of water and reached to carry my camera gear. Finally we reached the top, paused to catch our breath, and stared mesmerized at southeast France and northeast Spain below.

Our walk through the castle's ruins was undertaken in silence. Satisfied after shooting two rolls of film and noticing that Eric had ceased his note taking, we agreed that we had captured the essence of Queribus. With one last look at its proud splendor, we made our way back.

Near the parking area, we found a perfect picnic site. Eric broke open our picnic basket and spread out the mini-feast I'd fixed earlier. Raising a glass of wine he said, "OK, I want your impressions, and I don't mean photographic."

"In a word, 'awed,'" I said as I looked up at Queribus. "But as far as any strange feelings, I felt none." I hesitated before adding, "Well, maybe a little. Some sort of power, but more as a pull toward *them*—not specifically to Queribus itself. Mostly I felt deep sadness and immense respect."

"I understood why the Cathars that escaped from Montsegur were headed for Queribus with their treasure. Had they made it..." He looked perplexed as he gazed up at the phantasmagoria. Shaking his head, he continued—his tone awed. "Suffice it to say, this Cathar castle has me hooked."

"I know," I replied. "But the castle isn't truly Cathar." I gazed out at the surrounding valley. "The lords of the castles sheltered the Cathars because the lords, most Believers themselves, had family members high in the Cathar church." Melancholy filled me. "Because of the Cathar vows of poverty, nothing physical remains of them."

Eric nodded. He poured us both more wine, touched his glass to mine, and raised it upward toward the castle. "A toast to their spirit which remains—and to reverence for what they lived—not what they owned."

I proposed another. "A toast to our success in bringing them back to life."

We packed the remains of our lunch and drove toward our next castle, Peyrepertuse. My last comment had served as a reminder to ask Eric about his remark when we first met. "You said this assignment means a lot to you."

"Everything." He kept his eyes on the road, staring as though what lay ahead was the outcome he most desired, doubted and feared. "Not just everything in terms of my writing career—but that too. As for the writing, this is the most important assignment I've ever tackled. If it turns out well, I intend to expand it to a book." He took a deep breath. "But the greater importance is harder to put into words."

He fell silent, staring down the empty road until we rounded a bend and met with a stray group of cows meandering their way across our path. They milled around our car, definitely focusing us on the here and now. Eric inched the car forward to avoid a cow and her calf. Once clear, Eric sighed. "Now, how about our next stop?"

After I'd read him an account of the height, size and importance of Peyrepertuse, Eric glanced at the clock. "It's two thirty already. Time to reach an agreement on our castle visits—quality versus quantity? I vote quality."

He seemed surprised when I didn't offer resistance. "I'm satisfied that Queribus spoke for its neighbor, Peyrepertuse." I said as its ruins loomed in the distance. "A drive-by should suffice."

Eric laughed. "I venture to say your calves had some input to that decision." We stopped long enough to admire Peyrepertuse, an exceptional structure that gave the appearance of a gigantic ship stretched across the mountaintop. The castle's length was comprised of two castles connected by elegant curving walls containing spacious living quarters, a church and a vast reception room for the entertaining of knights and lords. Even in ruins, it conveyed its grandeur.

As we drove past, the echoes of troubadours ballads were almost audible on the cool Spring air, their ghostly refrain sounding an elegy to a vanished society.

"OK navigator, I'm counting on you for the quick route back to our *gite*," Eric said as he looked at the clock. "Our dinner invitation is at eight and it's nearly five."

"Let's try a different route." I said, holding the map to find an alternate. "This takes us by some gorges and Durfort and Termes castles."

"I'm game," Eric said, turning at the next junction. We soon were passing the Galamus gorges, amazed at the engineering feat that created the road. It clung to a steep hillside perched over rushing water in deep ravines. Our route became slower and more tortuous than expected. As we neared the turnoff to Durfort and Termes castles, he glanced at our time and opted to press on. "Not much left of them, but we should find Villerouge-Termenes Castle viewable. It sits right on the flatlands."

"I know we should see it," I said. "But I'd like to take a few shots from here for now, and, since it was the place where the last Cathar was burned, leave it for last." I felt I could hardly breathe.

"Righto, then. Get your shots and we'll drive on." Eric studied my expression. "You don't have to even think about it until then."

I buried myself in my professional role, taking a half dozen shots before I repacked the camera, climbed in the car and slammed the door. Eric drove on, silent until we made our turn toward the village of our gite. "You OK, Dana?"

"I think so. I feel more rational anyway."

Eric laughed. "Rational—your feelings. Right."

"Alex always told me to attack my emotions with rationality."

"Hmm." Eric studied my expression. "You haven't mentioned what Alex thought of your Cathar passion."

"He thought—rationally of course—that it was my overactive imagination." I looked away. "Mostly he didn't very much care. His focus was elsewhere."

"That's the worse kind of 'irreconcilable difference,' married or not. I should know. I was married for three years after I left the seminary."

My surprise showed in my voice. "*You* were married?"

"Yes, and happily at first. She was my first love." He stared blindly as we retraced our morning's route alongside the path of the storm. His jaw clenched as if to stifle the pain that filled his eyes. "Peggy was the stereotypical dream girl—blond, thin and vivacious. She seemed to dote on me, at least for the first year or so."

"And then?" I spoke softly, feeling the fragility of his account.

"And then I discovered all the many layers beneath what we call love. I discovered that Peggy had a pattern of being a victim. I should have known. As a member of St. Stephen's parish, she was often described as tragic—which I discounted." Eric looked over at me with the same look I must have given him earlier. I remained silent, my gaze neutral.

"With my priest's training, I thought I could help her change that pattern. But no matter how I treated her, I couldn't get beyond her distrust of men. She'd learned early in life to control it with seduction. It was that which finished us up."

His knuckles whitened as he gripped the steering wheel. "I came by her office one day to surprise her for lunch. As I pulled into the parking garage, I saw a parking space next to her van." His voice lowered, choked with anguish. "It was like a vivid, painfully slow-motion nightmare. I felt dizzy as I watched her van shake and heard voices. I stared through the windscreen, through her legs and the legs of the guy on top of her." He gave a sardonic laugh. "It turns out he was just one of several colleagues that she had seduced with her tragic little girl act."

"I'm sorry."

"I'm the one who's sorry—and it isn't over Peggy. Her life remains unchanged—tragic, if not monstrous." He turned toward me with a look mixed with bitterness and shame. "I'm over the anger. But I seem unable to cure myself of the quest to know Love. Love of God seems more illusive than ever. I gave up thinking that love of a woman might be the path." He looked away. "But I can't seem to relinquish my compulsive search for that which I no longer believe exists."

The rawness of his truth silenced me. My impressions of him as a dissolute charmer, who diluted his failures with alcohol, faded. I looked away, choosing to focus on the wreckage left in the wake of the tempest. It was only as we neared our gite that he spoke. "Thanks for hearing my confession. I promise to be more circumspect in future." His voice was lighter than his look.

"No need to apologize. We both needed to clear the air." I hesitated as we pulled into the drive. "Eric—don't chalk this up as airy-fairy but I feel…" I halted.

"You feel irrational, I hope—as did I." He reached over and took my hand with a gesture that urged me to agree.

"Irrational maybe, but I feel compelled to add something. Hear me out." I continued slowly. "It has to do with love—the love the Cathars knew—maybe even the love you're searching for. Something is here that's prompting us to let go of everything *not* love—of fear, anger, whatever blockages that have created a society on the brink of destruction." I felt sheepish, took a deep breath and muttered "'Nuff said," as I sprang from the car and headed for the shelter of my little cottage.

Eric halted me at the door. "Right then. I'll come by in twenty minutes or so and we'll head on over to meet our hostess." I closed the door, feeling a rush of relief at the thought of being in the company of the urbane and rational French.

The evening began with such promise. We entered to a babble of animated conversations in several languages, French and English predominating. The cozy dining room greeted us with heavenly scents. Our hostess, Madeline Villar, was the epitome of French charm as she greeted us with effusive kisses. A woman of a certain age, she nevertheless had kept her girlhood—in her laugh, the way she used her fine-boned hands to describe something—certainly the practiced way she would reach out to touch someone—flirtatious, but in a harmless way.

I studied her in admiration. She held her pixyish blond head at an angle, smiling encouragement, her accent enchanting as she stumbled through English. Sophisticated definitely, but with a *joie de vivre* I found captivating. And from the grin on Eric's face, so did he.

After pouring us a glass of wine—"From our own grapes"— she rushed to retrieve Madame Vorshenko's sweater and, with perfect etiquette, extended them a parting gift of a bottle of wine and bonbons as she bid them farewell. She reentered the house, cheeks bright with the chill of the night air.

"I am so sorry to be away when you arrive." She rushed to explain. "My daughter, Celine, she is on Easter holidays from university in Toulouse. We go to visit her *grand-mere* in Albi. *Apres nous, le deluge.*" Her laugh was that of a surprised child. "The heavens poured. But I am here now and your dinner awaits."

Dinner was superb, attested to by our wholehearted focus on each course. Having finished a delectable soufflé, Madeline escorted us back into the living room and poured us an aperitif. "Ah, Mademoiselle Dana. About your email of your Cathar project," she reached for my hand. "I am so excited to receive it. My roots are in Occitania's Cathar world. You will discover it is still very much alive here." Her excitement intensified as she turned to Eric. "Tell me of your project."

"I am a writer and Dana is the photographer for a series on the Cathars. Our magazine wants us to discover why the resurgence of interest in this heretical sect."

I watched her eyebrows lift and her look briefly darken before she responded. "'Heretical sect'—or the keepers of a Light that the world needs now?" She reached for the decanter, her tone light, as she turned to pour. "A topic that surely calls for a refill." She raised her glass. "To your success." After a moment of silence, she looked from me back to Eric. "Do tell me of your journeys."

"We're moving west for now, in the direction of Montsegur, with perhaps a stop along the way at Rennes le Chateau," Eric said.

"Montsegur but of course. Rennes, perhaps." She lowered her voice. "But it is Coustaussa, Rennes' neighbor, which may compel you. And perhaps I may persuade you as to why." She motioned to a low table facing the fireplace as she drew a chair closer to the fire. "Do come sit here, Dana, nearer to me." She eased me into its plush corners and reached for a bottle. "Armagnac. You must try it."

Whether from the heat of sitting so close to the fire, or the warmth of the Armagnac, I began to perspire—so much so that I shed my black cardigan sweater.

Madame Villar had just turned from pouring Eric *un petit verre*, just one small glass. One more than he needs, I thought, as she stopped, the decanter nearly falling from her hand. The other hand moved to her heart as her eyes fixed on my throat. Slowly replacing the decanter, she stared. "Where did you get your necklace?"

I hesitated, inhibited by her intensity. "It was my grandmother's. I always loved it, so she left it to me in her will." I lifted the chain for her closer look at its faint design of a cross within a circle, etched in common metal, with a dove on its reverse. "It's been in our family forever," I said, confused as Madeline lifted it and turned every corner to her gaze. I darted Eric a mystified look.

Madame Villar, still grasping the chain, looked up at me. "Your grandmother's name is?"

"*Was*—'Plante' with an 'e.'" I smiled at the memory of the tiny lady I adored. "She shortened it on arriving in America, saying 'Plant' was easier than Plantangenet. My grandfather shortened De LaSalle to Dissell, and 'Palmer' was the Americanization of my father's name, 'Palmier.'" I felt uneasy as I prattled on, "I never knew that until my Aunt Phillipa, who traced our family tree, gave me a copy."

Madeline reluctantly broke her rigid focus on my necklace as she asked, "Did your grandmother, or your aunt, give you anything else?"

Disturbed at her question's intensity, I racked my mind. "No."

"This family tree—do you have it with you?"

"With me? No, of course not. Anyway, the genealogy ended with the thirteenth century and…" I stopped as she released her hold.

Madeline gave one of her coy looks, taking a sip from her glass of Armagnac before saying, "I find family history fascinating." Her easy charm resumed as she added, "Perhaps you have some roots of your tree here." A deep laugh escaped. "Such a funny expression, 'tree.' If you provide this tree, I can perhaps search further for you." She waited for my response.

"I'll email it when I return home" seemed to satisfy her as she turned from me to Eric and said, "And now back to your journey. I recommend Coustaussa because of its importance to the Cathars as a castle offering refuge."

"Interesting," Eric responded, "but I read that little remains of the castle."

"True, Monsieur Taylor. But it is not just the ruins that speak. Before you reach Coustaussa, you will pass through Arques. There a man, very wise about Cathars, will tell you more." Her voice added sparkle as she spoke his name. "Pierre de Lahille. I mentioned your series and he is most eager to meet with you."

"*Two* experts on Cathars in one week!" Eric exclaimed as he turned to Madeline. "Perhaps Monsieur de Lahille works with Benjamin Carter."

Her sparkle dimmed. "Benjamin Carter—you know him?"

I rushed to reply, "He is a friend of a good friend of mine. My friend arranged for us to attend Dr. Carter's lecture in Carcassonne. He mentioned an upcoming announcement of his important new discovery about the Cathars."

Madeline's expression suggested we'd committed more than just an unpardonable gaffe. With a fearful look, she returned her gaze to my necklace. "I trust you did not show him your necklace."

I recalled the strange look Benjamin had given me. "He may have noticed it."

"My dear child, I know we have just met, but I ask your indulgence." She rose abruptly, her gamine stature suddenly imposing. Gone was the coquette, and in its place a voice, a tone and a look that commanded attention. "Mr. Carter is making a name for himself, but not for his efforts on behalf of the Cathars." She took a deep breath. "I cannot say more. Monsieur de Lahille will explain." Before either Eric or I could respond, she stretched out her hand, lifted my necklace to her lips, and said, "Meanwhile, you *must* put this in a safe place where *no one*—especially Benjamin Carter—can observe it." The hairs on the back of my neck prickled as she turned.

"My dear Monsieur Taylor, one more toast." She held her glass high, the solemnity in the atmosphere deepening as she waited for us to raise our glasses. "May your Cathar quest reveal all you seek." A loud snap of flaming wood exploded from the fireplace as we touched our glasses.

Nita Hughes

TEN

Mirepoix, France-April, 1243

Clotilde stopped her hasty movements, aware of the anxious beat of her heart. She frowned as she remembered how it had seemed to cease its beat the moment Fabrisse and Jean had ridden away—Fabrisse to Montreal and Jean to an undisclosed destination. Jean's recent return restored it, but it hadn't breached their impasse.

She slid a tray of bread loaves into the oven before heading upstairs for her self-imposed sentinel duty. She shivered as she opened the shutters. The breeze seemed to have originated in the frigid North, reluctant to give way to spring. Her gaze settled on her lilac bushes, their massive blooms bowing under the weight of the winds. I must pick them, Clotilde thought as she watched the roses, jonquils and poppies ride the winds with cheeky challenge. The distant hills drew her attention as she stared along the path Blanche had taken to gather herbs, moving on to the hills, skirting the rooftops, and fastening on the path from the town square. She leaned out, hoping to catch sight of Bernadette, who had gone to fill the water jugs. No sign of anyone, and still too early for Jean's return.

As Jean prepared to leave this morning there was less strain in his face, even some anticipation at intercepting Bernard. She contrasted his ease with the intensity of his earlier journey, its enigmatic destination still undisclosed. When she asked, his reply was always the same, "I must fulfill my promise to complete an agreement."

He'd withdrawn, his steely determination visible in his erect stance, his shoulders squared, his sentences abrupt. Such fierce resolve highlighted the deep lines in his forehead, exposed by the rapid withdrawal of his once-abundant locks. Her pain at his empty answers took on an added dimension of concern for him.

She recalled how he had fought his instinct to reach for her by turning away, uttering words that widened their breach. "Cease questioning that which I am not at liberty to reveal."

Silenced, she had accepted his declaration as broaching no alternative. Bernard did not. No sooner had Jean's words left his mouth, Bernard rushed into the room looking like a wild boar that had just felt the thrust of a lance. Clearly eavesdropping, he repeated Jean's "not at liberty to reveal" remark with a sneer, slamming his fist into the wall with such force that it sent a metal goblet ringing to the floor. As he lunged at Jean, Clotilde's cry rang out, silenced only as Bernard kept on going, out the door.

Jean's reaction had stunned Clotilde. "Let him go. He'll be all right once he has nursed his wound." Without another word, he walked away.

Clotilde drew the shutters closed as a sigh escaped. She still remained certain that Jean's mysterious departure had to do with his rendezvous with Fabrisse at the fairy mound. Her own wound to nurse lay in her inability to confess that she had overheard them. She was poised to mention it just before Bernard's outburst and Jean's hasty departure. His only words had been, "I should return within ten days."

She recalled how every minute of every one of the nine days it had taken, she moved as a sleepwalker. Not even when his horse's hoofbeats, so familiar in her imagination as each day passed, had stopped at the stable, did her numbness lessen. For, as his body lowered itself from his horse—intact, although weary beyond picturing—she'd run into the arms of a man whose homecoming brought him no joy.

Clotilde sat on their bed, stroking the wool coverlet as if to erase these four nights since his return. Nights once devoted to lovemaking were filled with Jean's angry thrashing through restless dreams, rising in anger at having dozed. His alarm, as he pleaded with her to tell him what he had said, was relentless in eroding any closeness once shared.

Only yesterday did she brighten as Jean became animated on learning that Bernard was returning. He had shown no alarm when told his brother had vanished soon after his own departure. Today's news that Bernard was seen riding from the direction of Fanjeaux prompted Jean to intercept him.

Soon they should return, Clotilde thought, as she stood up and smoothed out the bed surface, saying a silent prayer that the brothers return reunited. She prayed for a greater miracle—of something that would reunite her and Jean.

Splashing a bit of water on her face, Clotilde tucked her hair beneath its wimple, tore off her flour-covered apron and walked downstairs. She removed the last of the bread from the oven, wrapped herself in a light cloak and headed out the door. As she stared she saw a puff of dust in the distance. As the cloud grew near, Clotilde could make out the large figure of Bernard. Blanche must have seen him also, she thought, catching sight of Blanche running headlong down the hillside, her skirts flying in the wind.

Clotilde puzzled over one rider, not two. Where was Jean? A chill shook her at the memory of Bernard's curse as he rode away, nearly a fortnight ago. His fury unabated, he said, "Go without me, will he. He'll live to rue his action." Never would she tell Jean of the threat, but fear filled her at Bernard's arriving alone.

Clotilde walked over to the stables to await Bernard and Blanche. Her brow furrowed, remembering how strangely Blanche had reacted to Bernard's words. Ignoring the threat, Blanche declared that Bernard had a more important mission of his own in Fanjeaux. Clotilde was shocked as Blanche added, "Let us see which brother returns with real information."

When no rider appeared, Clotilde approached a stable-hand. "Has Master Bernard ridden through?"

"No M'lady, although I heard a horse and rider approaching." He pointed to an open stall door. "I've even readied fresh straw for the beast."

"Very good," Clotilde said, deciding to walk in the direction that Bernard would have to come. Nearly at a run, she exited the town walls, crested a slight rise and stopped at the sight of a familiar horse grazing peacefully. Bernard and Blanche stood nearby, lost in animated discussion.

The strangeness of their action turned Clotilde away. Hoping she'd not been seen, she retraced her route home. It seemed ages before the sound of horse's hoofs resumed, increasing their volume up to and into the stall the stableman had readied. Clotilde fought to hold her curiosity in check as she headed for the stables.

She found Bernard splashing his dust-caked face with water from the trough. But no sign of Blanche. Her look must have betrayed her puzzlement. Bernard swept her in an embrace, saying, "I've news to wipe the worry from your brow, dear sister."

Clotilde replied. "I'm eager to hear, but where is Jean? He rode to meet you."

"He'll make his way soon enough on his own, I'll wager." The absence of the word "brother," as well as the bitterness in his tone, stunned her. He had to repeat his bigger concern. "I'm starving, I said."

"Sorry, of course. Let's move into the house where I've fresh bread and drink." Bernard reached the house well ahead of her, leaving her time to glance back for some sign of Jean, or even the sight of Blanche—to no avail.

Bernard had gone directly to the cooking area. "Bernadette," he shouted, "I smell your bread. But it's taste this tired man needs. Bernadette?"

"She went to replenish our water," Clotilde remembered, about to add, "and Blanche is…" but held her words in check. She gave Bernard a sidelong look as she handed him a loaf of bread and waited for him to inquire about Blanche's whereabouts. Bernard remained fixed on the bread he was shoving into his mouth.

Clotilde went to the larder for cheese and fruit. Adding a bit of cold fish from last night's meal, she placed the dish in front of him. She returned for three more, one for Blanche, one for herself, and a third in the hope that Jean would soon arrive.

Bernard reached for another slab of cheese, scarcely glancing up as Clotilde said, "Blanche is gathering herbs and should return shortly."

"I'm too hungry to wait for the king himself. I will, however, hold my news until she joins us." He tore another chunk of bread, slapped the cheese atop it and shoved it into his mouth.

Clotilde had just refilled his plate when Blanche and Bernadette entered. Bernadette, balancing two jugs of water, said, "Blanche helped deliver our water supply, Madame." She turned as Blanche followed with a third water jug. Clotilde felt a rush of relief at the obvious. Blanche had remembered that Bernadette had gone to fetch water, and decided to help her. Clotilde ladled food onto their plates as Blanche sat alongside Bernard and gave him a rare smile. He kept on eating.

"How good to have you safely back, Bernard. How was your journey?" Blanche's question baffled Clotilde, their tête-à-tête still fresh in her mind.

"Tiresome, long, and not altogether safe," he said, turning from Blanche to Clotilde, "but newsworthy." He took a long swallow of tea before he continued, speaking with uncommon hesitancy. "A full report of my news must await Jean's arrival." A sneer preceded his next words, "as it concerns him."

Clotilde longed for Jean to walk in the door and dispel her deepening confusion. She stared as Bernard poured freely of the mead, downing each refilled goblet without pause. Wiping his cracked lips with the sleeve of his tunic, he met their questioning stares. "But this much I can say. My journey revealed many villages empty of Cathars. Toulouse was a mix of smug conviction that Raymond VII was invincible, and growing doubt as they waited for word of the Pope's actions." Blanche sighed and put her hand on his. "You may take heart, dear Blanche. All Cathars are confident that God and Montsegur will protect them." Bernard rose, stretched and yawned. "Anything more must wait. I'm weary."

"Of course, Bernard." Clotilde walked to the stairway. "As to sleeping, I..."

Blanche approached. "Please, sister, my little bed is perfect for Bernard." She turned to him. "Come, Bernard. Let me show you to my sleeping quarters."

"I accept. But wake me when Jean arrives." Together they vanished up the stairway.

"If you don't need me, Madame, I'll run along home." Clotilde turned at Bernadette's leaden words. Head turned away, body slumped against the table, Bernadette choked as she added, "My mum's poorly."

"Dear Bernadette." Clotilde took her hand. "Of course you must go to her. Do take her some bread and soup."

Bernadette stood, tears flowing, and with no move for soup, ran out the door.

Clotilde was shocked by her lack of awareness of Bernadette's grief. Overcome by so much that she could not deal with, she forced herself to busywork, putting away the goblets and adding kindling to the fire. As she grabbed the beeswax and began a brisk polishing of the long wooden table, a sudden storm began. The fierceness of its lashings intensified her anxiety for Jean. Her

97

mindless polishing ceased as a shadow fell across the table. "Jean?" Her heart raced as she spun around.

"No my dear, it is I." Blanche's gaze fastened on Clotilde. Her recent smiles had been replaced so completely as to have been a dream. Clotilde stared. How absorbed she must have been, she thought, not to notice the changes in Blanche.

Blanche's usual high color had drained away, her plumpness no longer peach-ripe, her light-brown hair, streaked with gray, straggled from her wimple. Clotilde felt a sudden stab of sorrow that her sister could have aged so quickly.

Blanche took the beeswax from Clotilde, assuming the manner she'd always used to stay her little sister's impulsiveness. "Whatever work remains to be done, we shall do together." Blanche said. "All will be in order." Her repetition of the phrase matched her stare as it took in the room, as though for the first time—or the last. "There is naught to fear as long as we remain together, dear Clotilde." Blanche said, drawing Clotilde into a too-strong embrace. She broke it to hold her at a little distance and examine her. "Those ribs poking through your tunic, do say you've not continued your fast."

"No, dear Blanche. Yesterday saw its end."

"And fortunate it did. I've made us a lovely tart with the last of autumn's apples." She took Clotilde by the hand. "Do come share a little portion with me." Blanche called out, "Bernadette, please join us."

"Bernadette left for home. Her mother is ill."

"Oh, dear, village gossip says Bernadette's mother's time is near." Blanche words lingered as she left to fetch the apple tart.

Clotilde followed, suddenly feeling her weariness. She sat beside the fire, inhaling the warmth of the aromatic chestnut wood and letting the scent of apple tart trigger a long-withheld response from her salivary glands.

Blanche poured out a warm mug of cider and offered it to Clotilde, saying softly, "Rest now, Jean will return soon." Clotilde was moved by her concern.

"Forgive me, Blanche. I've been so self-absorbed that I've forgotten your worry." Clotilde embraced her. "Your dear husband has so long been away. But soon now you shall be together."

Silence hung in the air as Clotilde studied Blanche. Oblivious, a blend of emotions washed over Blanche's features, making them almost grotesque. Her blank stare sent a sudden fear through

Clotilde. As she spoke, Blanche's tone was bleak, her words heavy, "Whatever comes, I must join my husband."

Clotilde put her arms around her. "Yes, and Montsegur, with its head in the heavens, will surely protect us all."

The door swung open, ushering in a blast of cold, wet air and a bedraggled Bernadette. Clotilde rushed to her. "Bernadette! What is it?"

"You must help me." Bernadette grabbed Clotilde's outstretched arms as she renewed her entreaties. "It's mother. Her dying wish is for a Parfait and the consolomentum." Bernadette's tears began to flow. "I must find them."

"Sit here." Clotilde drew Bernadette over to the fire.

Immobile, her anxious gaze remained on Clotilde. "Help me, Mistress."

"Have no fear." Clotilde turned. "I will go to the weaver's cottage and find those whom you seek. Have a hot drink and return home, where I shall join you. God willing, not alone."

"Let me accompany you." Blanche said. "Or Bernard."

"No, Blanche." Clotilde said, "Stay here in case he wakens. I'll go."

"I must go back." Bernadette pushed the goblet away.

Clotilde threw a dry cloak over Bernadette, swaddled herself in another and both hurried out the door. At the road's first forking, Bernadette hastened toward her mother's cottage. Clotilde bore away to the left and the weaver's settlement. Within the half-hour, three figures moved silently toward the home of Madame Rives. Two men, one quite young, the other much older, accompanied Clotilde.

Clotilde looked at their gaunt forms, enshrouded not in the usual dark blue hooded cloaks of their order, but in the less conspicuous, brown tunics of weavers. Clotilde hesitated to undertake the ritual of the adoratio, a simple bow in honor of their holiness. It was unsafe these days and risked exposing them.

Bernadette's mother's hut was of basic thatch construction, known by the familiar Occitan name as an *ostal*. Its strength was more than mud and wattle, its warmth that of pride of ownership, its few worldly possessions, treasured. As Clotilde and the Perfecti entered, they found Bernadette on her knees in prayer. Her face shone with relief. "Thank you, Madame—and you, dear brethren." Safe indoors, Bernadette and Clotilde undertook their bows, concluding with, "Pray God to make a good Christian of me and bring me to a good end."

The Parfaits held out their hands in response, saying, "May God make a good Christian of you and bring you to a good end." Clotilde followed Bernadette's stare to the figure lying in a small bed, alongside the warmth of the fire.

The older of the two men gently directed his question to Bernadette. "Your mother is conscious?"

"Yes, come." Bernadette's mother smiled as the Perfecti approached and began to administer the consolamentum. Although the full ritual included baptism, confirmation and ordination, her approaching death mandated an abbreviated version. Clotilde listened as the Lord's Prayer ended with a calling forth of God to send his Holy Spirit upon her. Madame Rives smiled, closed her eyes, and her gentle breathing ceased.

Bernadette surprised Clotilde by the grace and strength that seemed to descend upon her as she placed one last kiss upon her mother's peaceful brow before turning back to the Parfaits. "Thank you for coming. May I offer you food or drink?"

"No, Mademoiselle. It is not needed." They answered in the unison of *socius*, companions paired to share and support one other in their labors and religious observances. "We are grateful to have provided comfort to her special soul." Acknowledging the adoratios, they disappeared into the night. Their shaved beards, another sign of the caution taken to make them indistinguishable during these times, struck Clotilde as they left. It occurred to her how much harder it was to disguise their modest utterances, constant prayers and selfless giving of themselves to others.

Clotilde watched Bernadette climb up to take down a small box from a high corner cupboard. "I must return, Bernadette, lest Master Jean has arrived. Do you wish me to send Blanche to stay the night?"

"No, Milady," she said as she placed the box on the table. "I shall honor my mother in protecting the luck of our house." She pulled out a scissors and a small cloth from the box. "I must attend to laying her out alone. If Blanche would be so kind as to come on the morrow, I would be grateful."

"Of course." Clotilde went to the door as Bernadette turned back to her mother, eager to begin a time-honored tradition.

Clotilde drew the hood of her cloak down to shield her from the rain as she hurried along the path to home. Images rose of Bernadette alone with her dead mother, observing a ritual all villagers honored. The ritual of protecting the "star," or the luck of the house, was essential to its heir. Bernadette would sprinkle her mother's forehead before taking clippings from her fingernails and toenails. She would then place them in an honored location to assure that the house remain protected from any loss of its beneficent energies.

As Clotilde neared home she studied her own abode, a sinking sensation of luck having abandoned it when she saw no sign of Jean's return. Blanche and Bernard were lost in conversation until a gust of wind slammed the door closed. Blanche jumped, her look strange as Clotilde shed her cloak and went to join them.

Taking a place alongside Bernard, Clotilde felt his remove. Her words made an attempt at normalcy. "Bernard, dear brother, how you slept through a household in turmoil, I'll not know, but I'm pleased that you did."

His slow response came with effort. "Yes, that I did."

Clotilde turned away, feeling depleted, her eyes prickling with tears. Blanche filled the silence. "Bernadette's mother?"

Clotilde's, "She went peacefully," was filled with exhaustion that left her slumping down onto the bench as lifeless as an abandoned marionette. A hand held out a steaming mug of cider.

"Drink this. It'll restore you." Blanche said. "I told Bernard you'd gone to be with Bernadette as her mother lay dying."

Bernard mumbled, "She's better off dead in these times." He looked puzzled. "I'm surprised you found any perfecti remaining in Mirepoix."

"They live like moles and vanish into the night."

"Hmmph." Blanche said, "Better for all of us if they had vanished long ago."

Blanche's bitterness shocked Clotilde. She stared, as at a stranger. "Blanche, you can't mean it." Convinced such words could only come from fear and exhaustion, she enfolded Blanche in her arms. "It was you, dear sister, who taught me the blessed teachings of the good men."

Blanche looked up. "I feel so alone and so helpless. Mother died, you left with Jean, and now my husband, I…" One hand rose listlessly and dropped.

"Shush, dear Blanche," Clotilde murmured. "We are together now. Jean will soon return and help guide us through this terrible time." Clotilde brushed a lock of hair from Blanche's damp eyelids, aware of their roles shifting.

Bernard scowled at the mention of Jean. "Jean needs a minder!"

The door flew open, halting Clotilde's defense.

"Jean!" Clotilde rushed into his wet embrace. "I didn't hear your approach and I'd know Coeur de Lyon's hoofbeats a village away."

"He bolted at a snake in the path and reared into a ravine." Jean caught the distress in Clotilde's eyes. "His leg isn't broken, only badly sprained. I managed to lead him to the cottage of the animal husbandry man outside the village. He claims his liniment will set the steed prancing by the morrow."

Suddenly his eyes locked on Bernard's. "And you, dear brother. I see you made it safely—but as to what route, I'd dare not hazard a guess. I retraced the entire journey to Fanjeaux with no sign of you."

"I'd not have made it by cleaving to the main route." Bernard's faint scorn turned solemn. "Two thugs followed me, so I detoured via the forest."

Jean looked alarmed as he clasped his brother to his side. "How glad we are at your safety—and eager to hear your news."

Clotilde took Jean's dripping cloak. "There's naught he'll reveal until you've shed your wet clothes and had a warm meal."

Warmed by a fresh cloak, a seat by the fire, and a large bowl of soup, Jean turned to his brother. "And now Bernard—please share news of your journey."

"My journey to Fanjeaux"—Bernard's eyebrows furrowed as he studied his brother—"was like a hornet's nest. Rumors buzzed from every direction, most concerning the Count of Toulouse. His excommunication has left the city stunned. So cowed they say, that they fear he'll be obliging to all the Pope shall require."

"No!" Jean's shock didn't halt Bernard's tale.

"Repercussions from the massacre at Avignonet are growing. The Pope is enraged. It doesn't look good for the Cathars, nor for Pierre-Roger de Mirepoix." Bernard's tone turned ominous. "I've reason to believe you are in danger." Clotilde's hands began to tremble.

Jean reached out a hand to steady Clotilde's as he glared at Bernard. "What hear you—and from whom?"

Bernard paused. "More rumors I expect, but your name was singled out, implying something of great import and certain danger." Bernard shrugged as he opened his hands. "Nothing specific. To do with your latest trip, methinks." His comment ended with a bitter twist that caused Clotilde to bristle. She stood up, walked nearer to the fire and felt her anger ignite. Turning away from the sparks, she met Bernard's hardened-to-steel look with her own.

Jean reached for her, his expression holding a message that curbed her remarks. Turning from Clotilde to Bernard, Jean replied, "My trips are routine…" He looked from his brother to his wife, "…and no cause for danger."

Bernard deliberated before responding. "So you say, but rumor abounds."

Jean placed a hand on his brother's shoulder. "Such comments are pure speculation." Clotilde released a breath she'd not known she'd held as Jean continued, his words level, "But do tell us more of your journey."

Bernard avoided Jean's gaze as he continued. "Any optimism, I fear, vanished at the volume of rumors that offered little encouragement." Clotilde was struck, not only by the bleakness in Bernard's words, but also by the strange metamorphosis that seemed to be taking place. Bernard had long filled the role of the big brother. Solid as an elephant, his fearlessness lent any room the assurance of having a giant guarding its gates. No longer—fear shone from his eyes. His hands lay limply on the tabletop, empty of any ability to shield.

Jean must have felt it, she thought as he spoke. "My brother, your journey was a brave one. If anyone could separate truth from rumor it would be you." As Bernard's head rose, Jean added, "Your trip was invaluable in affirming the extra caution we must take."

Bernard shrugged and stared around the room as if seeking a quick exit. Clotilde spoke, hoping to further restore his dignity. "Dear Bernard, your counsel has shown us that we must place our trust, not in the Count's hands, but in God's."

"God's!" Scorn filled Bernard's voice as he stood, squared his shoulders and strode across the room. "I've seen where his guidance leads. Few remain alive."

"Alive…" Blanche's response was bleak. "Then perhaps Bernadette's mother has chosen the better course."

"What's this of Bernadette's mother?" Jean asked.

"She has gone peacefully to God this very night, my love." As Clotilde spoke, she took Blanche's hand. "I know you did not mean what you said."

"Forgive my mood, dear ones. I am tired. Do permit me to withdraw to my bedchamber." Blanche's "Bonne nuit" faded as she walked away.

Bernard rose slowly to his feet. "I too am weary." He looked at Jean. "Enough for tonight." He wiped his soot stained hands against his trousers, and frowned. "Unless you've brought word of a miracle, or..." He let his words trail behind him as he made his way to a cot in back of the scullery.

Clotilde felt something extinguished—the loss of two pillars of her own support. Jean seemed aware of her feelings.

"Strange how fear can peel back the façade we each use to make it through our lives." He tipped her face up to his.

She looked deeply into his eyes. "For Blanche to so bitterly denounce her faith..." She turned away. "It grieves me so."

"Fear, my love, is covering the whole of the Languedoc." Jean pressed a kiss to her cheek, his action rekindling her own faith in him.

She began to describe her experience with Bernadette's mother. "Not all are consumed by fear. The faces of the two Perfecti, who of all people should express fear, radiated deep peace and love." Clotilde felt comforted by the memory as she completed her account of Madame Rives' death.

"I wish I could have been with you, my love," he said as she burrowed deeper into his embrace. Although only absent for a brief time, his tenderness reminded her of how far removed he had been.

She stared into his eyes. "I pray that, whatever your mission, you find peace."

"This has been a hard time for us both." Jean drew her toward the stairway, his voice falling to a whisper. "Let us speak in the privacy of our bedchamber."

As they entered, Clotilde watched the candle flame flicker over the lines of exhaustion etched in his face as he spoke. "I've feared betraying my vow."

"Your vow?" Her question fell softly, aware of the fragility.

"I swore to secrecy. Until now." He lowered his voice to a whisper. "When Fabrisse has given me leave to share my mission with you." He eased her onto the bed, sinking beside her in relief. His voice was so low that Clotilde leaned in to hear the words spoken. "I've been asked to journey to certain places to retrieve treasure belonging to the Cathars. And to take it to safety."

"The Cathars have treasure?" Her shock made her voice rise.

Jean placed a finger gently against her lips. "Yes, a treasure of immense value. More than that I cannot reveal." His words were scarcely audible, requiring him to bend closer to Clotilde's ear, and whisper, "Knowing your distress, I rejoiced when Fabrisse gave me leave to tell you. Because..." He halted, locking his gaze with hers. "The success of my quest depends on you as well." He halted. As he returned his gaze to Clotilde, his voice, although barely audible, had added intensity. "Indeed, upon which the entire world depends."

"The world." Clotilde felt the same sinking sensation that phrase instilled in her before—the magnitude incomprehensible.

Jean's solemnity etched each word indelibly into her heart. "Yes. Ultimately all the world depends on us, my love. Consider it well before responding to my question." With a long inhalation, slowly released, he spoke each word as though it held the entire import. "Can you, without a full understanding, agree to honor its importance with *total* secrecy?"

"The world." Clotilde repeated, still stunned at the concept.

"Not just *this* world—" Jean's emphasis shocked her. "But one to come."

Confusion warred in Clotilde, but acceptance solidified as he repeated his question. "Will you honor such an important mission with total secrecy?"

Her response was as firm and clear as the question that prompted it. "I can, I will and I do, accept our mission. And I swear to honor and fulfill it with total secrecy." Her words' solemn resonance was to echo throughout time.

ELEVEN

Coustaussa, France- May, Present

"You're going back for what?" Eric asked, his eyebrow raised as I turned from placing my camera bag in the trunk of the car.

"To get a stronger flash and an infrared camera lens to take photos in the dark. I'll be right back." I headed back to my room.

Eric looked perplexed as I returned, flung open the trunk lid, and shoved his gear aside. "Why would you film something you can't see?"

I rearranged space for my added gear and replied, "Rumor says the Cathar treasure may be hidden in…"

"In one of the caves this area is known for." He broke in, his look brightening as he watched me close my camera case. "And that lens works subterranean?" He sounded unconvinced.

"That it does. Should we come across a likely cave, I'm ready."

He grinned as he held the car door open. "Clever. I guess that would also explain your shoes." He stared at my hiking boots as I tried to fit them within the crowded floor space. I picked up pamphlets, books and maps, and nearing the end of my organizing, looked up at the sound of gravel crunching. Madame Villar approached, her loud "Bonjour" ringing on the air.

Madeline gave a big smile and brushed my cheek with kisses. "I'm happy you have not yet departed." She waved the bit of paper in her hand, handing it to me with a flourish. "Mademoiselle

Evelyn Arnstein called and left a message." I felt a ripple of guilt at remembering that I'd not called Evie to confirm our schedule

I read it aloud. "Arriving Wednesday at 2:45 in Toulouse. Benjamin suggests you join us Thursday. Plan on staying the night. He has special information for your Cathar research. Call me: 62-45-6512. See you soon!"

"You may phone her from here." Madeline offered.

"Thank you, but I'll need time to think it through. I'll call her from Arques." I looked at Eric, my mind racing with options for rearranging our itinerary.

Madeline stared at me, concern replacing her jaunty greeting. "Forgive me. But I cannot refrain from a word of caution." She looked down at the message in my hand. "Monsieur Benjamin Carter, he is…" She hesitated, abandoning her effort at the proper English description in her flustered explanation, "knowledgeable concerning *la chronologie de l'histoire des cathares.* As such, he may be able to provide some information for you." Madeline stopped, looking pleased that she had managed the difficult job of giving the man some credit.

Seeing her hesitation, I rushed to agree. "We are fortunate that he is a friend of my friend, Evelyn." I glanced at the note. "He has been very generous in offering to help with our research. Even invited us to stay at his home."

Eric looked deep in thought as he took the note, re-reading it aloud. "Perhaps a bit too generous," he said. Madeline nodded vigorously.

"For Benjamin Carter—yes, without a doubt," she said.

There it was again, an indictment. But why so strong, I wondered, turning to Madeline. "You mentioned 'caution.'"

Her response was emphatic. "Yes, be careful. I do not know personally this Mr. Carter. However, there are many who question his motives." She gave a Gallic shrug and smiled. "He is described as self-serving by those kind souls who reserve judgement." A full-throated laugh escaped as she added, "Unscrupulous and vile, by those, like myself, who are outspoken."

Eric's response was light but his expression serious. "We will be cautious."

Madeline's relief was transparent. "Very good. I shall be most interested in hearing your opinion when you return."

Eric reached for our map. "Here is our route for the day." He spread it where all three of us could study it. "We're scheduling only castles that are important to our series." He moved his finger along our westward route. "As to stopping in Rennes, you suggest we see Coustaussa instead." Eric looked up at Madeline.

Madeline stared at our circles on the map. "Rennes is a powerful place to visit." She hesitated. "Many speculate that the four Cathars that escaped Montsegur with the treasure were headed for the caves near Rennes le Chateau." She looked up. "It has added to the many mysteries of Rennes. But Pierre is better at explaining why you should resist it for now." Her eyes widened as she said, *"D'accord?"*

"D'accord." The French phrase burst from me. I loved its emphatic feel. Not a limp "sure" or "OK," nor even the amiable, "I agree," but a resounding "dahh cord" solidity that sliced through any equivocation.

Madeline grinned as Eric returned to the map, moving his lips in silent calculation of the mileage. "If we skip Rennes, we could stay the night near Fanjeaux. It puts us closer to Toulouse and our rendezvous with Evie and Benjamin." He looked up, waiting for my response.

I turned to Madeline. "That means we wouldn't return for a few nights."

"Your things are safe in your little home until your return." A sly smile lit the corner of her eyes. "I know a perfect place for lodging. A friend of mine has rooms in his twelfth-century Cistercian Abbey, a little north and east of Toulouse. If it is on your route, I recommend it. *Très charmant.*"

I handed her a notebook and pen. Madeline jotted a few lines and returned it. I glanced down, smiling at the little heart she'd drawn around the name, *"L'Abbaye de Sainte-Marie de Villelongue."* Eric remained oblivious.

He stopped rummaging through the back seat long enough to say, "We'll need to take a few more things with us." Eric turned to Madeline. "Excuse me while I head back for them." As soon as her *"Certainement"* was given, he hurried off. As I placed her note in my purse, Madeline spoke.

"The man in Arques." She took the note from my hand and wrote: "Pierre de Lahille-dans la Marie-Arques." She let out a long sigh. "He will prepare you for Coustaussa—and more." A phone's loud ring, a quick '*Adieu,*' and she was gone.

I pocketed the note, amused at the fates having reshuffled the deck, and walked back to my room to pack for our extra days away.

Eric's efficiency inspired me as he headed for the car, carrying a sports coat, slacks, shirt, tie and a small plastic carry bag. "That should do it for me."

"Right. I'll join you in ten minutes," I said. I gathered extra clothes, and with minutes to spare, returned to the car. "Afraid the fridge was empty of any food to take with us," I said as I stored my things.

"I think *International Horizons* magazine will spring for proper meals along the way." Eric's smile remained in place as I murmured, 'right' and we pulled away.

It was the last word spoken for some time as we retraced part of yesterday's route on our way to Arques and Coustaussa. I opened the guidebook and sighed at Coustaussa's ruins. In contrast, the castle of Arques in the photo opposite seemed almost new. I silently read their description. "The castle of Arques was built in 1268, after the Cathar massacre. Simon de Montfort conquered the territory belonging to the Lords of Termes and handed the castle and its lands over to one of his henchmen. Coustaussa, much older, was built early in the eleven hundreds by the Trencaval family and conquered during the Inquisition. The thoroughness with which it was destroyed, given its strategic positioning, remained a mystery."

I gazed out the window, lost in the mystery of why Coustaussa wasn't assigned to one of Simon de Montfort's favorites. A sign, *Arques—fifteen kilometers,* broke my reverie and I turned to Eric. "I hate to break the silence, but..."

He laughed. "I've been giving you sidelong glances for at least the last ten kilometers. I even nodded and pointed to some ruins, and still couldn't break your hypnosis. Where did you go?"

"Deep into the mystery," I said as I pointed at a ruin we were passing. "The Cathars call out from every village and ruin." Eric looked at the lone tower silhouetted against the sky. "Can't you feel the sense that the past still lives here?"

"It's drama unfinished. Well, I'll give you one thing—the deeper into the Corbieres we go, the more I'm inclined to agree." He glanced out the window. "Arques ahead. Read what our guidebook says."

I read him the section that I had read earlier, adding, "Arques is near Rennes and Coustaussa." I stared at the photo of the castle's ruins.

Eric looked down at it. "Arques seems fully intact, but I confess I'm more intrigued by Coustaussa's pile of rocks. Maybe

Madeline's mysterious friend, what's his name, can shed light on why it was demolished."

"'Pierre de Lahille.' He has an office at the town hall in Arques. Madeline says he'll fill us in on Coustaussa—and more."

"And more." Eric mimicked my attempt to capture Madeline's inflection.

"Whatever the enigma, we'll soon find out," I said, staring out at the stately avenue of flowering chestnuts as we approached Arques.

Eric looked over at the map in my lap. "Check where Coustaussa is in relation to Arques and while you're at it, have a look at the mileage from there to Fanjeax. I'm trying to get a handle on our schedule."

I did a quick calculation. "Seven kilometers from Arques to Coustaussa, forty-five to Foix, thirty to Mirepoix, and fifteen to Fanjeaux. A total of one hundred twenty kilometers, give or take a few."

"Not as much as I thought." Eric slowed to make the curve ahead, smiling as he said, "I say we trust to serendipity. Since we seem to have a mystery tour guide—what say we just go with it?"

"Sounds good to me," I said.

"Good." Eric smiled. "It's the mood of the ruins and the essence of the Cathars that I'm after. The books, those photos..." Eric pointed to the opened pages on my lap, "may capture what remains, but not their story. I'd rather steep ourselves in a few sites that, whether intact or not, have a subtle message for our series."

"I'm with you. It's exactly that ephemeral quality I hope to bring to life with my photos." I rolled the window down as we entered Arques. "I'm feeling goose bumps even before we meet with Pierre."

Eric reached out a hand and lightly touched my flyaway hair. "Your hair matches your expression, wild and willful."

I made a quick move to anchor it behind my ears as we slowed down at the town center. "I'll look for a sign saying 'Marie.'"

Eric slowed the car. "There it is, it looks like a church," he said as he parked.

As we walked up to its double doors, I turned to Eric. "I don't know how much English Pierre speaks."

"You'll have to serve as translator. Seems my British insularity got in the way of my learning French." Eric pushed open the door to a darkish space, empty of people, but filled with bulletin boards with pamphlets and notices.

I looked closely for an attendant or at least a sign indicating hours open. Eric walked to the counter and rang a bell. A doorway alongside opened and a little man, almost wraithlike in his silent movements, approached.

"*Bonjour,*" The figure whispered.

"*Bonjour,*" I replied, adding, "We are here to see Monsieur de Lahille."

A smile lit his features as his voice rose in response. "You must be Madeline's friends, Monsieur Taylor and Mademoiselle Palmer. Do come in." His English was as smooth as his movements as he led us into his office. "Madame Villars called to say you'd soon arrive. We discussed your Cathar project." He waved his pale white hand toward a well-worn sofa, whose cracked brown leather was dominated by a ginger colored Persian cat. Her sleepy eyes scarcely opened as he moved her. "Down, Colette." He turned. "Please take a chair. I have tea or coffee."

"Just water for me, thank you," I said, staring into his deep, dark eyes, completely captured in their depths. I had a sudden image of their having once stared out from the depths of a hooded robe.

"Monsieur?" Monsieur de Lahille turned his gaze on Eric.

"Nothing for me, thanks." Eric replied. "But I detect a bit of my homeland in your accent."

"I studied for many years at Oxford. I lecture there on occasion even now," Pierre replied as he poured a glass of water from a pitcher on the sideboard. "But I'm more interested in you." He handed me a glass. "How may I help you?"

Eric began his account of our magazine series, pulling out the opening segment and handing it to our host. I watched as Monsieur de Lahille began to read, waiting for his frown. When nothing happened, I glanced at Eric, who whispered, "I added a prefatory caveat."

Pierre finished reading, laid the manuscript aside, and gazed from the pages to us. "I sense that your sympathies, even given your attempts to be unbiased, lie with the Cathars."

"Yes, I suppose so." Eric's response was slow and deliberate, while my loud "*D'accord*" filled the room.

Our host smiled and asked, "How much do you know of Cathar history?"

"Not nearly as much as Dana knows, but I've bought every book in English available." Eric motioned to me. "I cede the floor to my colleague."

"I've read everything in English that I can find. And some in French..." Reading seemed so remote from my deeper involvement. "But..."

"But there is more, I would venture to say." Monsieur De Lahille's words were as gentle as a benediction. "Do continue, Mademoiselle Palmer."

Eric's stare held the wariness of one ready to intervene at the slightest signal. Whether to moderate my words or to come to my aid wasn't clear.

"Yes, Monsieur de Lahille, much more. But not that which stems from research." I sighed and fell under the spell of the compassion in his eyes. "Some might say that I'm obsessed by the Cathars. I feel them, dream them, have visions of them, and know things that I've no way of knowing. Such sadness"—my hands curled into fists—"and rage consumes me at the brutality of their destruction." Uneasy, I looked at Eric. He was studying Monsieur de Lahille's reaction. I opened my still clenched fists, held out my hands and stared at them. "I can't explain it—my being here, what lies ahead—I only know that it captivates me in every sense."

"Are you a Cathar?" A smile spread across Pierre's face as he took my empty water glass. "Think on my question while I go bring some tea."

Pierre nodded and moved, or, more like evaporated, leaving his smile, like Alice's Cheshire cat, hanging in the air. Eric and I exchanged a bemused look that segued into smiles as Pierre returned.

"Thank you, Monsieur de Lahille," I said, as he poured my cup of tea.

"Please call me Pierre." He extended a cup to Eric and turned back to me. "Now, as to my question, let me explain its genesis. Yves Rouquette, a brilliant poet who writes in Occitan, the ancient language of the Cathars, our Lanque d'Oc," has published a book called *Cathars*. He began his book with that question having been posed to him. No was the only answer he could give, appropriately so because nothing exists—no Cathar church, no doctrinal teachings and no Cathar sect." Pierre reached down and began stroking his cat.

"We know better, don't we, my pet?" He turned from the cat's silent wisdom to us. "As you say in your article, there has been an extraordinary resurgence of interest in this group, a fascination with everything Cathar. There's a plethora of books concerning the Cathars and their treasure, thanks to a dedicated group of scholars sifting through their history. Their research attempts to avoid mystical avenues in their efforts to restore the Cathars accurately." He held out the teapot to refill our cups. "And yet that question lingers in many hearts, resonating agreement with Yves Roquette's final response: 'Yes, I am a Cathar.' His answer emerges gently, crystallized by solemn consideration and illuminated by Grace, by God, by Goodness, by Light—surely by all that the Cathars held sacred." Pierre's expression seemed to be lit by images of joy. He shook his head and turned to Eric.

"Why are so many interested now?" Eric's solemn question hung in the air.

"A good question. There is no clear-cut, rational answer." Pierre cleared his throat and continued. "The esoteric answer might be that those Cathar souls have returned. The pragmatic answer is that some marketing guru has decided that the Cathar legend draws tourists." Pierre looked at me. "What do you think?"

I took a deep breath before replying. "I feel the answer lies with society's yearning at this turbulent time, their search for Goodness—for God. Perhaps such a longing has rekindled an interest in a time and a people who held an antidote to greed, destruction and alienation." I fell silent, lost in a place that felt deep and sacred, but too tenuous to do justice to with words.

Eric filled the void. "Certainly the new millennium has shaken old systems to the core, leaving everyone fraught with fear. Terrorism exposed our deep vulnerability as stock markets plunged, technology and genetic engineering pose uncertain outcomes, and environmental problems mushroom. As a former priest, I hear many express a longing for re-connection to God, to service and to simplicity." He looked up, sobered at his words. I tried for lightness.

"At least we didn't have to deal with any millennium bug crisis."

"Sounds like a more insidious millennium bug may have hit." Pierre said as he smiled and headed to the door. "Let's walk. We can talk as we go."

A short stroll down cobbled village streets overshadowed by blossoming trees brought us to the base of a gentle slope, on top of which perched the castle of Arques. Its location, within the town and not on a mountaintop, was unusual. But more unusual was its shape. A rectangle of stone walls enclosed an extraordinary and imposing keep. The keep dominated the landscape, daring any to broach its inner sanctum. Its four circular corners, architecturally elegant with their opera-curtain curves, rose twenty meters high and encompassed three soaring floors.

"Let's go have a look," Pierre said. As he led the way, he was met with smiles and greetings from villagers. Our gentle hike ended in front of the enclosure walls. Entering, I gazed at the graceful keep's design and broke into a grin. "I can almost envision a bank of elevators, one in each circular corner, taking us up to the Lords and Ladies' private apartments."

"And right you are, except they used circular stone steps instead. Come," Pierre said as he moved for the narrow stairwell. As we neared the first landing I whispered to Eric, "Let's pay attention. I swear his feet never touch the ground."

Pierre went over to a graceful window opening and stared out across the fields below. He seemed not the least bit winded as he spoke. "The keep was perfectly designed to be both a citadel and a castle—with all the comforts." He pointed to a fireplace and a long trestle table that fronted it. "That table reminds me that I'd like to invite you to lunch. Arques is famous for its cuisine. Please say you accept."

"Of course, but we insist on you being our guest." Eric rejoined.

"*D'accord.*" Pierre's response, accompanied by a broad smile, was directed at me as I set up my cameras. Absorbed, I'd decided to shoot using my collapsible tripod and a macro lens. Longing to capture the atmosphere, I quickly went through three rolls of Velvia 220 film. Looking out through the window slits, I became lost in taking shots of the castle and the surrounding countryside.

* * *

We ate lunch in a restaurant just outside the village, a setting whose beauty was different, but equally as phantasmagoric as that of the Chateau d'Arques. Sited in a moss-covered cottage by a stream, the restaurant's interior was dominated by a fire crackling vigorously in an ancient fireplace. Nothing old fashioned, however, about its kitchen or its chef's skills, I thought, as I savored my incomparable trout meunière. We all fell silent, entranced by our surroundings and the surfeit of wonderful food.

As soon as the waiter arrived with dessert and coffee, we let out a collective sigh and resumed our more serious conversation.

I turned to Pierre. "Earlier, Eric and I were discussing our attempts to capture the mood that each site conveys."

"Yes, of course. Tell me of your success." Pierre waited.

"Well, take Arques, for example. There's strangeness about the chateau. It's like someone with nothing to hide. All bold and stalwart, it commands you to look at the keep. And yet I found myself drawn to photograph the landscape surrounding it. Like someone offstage whispering to draw my attention." I gave a slight shrug, feeling, as he stared, that it might be too vague, even for Pierre.

"Not surprising." He deliberated with his words. "There is much speculation in the area over what is called sacred geometry—a means of laying out structures along certain natural lines of energy. The arrangement of hills, valleys and forests created a composition that once spoke to ancient man at a very significant level." Pierre looked down at my cameras. "Since Arques was a major point within such a composition, the landscape may well have dictated your photographic choice." Pierre turned to Eric, who began an animated stirring of his coffee as he spoke.

"I think I know what you mean. I've been reading about Rennes le Chateau being part of such a mystery." He gave me a sheepish look and continued. "Dana and I want to stop there, but after Madeline's comments, we feel conflicted."

Pierre smiled. "True. Its mystery is deep, not entirely Cathar, but connected."

Eric nodded his head vigorously. "Right. I'm intrigued by the 'Tomb of Arques' and its significance to the Rennes treasure."

"The Rennes treasure, yes." Pierre gazed out at the sparkling stream, falling silent for a moment. "So much has been written about the priest Sauniere's sudden wealth and the sacred geometry surrounding Rennes le Chateau. Much is speculation, but the tomb of Arques is real, existing in Rennes until the late 1970s. It was ancient, with inscriptions older than Visigoth, Roman, Merovingian or Carolingian."

"Inscriptions regarding the priest's treasure?" Eric asked.

"Maybe, or at least someone thought so. Its distinctive markings were carefully effaced. But fortunately the tomb's exterior had been reproduced in some rather enigmatic paintings.

Perhaps you've read of them." Pierre sipped at his tea, glancing over the rim of his cup at Eric.

"Enough to be intrigued." Eric looked intently at Pierre. "An entire chapter referred to the painter Poussin's inclusion of the tomb in his paintings of the '*Et in Arcadia Ego*' theme. It claimed the tomb served as the model for two versions of Poussin's paintings, one currently in England, the other in the Louvre."

Pierre nodded solemnly. "That the tomb should find such prominence in the art of a painter of renown has provoked much speculation. Interestingly, one of the many drawn to the tomb was Louis IV's minister of finance." Pierre drew a deep breath and motioned for the waiter. "Would you care for more coffee?"

"No," we choroused, as we waited for him to continue.

"Well then, while the waiter prepares our bill, let me just say that to speculate at this point on the tomb's mystery, or on Rennes' treasure, is precipitate. I've a book I'll leave with you. Do read it before you make any visit to Rennes."

"Oh." I sat suddenly forward. "Would you excuse me while I make a call?" I drew out my note for Pierre. "Do I need any special prefix to dial this number?"

"You are meeting with Benjamin Carter." Pierre's expression darkened, as he looked from my notation to Eric.

"Actually a second meeting." Eric frowned as he added, "Madam Villars indicated you both share some concerns about this chap. "

"Enough to caution you about divulging anything to him." He hesitated, his solemn stare highlighted by deep ridges in his forehead. "Focus on asking questions, not answering them." His frown deepened as he turned to me. "I couldn't help but notice your necklace." He reached out a hand. "May I examine it further?"

"Yes, certainly. I assured Madeline that its value is only sentimental."

His eyes widened as he turned it back to front, holding it with great care, almost reverence. "On the contrary, it is of great value." His stare made me uncomfortable. "You must guard it from all eyes—especially Professor Carter's."

"He may have seen it in Carcassonne the other night." I looked over at Eric. "I can't remember if I wore it." His silence prompted a deep sigh from Pierre.

"In any case, do not wear it in his presence. I cannot say more at this time. I'm sorry." His focus remained on the necklace.

"Please trust my advice to protect this with your life." He stirred the remnants in his cup like a gypsy studying tea leaves. "You might think me unreasonable. But, until I meet with certain others, I am not at liberty to reveal the basis underlying my words."

Eric leapt up. "I'm getting impatient with such vagueness." Eric thrust his hand in his pocket, drew out a cigarette and tapped it against the table. He made an effort to moderate his tone as he added, "But I'm trying, for the time being, to go wherever such strangeness leads." He looked contrite as he reached for his lighter. "Sorry, I'll go outside." As Eric turned, he asked how soon I'd be ready to leave.

"Soon, but first I have to make that call." My answer was met with a shrug as he hurried away. I turned back to Pierre. "Sorry. We're both tired."

Pierre touched my hand. "It's understandable." He glanced across the room. "Let me show you where the phone is."

As I followed Pierre, I gave a quick glance outside and saw Eric standing motionless against an ancient wall, an unlit cigarette dangling from his lips.

Within minutes we were all seated again, Eric studying the bill and me studying Pierre, who had asked if my phone call went through all right.

"Yes. Thank you."

"Good." Pierre picked up a mint from the bowl the waiter offered and began to unwrap it. "I understand that you shall visit Coustaussa next."

I nodded. "Madeline insists. She said you would explain why."

"Must feel rather than see, I'm afraid." Pierre let out a sigh. "There is so little left. Feeling it is more critical, especially in light of the thoroughness with which Coustaussa Castle was destroyed after the Montsegur massacre."

"Their timing is provocative," Eric chimed in. "Our book says little remains."

Pierre looked solemn. "The destruction was as complete as humans could eradicate anything at that time."

"I suppose you have a theory as to why it was destroyed." Eric reached into his briefcase and drew out a pen and tablet, poised for Pierre's response.

"Because it lay on a direct path, not only an energy path, but a practical path between the regions of Ariege and the Corbieres, a path that led from Montsegur to the caves, to Coustaussa and on to Queribus." His eyes lit up as he added, "A path the sheepherders used as a conduit of information. Traveling great distances to Coustaussa, they brought their flocks to nearby pastures both winter and spring." Pierre grinned as Eric whispered, "Shepherds."

"Right. The 'shepherd' allusion again. The castle was a vital crossroad, not only for shepherds, but also for Cathars. Think on this as you stand among its ruins."

We thought of it all the way back to the town hall, where Pierre held out two books. "Eric, this is the book I mentioned on the sacred geometry of this area. You'll find it interesting, I know." Pierre placed a book of troubadour poetry in my hands.

"And this is for you, my dear Mademoiselle Palmier. It is in English, translated from Occitan. It is very lyrical, yet strong and indomitable. Like you, my dear." He grinned at my surprise and walked up to Eric.

"Two last suggestions before you depart, Monsieur Taylor. The Deodat Roche Museum in Arques is well worth a stop. As you leave Arques, take a quick glance toward the southeast, where you will catch sight of Rennes le Chateau and the Magdala Tower. Resist its draw, another more important treasure awaits."

Pierre's tone deepened as we turned to leave. "I suggest you remove your necklace." I pulled slowly at the chain until the hook was visible. Releasing it, I removed the necklace and placed it in my camera bag.

Pierre's gaze never wavered as he studied every movement until the zipper closed. Giving a slight nod, he bid us goodbye, adding one last request. "Say nothing of visiting me or Coustaussa when you meet with Dr. Carter."

Nita Hughes

TWELVE

Mirepoix, France-May, 1243

A fierce constriction filled Clotilde's chest as she opened her eyes, knowing it could be her last such look at her home. Long-held emotions threatened to explode as she thought back to four nights ago.

As the crowd listened to Fabrisse and Jean describe the growing massacres, most resolved to join their fellow Cathars at Montsegur. Relief had filled their faces as they returned to their homes. For her, relief was restored by Jean's revelations. Once shared, although overwhelming, her heartache had eased—until now.

She sat up, determined to conquer her sense of feeling ambushed by deep sorrow. The realities of never seeing her home again had brought back childhood memories and triggered an urge to action. She moved quickly to the window ledge, pushing wide the shutter to breathe in a long draught of air.

She caught sight of Jean leading Coeur de Lyon around the edge of the milling throng. He had organized their departure party, agreeing to ride ahead to safeguard their journey. She and Blanche, Fabrisse and her socia, Esclarmonde, and Bernadette would be in the first wagon behind. Bernard had volunteered to remain at the back of the many wagons. Each was piled high with the household items of the families. All testified to the finality of their decision.

"Madame—are you awake?" Bernadette's question rang up the stairwell.

"Only just, Bernadette. I'll take care of locking all the upper shutters."

"Very good, Madame. I'll tend to the ones down here."

Clotilde put on the shift she had laid out the night before, reserving her heavier tunic for chill of the nights. Within minutes, she had secured the shutters, latching them as firmly as she closed away her earlier emotions.

"All is secured downstairs, Madame." Bernadette's voice carried an extra reassuring ring this morning, Clotilde thought, as she replied, "Very good." Clotilde appreciated Bernadette's thoroughness, noting that she was as conscientious on leaving this house as she was in providing protection for her mother's home. The thought filled her with a sudden urge to leave a good luck charm to protect her own home. She walked toward the small chest alongside her bed and examined the remaining personal items—two hairbrushes, a small box with their family seal—and her dearest possession, the egg-shaped stone Jean had carved with their initials.

She held the ovoid warmth of the marble to her cheek before pulling the scarf from her hair and prying loose hairs from their brushes. She carefully entwined his hair with her own and wrapped them around the stone. Placing her amulet atop her scarf, she pressed their seal onto the fabric and looked for the perfect hiding place.

Minutes later she stood back from their bedroom fireplace, staring at the sturdy stone she had removed and carefully replaced. Jean had long ago created a cache for securing valuables and had carved a box to fit within. The box now held her dearest talisman. With a prayer for God to bless the safety of their home, she gathered her remaining belongings, and, with a heavy sigh, hurried down the stairs.

"I've seen to the locking up, Madame." Bernadette grinned. "Even put that sly cat out. She knows something is going on, so deep was she within her hideaway."

"Will the stableman take her in?" Clotilde's brow furrowed with worry, as much for the wellbeing of their animals as for the humans. "I feel as though I'm abandoning part of our family."

Bernadette pointed in the direction of the stables. "Never fear. The stableman's wife has already claimed our spoiled puss as her own. I've taken our leftover foodstuffs to her, along with several basins for water. Puss is fine."

Clotilde felt pleased—for the cat's safety and for Bernadette's decision to accompany them. With the burial of her mother only four days ago, Clotilde feared she might remain. As they walked out, Jean approached them.

"I thought I would make one last inspection." Jean said, his gaze locked on hers. "Say you are all right, my love."

"I'm all right, my love—now that I've left my blessing." Feeling tears threaten, she pushed him toward the doorway. "Do go and add your blessing."

* * *

For the first few hours of their journey, Clotilde focused on Jean's horse, well forward of the partially covered wagon that she shared with the others. Fabrisse, Blanche, Esclarmonde and Bernadette were locked in their own thoughts. Hers were too fragile to explore. Refusing to look back, she wanted only not to think or feel.

"We are going to stop at Foix." Jean's shout interrupted her restless doze. Clotilde blinked, confused as to where she was. Jean glanced across the sleeping Fabrisse to ask Esclarmonde, "Is Foix prepared to have us?"

Esclarmonde's response was strong. "Yes. My father extends his protection with that of the Count."

Fabrisse woke, Jean's silence telling her his tension remained unabated by Esclarmonde's assurance. "I take it you anticipate problems," she said.

"Perhaps," Jean replied. "None that are evident for the moment. But at our last stop, a shepherd warned us not to use the South Gate into the city."

Esclarmonde and Fabrisse exchanged a glance before Esclarmonde spoke. "The Inquisitor, William Pelhisson, a Dominican monk sent to intimidate Foix, has offered dispensation of debt for anyone revealing a Cathar."

Jean snorted. "So the Church now offers dispensation of debt along with sins. Surely the people don't trust such a claim." Jean looked out along their route. "Whatever others may do, we shall take it seriously and remain on the alert." He swung Coeur de Lyon around, his parting words ringing out, as much, Clotilde thought, for the avid listeners he passed, as for her. "I trust God's guidance."

Clotilde watched the dust swirl in his wake, thinking how changed he had become. Once God's studious scholar of the Cathar faith, now a warrior, a man of action, ready to defend not only his faith, but also those he loved.

The women found sleep impossible, so alert were they to any movement. Except for Blanche, who had scarcely registered Jean's arrival and departure. Clotilde turned to her.

"Dear Blanche, you must be lost in thoughts of your husband."

"Yes, but..." Blanche turned toward the rear of the caravan. "It is Bernard and Jean of more concern. Bernard so shuns his brother as to ride at the rear."

Clotilde lowered her voice, aware that Fabrisse and Esclarmonde had closed their eyes, either in sleep or prayer. "It pains me to see their coldness. They need each other so much—now and when we arrive at Montsegur."

"Perhaps at Foix they may reach a peace." Blanche halted, puzzled by Jean's turning the caravan away from the main route to Foix. "We are detouring."

"For safety, Jean is keeping well away from the city's outer walls." Clotilde sounded more confident than she felt. All fell silent as Jean led them in a circuitous approach to Foix. As they neared the city, a horse and rider approached. Jean halted the caravan.

All eyes watched as the two fell into conversation. When the rider moved on, Jean approached the lead wagon.

"He is a representative of the Count," Jean said. "He assures us that the Inquisitor made for the Abbey Fontfroide two days ago."

"Does that mean we are not at risk in entering Foix?" Fabrisse asked as she scanned the anxious faces craning out all along the length of the caravan.

"To make certain that we are not, I've decided to delay our entry into the city until after dark." Jean studied his entourage, knowing all were concerned. "I must ride back to notify Bernard and the others."

As moments passed and the women prepared to disembark, Jean rode back. "Stay in the wagon until we move into the forest ahead."

The party seemed relieved as each wagon was secured deep within the shelter of a dense glade of trees. This should have calmed her, Clotilde thought. But as Jean gave word to dismount from the wagon, her uneasiness grew. A few, accustomed to a nomadic lifestyle, started small fires, but kept them low and contained. Clotilde stared, aware that they had traveled from shelter to shelter, only to have them destroyed by the inquisitors.

Even the grave was not safe, Clotilde thought, having heard news that the Church had begun to dig up deceased Cathars and burn their remains on the stake. Clotilde snapped out of her grim reverie at the sight of Bernadette scurrying to offer flagons of mead. Esclarmonde and Fabrisse partook of nothing until all were provided for. Clotilde watched Fabrisse's socia, Esclarmonde, tending to the flock as though they were her army.

She was a model of intelligence and courage just as her namesake, Esclarmonde, the elder—venerated in song and story— had been. It wasn't just the Cathar Parfaites that enjoyed such honor and respect, Clotilde thought. All women in Occitania were accorded full rights: entitlement to hold lands, bear children, have an education, leave their husbands, become Parfaites, and to enjoy all the entitlements accruing to men. But of all women Esclarmonde, the elder, the sister of the Count of Foix, set a high standard for this Esclarmonde to follow.

Clotilde heard tales of the uproar this venerable lady had created when St. Dominic's companion, Brother Stephen of Minia, addressed her in an unconscionable manner during a religious debate. "Go tend your distaff, Madam," he had shouted. "It is no business of yours to discuss matters such as these." The swell of indignation that had filled the city at this boorish remark was not his only comeuppance. Esclarmonde, the elder, or so the story tells, ignored him as one would the braying of an ass. She was cheered and the tale passed throughout Occitania into history.

Although equality of women was beginning in the north, a far greater degree of respect flowered in the south of France. Clotilde knew that it was partly owing to the skill with which the Provencal woman commanded equality. The troubadours honored such women by developing their traditions of *amour courtois,* a practice fast spreading throughout the land.

The castle of Montsegur, Clotilde knew, was once part of the elder Esclarmonde's inheritance. She had it placed under the control of Raymond de Pereille, vassal to the Count of Foix. He'd seen to it that the castle was rebuilt, its fortifications strengthened. Raymond named his own daughter "Esclarmonde" in honor of the Count of Foix's noble sister.

How apt the honor, she thought as she watched the namesake move among the crowd. A palpable lift in morale was felt when Esclarmonde neared. Optimism grew.

Later, as Clotilde lay deep within the castle of Foix, unable to sleep, she shuddered at her earlier optimism. She rose and walked to the fireplace, warming her hands to ease her chill, anxious over the outcome of the conversations with the Count of Foix. Jean yet remained in discussion with the Count, Raymond de Pereille and his son-in-law, Pierre Roger de Mirepoix. Clotilde felt reassured at learning that Pierre of Mirepoix would be in charge of the defense of Montsegur.

It was the last time that she had felt encouraged. Her unease was felt from the moment she sat down at the dinner table. Not even the opulent expanse of the dining area, the fine tapestries gracing the walls, or the aromatic aromas of the food, eased it. In spite of the abundance of candles, the room seemed cloaked in a pallor that dimmed any warmth or comfort. Absent were the troubadours, strumming their harps and singing the songs of Raymond of Miraval. Even the tapestry colors seemed to fade, as did the hope on the waiting faces when Pierre-Roger spoke.

"Ever since the Count of Toulouse signed the peace of Lorris treaty in January, Montsegur has become the prime focus of the Catholic Church."

The Count of Foix cast a baleful look at Pierre-Roger before assuming control of the conversation. "Let me assure you that the Count of Toulouse's signing of the treaty was done in the hopes the Pope would appeal his excommunication. A foolhardy ploy, as it turned out. For, in doing so, he sealed the fate of Montsegur and further tied his own hands." A gasp went through the room.

Clotilde broke the silence, daring to speak for them all. "As to sealing the fate of Montsegur, my lord."

The Count of Foix's expression moved from surprise to pity as he turned to Clotilde and replied, "I am saddened to inform you that a decision was reached. All present at that ignoble gathering were forced to agree to exterminate the Cathar heresy. Unanimously, they seconded the Pope's edict: 'We must cut off the head of the Cathar dragon—Montsegur."

The room hummed with disbelief as Jean gave voice to the question rising to everyone's lips. "Raymond VII, the Count of Toulouse, actually agreed to such a thing?" A murmur of incredulity echoed his words.

Both Pierre-Roger and the Count of Foix began to reply—the Lord of Mirepoix yielding to the Count. "It is my understanding that Raymond's intent was to placate, once again, the Catholic powers. He'd gambled that, by showing evidence of his antipathy toward heretics, he could stop any further bloodshed." The Count of Foix stared long into the fire before continuing. "It seems the Church has had enough of Raymond's earlier rebellions and his steady mockery of them. It is deeds this time, not words, that they demand." He spoke slowly. "They have left him little recourse." The Count sighed, its depth more convincing than even his words. "Raymond has suffered too many defeats with his rebellions. Now, with the Church and King aligned in their decision to take harsh measures, well..." He looked across the table, fully aware of the atmosphere of despair that filled the room.

Before another question could escape, he stood and bowed to each woman in turn. "Thank you, dear ladies, for your patience in hearing me out. Please forgive my rudeness in overlooking how tired you must be." The Count took his wife's hand. "Do show the ladies to their rooms, my dear."

It was nearly dawn before Jean returned to their chamber. He found Clotilde on her knees in prayer. The look that passed between them spoke volumes. "I trust there are few options remaining to us." Clotilde whispered.

"Nothing but to proceed to Montsegur. The Count of Foix and his liege lords will do all possible to defend any attempts against it."

"But I thought it was impregnable."

"With its location at twelve hundred meters in the clouds and sheer mountainous walls on all sides, Montsegur is formidable..." He hesitated. "Except for the west wall. But Pierre-Roger's vigilance has anticipated such weakness and has posted guards there."

"And as to revealing such to the others..." Clotilde's eyes widened. "They are so confident in their decision to go."

"A cruel thing to do. There is no better choice for them." Jean took her hands in his. "We are safe at Montsegur—or safe nowhere."

"How is Bernard taking it...or are you two speaking?"

"Bernard is stubborn." Jean's face took on a sadness she'd only seen twice, at the change to his plans to become a Parfait and at the death of their child. "My hope is that Montsegur will fortify our faith in God and in one another." He sank down onto the bed. "Let us try to rest. Daylight is near."

"Will we ride on tomorrow?"

"No. There are others joining us. We shall depart the following day."

* * *

As the towers of the Castle of Foix faded from sight, the departing caravan focused on their arrival at Montsegur. Their eagerness reassured Clotilde that no word of the Count of Foix's revelations had reached their ears.

Even Blanche attempted a cheerful façade, although as Clotilde stole glances at her, it seemed more the painted smile of a marionette. She had a fleeting but fading thought that perhaps she should discuss some of what the Count of Foix had revealed. Clotilde wavered; she feared any release of Blanche's tightly contained emotions.

As they neared Montsegur, the group's curiosity grew. Clotilde strained to take it all in as it came into view. She'd heard that it had been built somewhere between the eighth and the eleventh century. But by whom, and for what purpose, was still unclear. It had fallen into ruins by 1204, although some Perfectae had established occupancy even then. Legends abounded concerning Montsegur's mysterious positioning and unique design. Without vital roads or commanding a territory, it was not considered a fortress as were other chateaus. Its architectural alignment with the sun prompted speculation that it may have been a temple to the sun.

Cathars simply considered Montsegur as their most holy destination, a center for God's Light. The dying were carried up steep mountain paths to receive the *consolamentum*. Wealthy counts and countesses—nobility of all ranks—came to Montsegur to practice their faith. God willing, such Light would be strong enough to vanquish the darkness overtaking them, Clotilde prayed as they slowed to a halt.

Slanting rays of the sun rose from behind the pinnacle of limestone rock and bathed Montsegur in a misty halo. All knelt in prayer. As the last "amen" faded, Clotilde cast her glance around the spring-green slopes lying peacefully under their blanket of cows, sheep and flowers. The lyrics of a troubadour's song burst from her. "The knowledge that makes me rejoice, teaches me to praise each day at sunrise."

"I taught you that song when you were just a wee one. How you loved to sing it." Blanche's words were interrupted by Jean's command to return to the wagons. The caravan continued until it reached the remaining third, a steep incline, which could not be traversed except by climbing. On foot, and supporting the elderly and ill, they continued upwards, exhausted and elated when they reached the top.

No medieval castle equaled the Great Gate of Montsegur. Many gasps were heard as they stared at walls two meters in width. And yet with no protecting tower or crenellation, Montsegur's purpose was not that of a fortress, Clotilde decided.

Jean, who had caught her puzzlement, agreed. "A fortress it is not, but Montsegur is as strong a sanctuary as any spot on this earth—and doubly blessed."

A sudden chill overtook her as Jean drew her to him with a fierceness that filled his voice. "Whatever comes, we shall face it together."

THIRTEEN

Coustaussa, France-April, Present

"There it is—the Deodat Roche Museum." Eric braked as he pulled the car into a parking space beneath a chestnut tree. He turned the ignition off and said, "I think a quick visit might add to my research."

"Right. And provide me a breather before going on to Coustaussa. Pierre expects it to connect with me—and I'm not sure I'm ready." Obviously not, I thought, aware that I hadn't made the slightest move to get out of the car.

"So, we buy some time in the museum," he said, as I opened my door.

The museum was a gem, an ancient structure whose interior had been skillfully converted into a cool, open expanse of well-designed displays. It clearly was a shrine to the work of Deodat Roche, renowned as an expert on the Cathars. More than just an expert, he was often referred to as the "Cathar Pope."

I wandered through the museum's spacious rooms, staring into glass cases containing voluminous writings, a number of photos, and a few sparse artifacts. I managed, with the aid of an English guidebook, to do a quick scrutiny of the lower level's exhibits—all testifying to the fact that scant evidence of Cathars remained.

After I'd seen the last glass case, I headed upstairs and over to a cushy leather couch in the room's furthest corner. Empty of people, its pristine wall space was dedicated to photos that chronicled Monsieur Roche's illustrious career.

Whether it was my profession, or the force that emanated from the images, I felt the photos to be the most compelling exhibit in the museum. The powerful black and white images of Deodat Roche's life commanded scrutiny. His intense energy, whether photographed alone or with others, hypnotized me. The huge eyes dominating his slight form conveyed an indomitable spirit. Every photo attested to his deep commitment to justice for the Cathars. I took my time examining each one. The last in the series showed him still vigorous into his hundredth year. His aesthetically lean form suddenly reminded me of Pierre.

My thoughts returned to our strange meeting. For all Pierre's warning that we not be deflected by mysteries, what remained was the larger mystery surrounding the man himself. One moment he'd twinkle with the enthusiasm and directness of a child, the next his comments conveyed the occult wisdom of an ageless soul who'd come from far away to occupy this body.

Returning to my corner, I sank back down on the couch and stared fixedly at Roche's last photo. Like the paintings whose eyes seem to follow you, his locked on mine, echoing Pierre's, "Feel Coustaussa—but discuss nothing with Dr. Carter."

* * *

"There you are." Eric's voice startled me out of a doze.

I opened my eyes to find him sitting beside me. His amused look suggested he'd been there for some time. "How long have you been here?" I asked.

"Not long, just a few minutes." He reached to brush a strand of hair from my eyes. "You needed what we Brits refer to as a little toes-up."

"I guess so. I was dreaming of Pierre in Coustaussa—only it wasn't destroyed." I gave a big stretch. "Strange, but I'm ready, I think."

"Me too. I found a couple more Cathar books in English." He held out a packet of books. "I'm particularly excited at this one." He drew out a slim volume that covered the Cathar religion. "I'm convinced that their treasure lay in their religion and...." Eric halted mid-sentence as he stood and walked up to the photos.

"Wow," he said as I joined him. "Even without much in the way of tangible discoveries, he accomplished his lifetime's quest—to bring the Cathars back to life." Reaching the last photo, he shook his head and said, "The old fellow knew that the treasure of the Cathars lay hidden in the intangibles." He pointed to the packet of books he'd left on the sofa. "I'm hoping these may shed some light on what it was." He picked up his package, glanced at his watch and said, "We'd better press on."

* * *

Soon after leaving Arques, Coustaussa's ruins came into view. A few remnants of walls gave a ghostly hint of what they had once enclosed. I reread the reference book's account: "Built by the Trencaval family in the early twelfth century, Coustaussa was strategically positioned to control the passage between the Corbieres and the Aude Valley. Its location allowed Coustaussa to serve as a base for travelers—Cathar Parfaits, shepherds, troubadours, and Lords of nearby castles." An intriguing sentence caught my eye. "At the beginning of the fourteenth century there remained a few Cathar Perfectae who came from Coustaussa."

I read the sentence aloud, adding, "Coustaussa sheltered Cathars fifty years after the massacre at Montsegur. Pierre said it was destroyed soon after the massacre." Eric shrugged as he parked the car alongside the castle ruins.

I sat for a moment, staring at the ruins as Eric turned the key off. "'Soon' could mean sixty years later."

"I suppose you're right. Simon de Montfort occupied it, delaying its destruction. Hmm—strange that such an important man set up camp in Coustaussa rather than turning it over to one of his lieutenants." I stared off into space.

"Maybe he found what he was looking for and obliterated any conjecture by destroying it." Eric said as he opened the car door. "Let's go have a look."

I grabbed my Leica, extra film and the infrared filter. My necklace fell out as I did, deciding me that it would be safer on my neck for now. It felt good to have it back on, but I vowed to find a safe hiding place before meeting with Benjamin.

"Hurry on over and have a look," Eric called out from one of the ruined walls. Fortunately the climb was easy, I thought as I joined him. I set up my tripod and camera, eager to get behind my lens before the sorrowful mood of the place got to me. Eric walked around what remained of the castle's interior, now scarcely identifiable as anything but a collection of rubble overgrown by grasses. I took a full roll of film of the ruins, but soon headed beyond the remains. Inching my way over piles of rock and down the sloping hillsides, I gingerly cradled my camera bag until I came to what once may have been an exterior entry. Wanting to capture the ruin's sense of being a sentinel, I unclasped my tripod, set it up and studied the scene.

Rennes le Chateau's Magdala tower hovered in the distance, prompting me to wonder whether the tower was designed to watch Coustaussa. I shook my head and turned my attention to what looked like a cave. Clutching my camera case, I positioned each step sideways as I inched my way down to the opening. Uncertain as to whether it was formed by the tumbling remains of the castle walls, or whether it was an actual cave, I entered. A cool draft of air beckoned me to go deeper into the cave's moist darkness, until a sudden cascade of falling rock forced my quick retreat.

I blinked as I exited and saw a haze of dust lingering on the air. Shielding the sun from my eyes, I turned full circle, expecting to see Eric as the cause of the slide. Nothing and no one stirred.

An uneasy calm prevailed, its hush pregnant with something that caused the hair on my arms to rise. I shook the feeling away by preparing the low-light lens and filters for shots of the cave's interior. Determined to explore deep within, I recalled that the entire area was riddled with such caves. My mind clicked as fast as the camera's shutter. An area riddled with caves, a castle whose strategic position was only a day's ride from Usson Castle where the escaping Cathars were last seen—could the Cathar treasure have been hidden near here, only to be discovered six hundred years later by the priest at Rennes le Chateau?

A sound of hoofbeats broke my reverie. I rushed out the cave's entrance to see a horse and rider speeding away, not more than forty feet below where I stood. My camera hung as though frozen to my fingers. Before I could focus, horse and rider were gone, leaving not a trace of dust cloud.

Baffled, I sat down on a boulder, remembering my mirage at Carcassonne. "Feel Coustaussa." Pierre's counsel returned as clearly as though he were here. I laid my camera aside and closed my eyes. I felt the breeze carrying the scent of blossoms, the afternoon sun on my face, the cool hardness of the rock beneath me, the faint soreness of feet unaccustomed to boots, and …

A bird's trill suddenly ceased as a piercing cry filled the air. The depth of its anguish froze me to the spot. A man, I thought, given the wail's volume and resonance. I was torn between opening my eyes and an instinct not to. Remaining perfectly still, an immense pain filled me as a word rang out.

"Clotilde!" The strange name reverberated with such suffocating pain that I felt as if my heart would break. I opened my eyes—to nothing. No sound, no man in pain, no horse. Nothing but a heart that beat too fast and a sorrow begging for release.

Tears streamed unchecked. Eyes tightly closed, I beseeched the man to return. A sound drew me—the now familiar sliding stream of falling rock. I jumped up as a shrill whine filled my ears and shards of rock flew through the air.

Gunshot! I spun around, one hand clutching at any handhold, the other gripping my camera case, as I raced up the hill.

Rounding a rise that shielded me, I came to a sudden halt, breathless and alert for the sound of gunshot. The silence was rent, not with another gunshot, but with what sounded like the tones used with the strange name that still rang in my ears. I must be wrong, I decided.

"Dana, are you all right?" Eric asked as he raced up. "I thought I heard a shot. When I found your tripod up above, I thought..." He stared. "Say something." I registered his alarm, but it couldn't pierce my paralysis. "You must be in shock," he said as he took my arm and guided me back to the car.

I moved like an automaton. In spite of the gunshot, I felt reluctant to leave. As we reached the car, I spun around. No one was in view. My voice returned as I got in the car. "Not a word, just drive."

"As you say." Eric's voice was gentle as the car sped away.

I kept returning to the haunting image of the ruins, feeling unbearable sorrow as they faded from sight. The reality of the gunshot brought a lump of fear and an awareness that the cessation of any further shots, as I scrambled away, was intentional. It was meant as a message—a "go away—stop what you're doing" edict. I turned to Eric, my voice hollow.

"There was a gunshot. I jumped. It chipped the stone I sat on."

"You should have said so sooner." He swung the car into a U-turn and headed back to the castle. "Someone shot at you. We can't just drive away." His rage grew as we drove into the parking area.

"Please, Eric. There was no sign of anyone—no car, no person and no gun. You were there and saw nothing." I reached over to him. "Let's just chalk it up to my imagination or a careless hunter, and move on."

Eric opened the door and got out. "Now that I know it was a gunshot, I want to have a look around." He glared, saying, "Stay where you are, lock the door and get down in your seat." Before I could respond, he was gone.

Slumping down in my seat wasn't an option. My eyes did a full scan of the landscape as I replayed the entire incident, trying to reinforce the belief that only Eric was anywhere nearby.

Something was stirring in the direction Eric had gone. My heartbeat quickened as a head darted from behind a boulder. I froze, my breath coming fast.

I ducked and screamed, "No!," preparing to resist as the car door opened.

"Dana, it's me. What happened?" Eric said as he entered.

"Where did you come from?" I needed to hear that he'd come from the same direction where the hidden figure appeared.

"From the rear of the car. I did a full sweep of the area without seeing a soul." He reached into his pocket. "But I did find this." He unfolded a piece of paper.

I began to translate it. "Archaeological Excavation. Observe restricted area signs. Keep out—Museum of Toulouse—Dr. Benjamin Taylor." I let it fall. "Our friend, Benjamin Taylor again. But we didn't see any such notice, at least I didn't."

"Nor I. And nothing resembling an archaeological dig." Eric started the car and turned it toward Arques. "And nothing warranting a gunshot or the look on your face just now. You were terrified by something."

I told him I'd seen a furtive figure staring out from behind the rocks.

"Damn!" Eric seemed torn between returning to the ruins and continuing on to Arques. "I'm headed to ask Pierre to call in the gendarmes."

"Pierre said he was leaving for a few days. Going back will prove futile. As for the gendarmes, such publicity could stop our series in its tracks. I'm fine, really. Whoever fired that gun just wanted to scare us away." I kept on talking as Eric frowned. "Let's move on for now and discuss it with Pierre when we see him."

"As soon as we see Benjamin I intend to have it out with him. If he ordered one of his goons to scare us away, I'll..." Eric screeched the car around.

"Except..." I began as Eric finished my sentence.

"Except for the fact that Pierre said not to mention anything to Benjamin about our stopping at Coustaussa. That's no longer an option."

We both fell silent until we passed a sign saying, *FOIX - 3 Kilometers*. "It'll be dark soon." Eric said. "Let's do a drive by only."

"Agreed. I'm more than ready for a glass of wine on the terrace."

"We could stop at a bed and breakfast in Foix, but I'd like to get a few more kilometers under our belt." Eric gave me a questioning look.

"Fine by me. Mirepoix's not that much further." I settled back into my seat and closed my eyes as he drove on. My thoughts returned to the memory of the man's anguished cries. They reverberated even stronger than the gunshot or the image of the man in the photo. Haunting, I thought as I fell into a half-sleep. Something prompted the sudden release of my sorrow, as Eric's voice penetrated. "It's all right. I'm here." I startled, unsure whether he'd actually spoken, but filled with peace.

* * *

Eric's attention was on the road as I came fully around. He turned and said, "We're about to enter Foix. Glad to have you back. I'll need your help navigating. This town's bigger than I thought."

The three spires of Foix's castle loomed into view. The chateau's hilltop perch, although not formidably high, seemed the perfect setting for the townspeople to admire it. Behind its modest hill rose much higher mountains, cradling the city at their feet. Foix glowed, rosy and smug, in the slanting rays of daylight.

The castle looked in good repair. I turned to our guidebook. "Thanks to the protection provided by the King of Aragon, the town of Foix was never really subjected to serious attack during the crusade against the Cathars—in spite of Simon de Montfort's threat to 'melt the rock like dripping fat and grill its master over it.'"

"Interesting, but I need you to watch for signs so we don't get swallowed up in Foix's narrow streets," Eric said as he slowed our approach.

I did my best. Using the castle as our target, I alerted Eric to roads that might lead to it. The streets were challenging, cobbled and walled on all sides by three and four story homes that dated back to the twelfth century. Soon we were enveloped in an endless procession of vehicles as the road narrowed and neared the castle.

Eric smiled as I craned out and took a few shots of the castle. "You did a great job getting us here. When you've captured enough shots…" He nudged the car along our interminable parade. "I say we head for Mirepoix."

"I'm ready and there's a sign," I shouted. "Turn right."

Eric adroitly made the turn, leaving me with fleeting impressions of tiny sidewalks packed with people moving in and out of shops filled with strange wares—sausages and in-line skates side by side.

"It seems so out of place in a setting frozen in the past," I said as Eric gave a quick glance out his window.

"I agree," he said. "I'm glad they didn't destroy Foix." He looked out. "A fascinating place, but we need to move if we hope to make Mirepoix before dark."

"Right," I said as the castle's towers disappeared from our rear view mirror.

A sky of deep rose with streaks of jade green and midnight blues took my breath away as we neared the outskirts of Mirepoix. I turned to Eric. *"Le heure bleue*, the blue hour, a time of transition—so poignant and evanescent."

He nodded—his look deeper than any words, before returning his focus to the road and a sign saying, "4 kilometers to Mirepoix." "Let's start looking for a *gite*."

I agreed and returned my attention not only to roadside signs but also to the countryside's hypnotic appeal. I chalked it up to the Ariege's contrast to the Department of Aude. Whatever it was, its soft, green landscape, bathed in the last rays of the setting sun, stirred a strange contentment as we approached Mirepoix.

"Lights are coming on up ahead." Eric said. "With any luck we should see signs indicating rooms available." He glanced over at me. "I know you'll spot one."

And he was right. We soon passed a sign. "Stop. I think it said 'Auberge.'"

Eric pulled off the roadway, leaving the car's headlights shining on the sign. *Relais du Silence. Auberge de Mystere—5 kilometres a droite.* "Turn right up ahead and let's go check it out. It's close enough to Mirepoix."

Eric smiled. "Great, since we can't see anything of the village tonight."

We drove down a long country lane, a field of sheep running at our sound, only to stop a few yards away and stare. I smiled at their solemn faces as the headlights picked them out of the growing dark. My smile fast faded.

"We must have reached the five kilometer mark, Eric, and..." I peered through the dark. "Wait, a think that might be a driveway up ahead."

A driveway and a sign, *Auberge de Mystere*. Eric drove slowly down the lane, past a stable and into a courtyard. We parked and walked up to the *auberge*.

"I think someone heard us." I nodded at a woman standing in the doorway and began my greeting. "*Bon soir, Madame. Nous voidrons une chambre...*"

"You're American." She looked from me to Eric.

"I am. Eric is from London. But you sound American." I looked her up and down—blond hair, very fair skin, a figure tending toward plump and deep blue eyes that focused their direct stare. "Wisconsin or Minnesota, I'd say."

"St. Paul." She turned as a man approached. "My husband is from Dijon," she said as he approached and held out his hand.

"*Bon soir, Madame and Monsieur.*" He looked from Eric to me.

"*Mademoiselle* Dana Palmer."

"Eric Taylor here."

"Andre Villeneuve. My wife is Lena. Forgive my English." He moved aside. "Please come in. We have a very nice room available. Dinner is at eight."

As we followed Andre and Lena inside, I froze. The house captivated me. So much so that it took me a moment to ask, "Might you have two rooms?"

"Surely." He looked from me to Eric. "One on the second floor, the other in back of the kitchen area."

"That will do for me just fine." Eric smiled. "I'll take the downstairs room."

"I'll show you the rooms while Andre fixes you an aperitif," Lena said as she guided us down a long hallway that skirted the kitchen and ended at Eric's room. "Will you be staying long?"

"Only one night," I said, a stab of pain at the simple phrase. She nodded and opened the door to a charming room, prints on the wall, a white coverlet on the bed and a bouquet of flowers on the desk.

139

Eric's smile widened at the large bed, good reading light and ample desk. An adjoining room with a small shower, toilet, bidet and basin prompted his, "Perfect."

Lena turned to me. "Very good, now to show you to your room. It can be a bit confusing to find. The chateau is old, its rooms added arbitrarily."

We followed her down the hallway, past the entry area and up a wide set of stairs. Lena pointed to the roof beams. "It is one of the oldest houses in the area, having survived the famous flood of 1279. The dike that held back Puivert Lake burst, causing terrible flooding that destroyed most of Mirepoix."

"I read something about a flood and a lake diverted." Eric looked up and turned to Lena. "But thirteenth century—the house doesn't seem that old."

"Older. It was built sometime in the late eleven hundreds. The flood missed it because it stood well back from the River Hers. They reconstructed the entire town of Mirepoix in 1289—except for this house and four others. It was a miracle it survived."

"And beautifully, I'd say." Eric studied the solid beams and flooring.

"Before we bought the chateau eight years ago, this level had been remodeled. It was considerably opened out, the stairs widened and four more rooms carved out of the original two. The floors above this one contain four good sized rooms as well."

"The house is bigger than it looks from the road." A deep sigh escaped my paralysis. "It's lovely."

Lena smiled as she hurried down the hallway and inserted a large key into the first door on the right. "Your room is one of our finest."

I stepped into the room and stopped, overcome by a feeling of belonging. The room was so big that the large bed, tucked lengthwise along a niche in the wall, seemed small. Rich draperies hung at each side of the bed, tied back with golden tassels highlighting a cream satin spread piled with masses of European style pillows. Lena saw my eyes go to the silk cornices. "It looks like a bed from Versailles."

"Luxurious yes, but practical also." She drew the heavy cords and the entire bed was enshrouded in draperies. "These houses were drafty and unheated except by the fireplace." She turned and pointed across the room. "Voila—the fireplace."

"I spoke too soon on my choice of rooms." Eric said as he walked over to the open fireplace and settled into a large chair drawn up to a table nearby. "I could write all through the night in this chair." He reached over to the rock front of the massive fireplace that extended into a wide platform. "Room to store my books and drink."

Both Eric and Lena looked at me, awaiting a response. I stared fixedly at the fireplace, feeling myself drawn, like the smoke— away.

"Are you all right?" Lena's touch startled me. I blinked, unable to respond.

"She's fascinated by fireplaces." Eric to the rescue, I thought, vaguely aware he had murmured something plausible.

"True," I said fumbling for a credible remark. "So much so..." I looked at Eric and back to Lena, "...that he'd have as much luck at getting this room away from me as..." I pointed to the ashes, "that burnt wood has of being restored."

"Well, then. I'm happy you like it." Lena smiled as she moved a vase of flowers away from the fire. "Please join us in the lounge area for an aperitif."

Lena seemed puzzled as I continued staring at the fireplace. She walked to the doorway and held out the room key. I took it and, with great reluctance, followed her and Eric down the stairway. "An aperitif would be lovely. Thank you." I forced the proper words while longing only to return to my room and remain there.

Lena paused when we reached the entry to the lounge. "I can have your luggage brought up." Absorbed in thought, I felt grateful when Eric responded.

"No. I'll bring it in and join you in the lounge soon," Eric said, giving me a strange look as Lena led me away to meet her other guests.

The lounge was spacious and welcoming, comfy-looking overstuffed chairs and sofas clustered around a fireplace even larger than the one in my room. The guests looked up and smiled. "My dear guests, it looks as though we are destined to have an English speaking gathering." Lena's cheeks dimpled as she turned to me. "Meet Dana Palmer, an American. Her friend, an Englishman, will soon join us." She turned to the gentlemen who stood, hands outstretched. "Monsieur and Madame Edwards are from New York. Monsieur and Madame Levi are from Jerusalem. Monsieur and Madame Everidge are from London." I hesitated, hand extended, as the wives brushed light kisses swiftly on both sides of my face. Lena, pleased with the group's welcome, excused herself to return to the kitchen.

I joined them around the fire as drinks were poured and toasts made. They had just asked me how we'd come to be in Mirepoix when Eric walked in. I introduced him and said, "I'll let Eric explain how we came to be here."

His accent expanded its rich overtones, very British with Scots remnants. Commanding, masculine and slightly pulling everyone's leg, I thought, as he began. "I'll have a single malt Scotch, thank you." He settled back with an appreciative look as his drink arrived.

"What brought us to Mirepoix?" He looked at me and grinned. "Mystery brought us here." Lena walked in just then.

"Oh, yes, our sign. But as to our mystery…" Hesitating, she turned to her all ears audience. "Let's hold that discussion until dinner. I've been sent to inform you that dinner is ready, and that our chef, my husband, allows no delays."

The corpulent Frederick Levi led the way, giving a nod as he said, "Andre's cooking would command haste from a king."

Dinner was unforgettable, as was the conversation. We enjoyed the progression from appetizer to entrée to dessert, with little or no comment except "Exquisite," "delectable" and "formidable!" Each seemed to savor every bite of salmon, potatoes au gratin, wild asparagus and tart tartin. Conversation resumed in earnest as the plates were taken away and cheeses, olives and bread appeared.

"Now, Mr. Taylor, if you will please explain your *mystery* comment, Andre and I shall reveal ours." Lena turned to Andre as he poured out Armagnac.

Andre extended a tray of the liqueur as he commented, "Lena named our auberge for its mystery, one that has never been solved. We must hope that yours is more accessible to explanation, Monsieur Taylor."

Eric smiled as he began. "I am a writer and Dana is a photographer. We have been assigned to do a series on the Cathars, one that will try to unravel the mystery surrounding the reemergence of interest in this group. Our series will include: Who were they? Why do they haunt this land? What was the mystery that threatened the Pope and Catholicism? Why was every Cathar killed? Is there a Cathar treasure, and if so, where is it and what is it?" Eric paused, lifted his drink and swirled its heavy richness against the glass before he drank.

"We heard of them for the first time in Carcassonne." Pamela Edwards looked intently at Eric. "Tell us more."

"The Cathars lived throughout this area during the twelfth and thirteenth centuries. The Cathars, however, had no land, few possessions and no vast cities or monuments to focus anyone's attention on. All those castles that you see lining the "Pays de Cathare" are not Cathar. But the group was important enough to destroy."

"All killed, you say, old man—by the Church. Unlikely the Pope would sanction killing anyone, I'd say," Ian Everidge said as he looked around, his color heightening at the silence in the room. His next words sounded part placating and part confusion. "I thought the Inquisition business..." He faltered. "I mean, weren't the Crusades in Jerusalem—noble knights to the rescue—purging the world of heretics?"

Frederick Levi's voice, iced with contempt, filled the room. "The Crusades didn't begin and end with Jerusalem. They went on to indict all non-Catholics. The Inquisition used the knights to continue the bloodshed by purging Europe of anyone threatening the doctrine of the Catholic Church. Nobility didn't play any part in it—greed did." Frederick's words were delivered with clipped statement of fact simplicity, but his eyes were rimmed with pain. "That particularly brutal pogrom not only destroyed Cathars, but also Jews, Gypsies and all suspected of being heretical to the Church's interests. It was then that the wearing of the yellow cross began, adopted later by the Nazis." Frederick looked unwaveringly around the room. "As to the Cathars, imagine," he turned back toward the Edwards, "one thousand years from now, someone asking, 'Who were the Jews? Why were they eliminated?'"

Ilse's eyes had never left her husband's, but seeing the emotion in them, she continued for him. "Fortunately, against all odds, we have survived as a people and as a religion." She turned to Eric and me. "Your Cathars must have had something very powerful to warrant complete extermination."

"*Goodness.*" Lena's one-word response silenced the room. The Edwards seemed reluctant to voice any comment. The Levi's held hands in wordless empathy.

Andre's voice lifted the atmosphere. "Goodness they certainly had, my dear wife." He shrugged. "But as to its being the sole cause of their destruction, it seems too much a mystery to solve over dinner." He gave his wife a slight wink. "Lena's eager to regale you with our own mystery." Lena nodded and began.

"You know that this house dates back to the early twelfth century. The original owners were Cathars, as was most of Mirepoix—including the lord of the area. We traced the house's provenance back to the original owners, the Armand de Fanjeaux's. Having moved from Fanjeaux to Mirepoix, a son, Jean, inherited the home, took a wife..." Lena paused. "Her name wasn't a common French name."

"Clotilde."

I jumped to my feet, knocked my drink to the floor, and let out a cry as glass shattered and everyone stared. Andre made a dismissive gesture as he cleared away the broken glass. Eric offered me his drink, saying, "You look as though you need it."

I faced their waiting stares. "I'm sorry, I..." My words stuttered to a halt, unable to form any rational explanation as I turned to Lena. "Please forgive me and do go on." I took my chair, feeling chilled as I waited.

She spoke softly. "At the time of the Catholic Inquisition, Jean and Clotilde, along with many other Cathars, escaped to Montsegur."

I grabbed Eric's hand as I whispered, "All were killed."

Lena must have heard me. "Not everyone died. Records show that four escaped." She looked at Andre.

"True," he said. "Four Cathars scaled the steep walls with the Cathar treasure." Andre's eyes filled with compassion. "I pray Jean and Clotilde survived."

"I'm sure of it." Lena smiled brightly and added, "Although I doubt they ever came back to their home. Because of the mystery, that is."

Andre rose to leave the room. "While Lena works up to the climax, I shall go and retrieve our treasure." My heart pounded as he walked away.

Lena smiled. "Now don't be expecting any gold or jewels. Ours is of no monetary value." She looked up as Andre returned. "You would agree, I am sure."

Andre nodded as he stood beside our table. "Yes, well, I thought so when I discovered it—until the folks from Toulouse began to trot down here to examine it." He carefully handed a box to Eric. "Be careful opening it. It has remained hidden for over seven hundred years, behind a boulder in the fireplace in Mademoiselle Dana's room." Andre seemed apprehensive as he gave Eric the box. "We rarely display it, but somehow it seemed fitting we do so this evening."

Eric laid the top of the simple box aside and lifted out a fragile square of silk enclosing something within. A look of puzzlement clouded his features. Silence grew as I leaned in to get a closer view.

"That marking, let me see what it is." Tears began, for I knew the answer even as Lena and Andre replied.

"It is Jean's family seal." Andre replied.

Eric looked up at me before going any further. I couldn't speak but nodded 'yes.' He resumed his unwrapping of the fragile silk.

"What is it?" Ian said as he rose to look.

"It seems to be a strand of hair tied with a ribbon—perhaps two different strands of hair." Eric's voice cracked. He coughed to clear his throat.

Andre, anxiety flickering in his eyes, bent to examine his delicately fragile mystery. "*Absolument.* There are two distinct colors of hair entwined together. Someone wrapped them in the silk, impressed the seal and hid it in the fireplace."

I leaned in closer—so far that my necklace fell outside my blouse, its pendant landing gently on the embossed silk— alongside the seal—a perfect twin to its design of a dove and a cross.

FOURTEEN

Montsegur, France-May, 1243

"Cut off the head of the Dragon." The phrase kept running through Clotilde's thoughts as she looked across the crowded courtyard of Montsegur and waited for Bernadette. The faces that passed by were those of ordinary people, simple souls seeking a place to study or pray. Clotilde spent her days helping the growing numbers of people arriving. It was getting harder to find beds for them. Bernadette, who lived in the makeshift village just outside the castle walls, often came to help.

Suddenly Bernadette's face appeared in the crowd, a group of people following her. "Dear Clotilde," she said as she neared, "the Maurs family has come from Montaillou. Have we a place for them?" She introduced the elderly couple, their two sons, one daughter and five grandchildren. "Their daughter, Raymonde, is a Parfaite. Her socia was too ill. I carried her to the infirmary."

"You honor us." Clotilde gave Raymonde the bow of adoration and said, "I know how weary you must be." She looked at Bernadette. "There is some room outside the keep, in the far corner. Do stop at the granary for food and drink." Bernadette nodded and led them over to the keep.

As she departed, Clotilde noticed the change in Bernadette. Gone were the lines of sorrow from her mother's death, her steps lighter and manner eager in her new role. Being of service added radiance to her features. Her latest charges, in contrast, were dusty, lean and barely of this earth.

An image came to mind of another Parfaite and her socia who had arrived yesterday. Like foxes pursued by hounds, they told of tribulations beyond imagining, living in first one forest and then another, each a target for atrocities should they be discovered and fall victim to the Inquisition. Help came from God via the many Cathar Believers who helped them escape to remote caves. Always on the move to find sanctuaries further afield, they rarely spent more than a day or two in any one place. Their joy at having arrived in Montsegur shone through their careworn bodies.

Clotilde let out a long sigh—for their exhaustion and her own. She'd spent many nights awake due to the noise and crowded conditions. Although their living space was small, at least she and Jean were together. Poor Blanche, however, had no sooner been reunited with Pierre than he fell ill and was taken to the infirmary. Pierre's mother had died shortly before Blanche arrived. And now his health was fast failing. Clotilde turned at the sound of Blanche's voice.

"Clotilde!" Blanche's tone held accusation and relief. "I've been asking everywhere for you."

Clotilde responded with a rush of irritation. "I was called to nurse the sister of the knight, Jordan Calvert. They arrived just before dawn, after journeying many days. A young woman, she received the consolamentum and died peacefully."

As Blanche's lip began to quaver, Clotilde held out her arms and Blanche fell into them, yielding as a fearful child, until she reared up. "We must stay together."

"Dear Blanche, we are together. I was headed to join you and Pierre at the infirmary. I pray he is faring well."

"Not well." Blanche wiped tears as she turned away. "The consumption is taking his last strength. He's had naught but liquid to sip."

"Perhaps his body needs a rest from digestion." Clotilde turned Blanche to face her. "Let's go make him a poultice of comfrey, dear sister."

"I fear for him." Blanche's gaze withdrew to some landscape of gloom.

"Dear sister, do go and rest and I shall go stay with Pierre," Clotilde said as she gently turned Blanche in the direction of her quarters.

Her own rest would come much later. The compound had long been asleep before she and Jean finally retired to their little space—exhausted but awake. In recounting her day, Clotilde confessed her despair that Blanche would return to her old self at Montsegur. "Her fear has only grown since Pierre's illness."

Jean enfolded Clotilde into a spoon-shaped embrace, feeling her heart beat as he said, "With Pierre's long work with tanning fumes, his lungs..."She buried her face deeper into his shoulder as he continued. "We must accept and rejoice as he meets his God." Jean began stroking her hair. So keenly did she welcome the soothing impact of his touch that she hesitated before revealing another deep concern. "I fear that there is naught ahead for any of us but death." Clotilde sat up, her steady stare meeting his. "A new arrival mentioned plans for a siege of Montsegur."

Jean got up and poured each a glass of wine, handing one to Clotilde before he began to speak. His voice was muted but firm. "The Cathar bishop, Guilhabert de Castres, returned today from a secret visit to various chateaux in the area."

"I'm dismayed that our bishop would risk the journey at his advanced age."

"He's done it before on several occasions, my love. He leaves Montsegur in the dead of night under much secrecy. He often returns jubilant at having helped his flock, but today he returned in great sorrow. A group of displaced lords of Languedoc informed him that Hugues des Arcis, the new seneschal in charge of guarding Carcassonne, and Peter Amiel, the Archbishop of Narbonne, plan to assemble an army large enough to lay siege to Montsegur."

Clotilde looked horror stricken. "So it is true. And what of our defenders, Raymond de Perella and Pierre-Roger?"

"They are aware and ready. A siege of Montsegur will prove more daunting than the soldiers of the Pope can foresee."

"We must do something." Clotilde began to pace the small confines of their bedchamber like an animal in a cage.

"With our current supply of water and food, we can hold out indefinitely." He took her hand. "Do come sit by me. Our benefactors vow to provide defenders valiant enough to defend Montsegur from any siege."

Even as Jean folded her in his arms, Clotilde felt the restless need for action more than solace. "Surely we can do more than trust," she said, looking into his tired eyes, stunned at how weary he looked in the candle's glow. His once solid features seemed emptied of that which had captivated her—his youthful curiosity, humor and confidence. It frightened her. She drew his hand to her heart. "You are all to me."

"And you to me," he said. "Remember that when I leave Montsegur."

"Leave Montsegur?" Disbelief filled her. "I fear for your safety."

"My safety is not important." His response alarmed her.

Jean rushed words of reassurance. "Trust that I shall be safe. Should a siege come, however, I must consider safeguarding our church and its leaders, Bishop Bertrand, Bishop Guilhabert and others." He drew her back down on their bed. "Even more important are the teachings of our Church. These must endure." Letting the meaning sink it, he waited. "Say I have your support."

"Always." Clotilde broached another concern. "Bernard—will he go also?"

"No, my love. I asked him to remain with you and Blanche while I am away." Disbelief rang in his words. "But he was so angered at my news that he left Montsegur." As Clotilde's eyes widened, Jean continued, "He intends to reach Toulouse and attempt to marshal the support of the many faidit-lords in the area." Jean sighed. "If he succeeds, he believes that Raymond VII's support for Montsegur would be assured."

"But it's said that Raymond VII is now a toothless tiger."

"It's true that he has been de-fanged. But to give the Count his due, he did what he could and, with such a show of support, may…"

"He did very little, in my opinion." Clotilde fumed, knowing that Raymond was the one man who could have united every count in the territory in support of him, including those of northern Spain. "He could have saved the Cathars, his castles and the whole of the south of France. But now he's reduced to…."

"You are too hard on him," Jean interrupted. "His latest efforts were to attempt to take possession of Montsegur."

"Take possession of Montsegur. Toward what end?" Clotilde frowned in an attempt to understand.

"Toward an end less painful for the Cathars, my dear. It is said that he spoke at great length to the Pope. He suggested that the Pope should consider having the Dominicans relinquish their Inquisitor duties. In exchange the Count gave his solemn vow, as a disciple of the Church, that he would assure containment of heresy."

"Is there any hope that such would be allowed?"

"It all backfired. The Pope not only ignored such a request, but also further humiliated the Count by extending his excommunication and relegating him to a non-entity. The Church is deaf to his protestations and seeks action, not vows, from Raymond VII. Only Blanche of Castille's intercession saved the Count's title."

"I'd have expected as much." Clotilde bristled, her reply fueled by rebellion as she added, "We shall not be as easily intimidated."

"It is for that reason that I must leave Montsegur for a time." He lifted her chin. "Say you understand."

"I do understand. I've not been blind at your many consultations with the Cathar Duke and Bishop. Only confused at exactly what role you play." Strength and determination suffused her silent question—and hope.

"What the Church and God wills. More than that, I cannot say." He blew out the candle, whispering, "Trust me, my love, you shall know as soon as I do. For now we must rest and reserve our strength for what lies ahead."

* * *

Within days the siege began. Hugues Des Arcis, at the head of the Inquisition's army of French knights and men-at-arms, pitched camp below Montsegur. The Cathars put their trust in God and Montsegur's valiant defenders, a garrison of men wholly committed to protecting Montsegur. That it dare be put under siege only heightened their resolve and strengthened their faith. They defended more than a structure, or even the people within. It had become their temple, the outward and visible expression of their beliefs. Not only had they adopted the Cathar faith and love of Montsegur, but also, as its defenders, boldly exhibited such valor in its defense that even some of their foes defected to become Cathar supporters.

There were by then, several hundred people in Montsegur itself, plus many more Cathars clustered outside its walls where a group of Parfaites and Parfaits had converted a cluster of shelters into a quasi-village. Their community soon expanded to incorporate the garrison of one hundred fifty men, the families of knights and men-at-arms and all Cathars who managed to make their way to the overcrowded fortress.

And fortress Montsegur had become. The one-time cathedral of Light was fast overrun by stone-guns, wooden propulsion machines mounted on the eastern barbican wall. Armed defenders rushed to and fro throughout the night, replenishing their necessary armament.

Clotilde marveled at the support that Cathars could and did give. While disapproving of warfare and not participating in the assaults, they found other ways to aid their valiant defenders. With all the cruelty imposed on those of their faith, the Cathars showed no rancor, hatred or retaliation. Morale was high and faith was strong. All went about being of service in whatever way was needed. Only one face came to her as being lost in darkness—that of Blanche, her beloved sister.

Through work, Clotilde prevented being engulfed by the deep depression that had overtaken Blanche. She moved from dawn till dark, often teamed with Bernadette, although less frequently of late. Bernadette was now responsible for overseeing the schooling of the children. It was the Parfaite Esclarmonde who aligned with her, challenging her to go beyond all boundaries in being of service. Sometimes Fabrisse joined them. But Fabrisse, as Mother Superior of the Cathar Parfaites, was held in high veneration, and her role became that of spiritual guide to the many seeking her day and night. Strange to comprehend was the change which allowed Parfaits and Parfaites to no longer travel in pairs.

The care of the sick, the distribution of foodstuffs, garments, candles and water made a continuous call on Clotilde's energies. Even her and Jean's private quarters had been, in part, conscripted as a storage area. Esclarmonde stepped across the threshold as she headed for their storage area. Clotilde studied the woman. She worked so hard, surely she would exceed the reputation of her namesake. Esclarmonde put down her empty baskets as she took in the dwindling supplies. "We are running so low on foodstuffs."

"More shall arrive soon, thanks to the courageous villagers below." Clotilde smiled at the thought of their resourcefulness in support of Montsegur. Their little village had become a giant Cathar market, with merchants from all around bringing conveys of wheat and corn to re-stock Montsegur. Clotilde smiled at Esclarmonde. "They are fearless in outwitting the army below. It will take more than the French army to staunch their bravery."

"Thank God for such loyal partisans." Esclarmonde gave a prayer of thanks.

"And not just food—fresh troops continue to arrive to help the Cathar cause." Clotilde's statement held amazement.

"A sign of faith for what the future holds," Esclarmonde said as she loaded her baskets, hefting them as though their weight was that of feathers. "Clotilde, my dear. I must be off to deliver the food. You are needed in the infirmary."

"Pierre—I fear he hasn't long for this world."

"His time has come. Fabrisse has gone to administer the consolamentum."

"I must go to Blanche." Clotilde hurried away, racing through the pentagonal courtyard of the fortress to reach the infirmary. Many from the village outside had moved within, leaving little space. The enormous courtyard had been taken over by storage sheds, stables and makeshift quarters for the defenders and their families. Scarcely acknowledging greetings, Clotilde arrived breathless at the keep. Entering its dark, cool shelter, she neared the area of the infirmary.

She froze at the look on Blanche's face. A mix of accusation, anger and despair seemed etched in the stony stare that greeted her. The silence in the room, the clean table spread with a white cloth, the almost palpable energy of sanctity emanating from Fabrisse, told Clotilde that the consolamentum had begun. Fabrisse gently touched Pierre's forehead with a copy of the Gospel according to St. John.

"How is he?" Blanche asked, tugging at Fabrisse's arm. Clotilde, knowing the answer, remained silent and available.

"Joyful now that he has entered God's kingdom of Light." Fabrisse took Blanche's hand. "Look how peaceful he is."

Clotilde took Blanche's hand as she looked down at Pierre, awed by the depth of joy on the lips of a man she'd scarcely known. Much older than her or Blanche, Pierre had always seemed busy and was, by nature, remote. Feeling at last connected with him she drew Blanche nearer. Blanche was unresponsive, her once pliant warmth cold, her ears deaf to Clotilde's, "Dear sister, I am here."

Fabrisse looked from Blanche's colorless face to the pain in Clotilde's. "Come, let us pray."

Hours passed as Clotilde sat with Blanche alongside Pierre's body. Neither Fabrisse's prayers or Clotilde's entreaties affected Blanche's decision to stay with Pierre. Her vise-like grip on Pierre's hand remained as darkness descended. Clotilde whispered, "Dear Blanche, you must rest. Let me prepare you a tisane to help you sleep."

"Don't leave me." The fierceness of Blanche's grip proved inarguable. Clotilde remained. Her mind turned to thoughts long held at bay by incessant activity. She wondered where Jean, gone for days now, could be. She'd heard rumor that he had been seen making his way to the fortress of Usson for a meeting with Deacon Clamens. Her thoughts filled the growing darkness with fear.

Suddenly a scurrying sound, a flickering light and a soft voice entered the room. "I feared you'd still be here. It's been over four hours since I left." Fabrisse gently took the hand that had welded itself with Clotilde's. "Come my dear Blanche, Clotilde needs her rest. I shall sit with you. Pierre's service is on the morrow."

"I will return in the morning, dear sister." Ignoring Clotilde's words, Blanche reached in panic to restrain her. Even with Fabrisse's solid restraint, Clotilde's backward glance left an image of Fabrisse struggling like a farmer leading a resistant bull to the pen.

The night seemed both short and endless. The peace that Montsegur offered when they first arrived, the vivid stars, the crystalline skies, the solitude of the night, long had been eclipsed. The nights now were filled with sounds of scuffling, of shouts, of soldiers running across the castle yard, and of stone guns being loaded. Clotilde's anguish grew at Jean's uncertain return. And as to Bernard, he had departed also, consumed with anger at his brother not needing him. Clotilde sighed, suddenly filled with anxiety at Bernard's attempt to prove he could take charge without his brother. She slid to her knees in prayer, silently asking for Jean and Bernard to return safely and Blanche's heartache to ease. Opening her eyes, she was surprised to discover she had slept. Sunlight was streaking through the slit of the tower window, falling in a crisscross of light across her bed. "Blanche. I must go to her," she said as she slipped on her tunic and sandals and departed.

The area where Pierre's service was being held had begun to fill with people. Her gaze found Blanche, or a deflated version of Blanche. Gone was the strong Blanche who nursed their mother through her illness and death, gone the gentle Blanche who raised Clotilde single-handedly, and gone the angry Blanche of last night. But what replaced it was harder to bear—a woman worn and emptied of all but her need for the one whose hand was held out to her—a hand gripped with such fierceness that Clotilde winced.

Fabrisse attended to the simple ceremony. Pierre wasn't of a level of importance to have a death roll, a document acknowledging his actions in this lifetime, but many knew him and lovingly attested with kind words to the gifts his life had brought them. Blanche remained silent as Fabrisse bestowed her blessing on Blanche and informed her that Pierre would be buried outside the castle walls after midnight. Clotilde listened, awed that any level ground could yet remain on their narrow strip of mountaintop. She looked up and caught the eye of the seigneur of the fortress, Raymond de Perella. He had waited until the end of the Cathar service.

"My dear Madame," he said as he offered Blanche his hand. "How sorry I am to hear of the loss of your husband."

Blanche, unable to respond, looked to Clotilde, who answered. "Thank you Lord Perella. Blanche is overcome, but she appreciates your honoring us."

"And I know how helpful you have been, dear Clotilde, especially with Jean away. Please give us the pleasure of joining us for dinner this evening. My wife and children will enjoy your company." He waited.

Clotilde looked at Blanche staring listlessly into the distance, giving no sign of having heard the invitation. "We are honored, Lord Perella, but my sister is grieving too much to be able to attend, and I shall wish to remain with her."

"Of course. Do let me know how I might be of help, Madame." Blanche averted his eyes as he spoke to her. Lord Perella turned back to Clotilde and lowered his voice, "Consider my invitation moved to Thursday evening when I trust circumstances shall allow for our sharing a meal together."

"Thank you. You are very kind." Clotilde felt a rush of excitement at the opportunity to hear word of Jean's whereabouts.

* * * *

Thursday night brought with it an evening breeze that carried a hint of summer. The moon was full and bathed in a celestial circle of silver clouds tinged with ruby red. It seemed magical, Clotilde thought, as she hurried toward the quarters of Lord Perella. Her long legs moved with youthful freedom, expressing her guilty joy at being alone, out of reach of Blanche or of any demands for the moment. Clotilde's anticipation grew at the thought of news of Jean. As she neared the Lord's apartments, she slowed her step and smoothed the soft folds of the one special dress she owned. Its green silk whispered against her hands. Giving one last tuck of her wind-whipped hair, she entered the rooms of Lord Perella.

Lady Perella smiled as she rose to escort Clotilde into the candlelit interior of their quarters. "Do come sit by me and my family. We are so pleased you could come, my dear Clotilde." Her Ladyship moved with dignity, head held high, eyes lit with warmth as she neared her family. Clotilde knew that she had recently left her marriage bed to take vows as a Parfaite. Such a decision endeared her even more to her family and impacted not at all her status. Lady Perella retained her lands and rights, only increasing her family with the addition of her socia. Clotilde watched as she turned to introduce the slight young woman enveloped in dark gray. Although they were no longer required to go in pairs, the friendship they shared was unbroken.

Clotilde smiled to see that, as was true of commoners in the Languedoc, the lord's entire extended family gathered together. Their unity heightened her admiration at their courage in the face of adversity.

The seigneur of the fortress, Raymond de Perella, had placed himself at the service of the bonshommes rather than over them as Lord and owner of Montsegur. His entire family stood beside him. Two of his daughters were married, one to Pierre-Roger de Mirepoix, and the other to Guiraud de Ravat, who was also present. The third was an invalid, another Esclarmonde, and true to her name, pledged to the service of God as a Parfaite. Corba, Lady Perella, was a Marquesa and greatly beloved of her children, who took great pride in her decision to become a Parfaite.

Clotilde lingered over a discussion with Pierre-Roger de Mirepoix. More than the lord of her village or one of the finest knights in the land, he was a friend. She lowered her voice to a whisper. "My lord, what news of Mirepoix have you?" She darted her glance around before braving the question that consumed her. "And Jean?"

Many eyes followed them as Pierre-Roger, now acting garrison commander of Montsegur, led Clotilde over to the stone window seat in the far corner of the room. "Not good news of Mirepoix." He kept his voice low. "As you may know, I was forced to join the ranks of my fellow faidits, my lands and titles ripped from me. I had the supreme ignominy of seeing Mirepoix given over by the Pope to be ruled by heirs of Guy de Levis." His wine-reddened face suddenly bleached of color. "The inquisitors have had a free hand with our kinsmen, I fear."

"No!" Clotilde, warding off shock, gazed out at a courtyard bathed in moonlight. "I'd hoped, that is—it must go hard with any

156

Cathar moving through the land these days." Her voice firmed as she looked up and added, "For Jean."

"Your husband is a brave man." Pierre-Roger replied. "And a safe one. We should have him back in our fold in less than a fortnight." He stood and offered his hand. "Let us rejoin the others."

Clotilde took her place at a table set with platters of fish, vegetables, fruits and bread. While less abundant than custom would dictate under normal circumstances, the lord had done his best to honor the esteemed members of the Cathar church. In attendance were Deacon Clamers, Bishops Bertrand Marty and Raymond Aiguilher. Clotilde stared at their Honors, Marty and Aiguilher, the venerable pair who had openly engaged in debate with St. Dominic fifteen years before she was born. They took scant sustenance or little involvement in the conversation. The latter due more to failing hearing, she thought, as one strained to decipher a comment from his partner. Undiminished were their unwavering expressions of peace.

The dinner moved too swiftly to an end, Clotilde's appetite for conversation scarcely slaked. Lady Corba explained it thusly, "Our commitment, as you can see, is to simplicity. We are far removed from the days of troubadours, artists or musicians playing on lutes." You may be far removed, Clotilde thought, nodding solemnly to the esteemed Parfaite, but not I. She felt so light-hearted at word that Jean was safe, that it was all she could do, as she headed home through the moonlight, not to burst into song. She softly sang the haunting lyrics of one of their beloved troubadours, Raymond de Miraval's, compositions—repeating its final stanza. "The ladies and lovers will recover the joy they have lost."

* * *

Hours later, restless, unable to sleep, Clotilde sat sipping an infusion of vervain as she stared out at the still-moonlit night. The shadows grew long, bringing with them a chill of pre-dawn anxiety. Such stillness was unusual. The past few nights had been rent by a predictable barrage of shots from the French army, met with a swift response from the besieged. Tonight's silence impaled her with its piercing point of uncertainty.

A shadow, moving stealthily through the faint light, drew her attention. She held her breath at the sibilant rustle along the stone flooring as a figure entered her room. Seeing it enshrouded in a cloak of midnight blue, Clotilde sighed in relief. The blue-black dye from finely ground purple berries was used for the robes of a Parfait or Parfaite. As the figure lowered the robe's hood, Clotilde exclaimed, "Fabrisse!"

"Yes, my dear, and not bearing good tidings." Fabrisse took Clotilde's hand.

Clotilde fought the ache in her constricted throat— unsuccessfully. Her anguished, "Not Jean!" reverberated through the room.

"Hush, my child. No, not Jean, it is Bernard that brings me."

"Bernard." Relief suffused her as she sank down on the bed.

"He was taken by the inquisitors."

"Oh no, poor Bernard."

"Poor Bernard has the wrath not only of the inquisitors, but of God as well." Fabrisse's tones implied a fate worse than death.

"Do tell all you have heard." Clotilde hesitated as she took Fabrisse's hand. "But before continuing, let me pour you some of this vervain. You look exhausted."

"Thank you, my child." Fabrisse accepted one cup and then another, seeming to seek in its depths an antidote for a world gone mad. With a solemn shake of her head, she continued, "Bernard killed one of the inquisitors, injured the other and made his escape."

"Then he is safe." Clotilde let loose a long sigh of relief.

"For now. He was last seen in the forest, hiding as he makes his way back to Montsegur." Fabrisse held Clotilde's gaze. "With the hounds of the Pope baying at his heels, I must caution you not to hold undue hope for his safety." Clotilde's look of shock prompted Fabrisse's expression to soften, but not enough to ease Clotilde's anger as she said, "How much hope for safety can be held out for any Cathar—you, me, Jean, Bernard, Lord Perella, Pierre-Roger de Mirepoix, or the faidit lords who support them? Surely it is only a matter of time before we are all tinder for the flames."

FIFTEEN

Fanjeaux, France-April, Present

As we drove through the village of Mirepoix, I returned to the events of last night. Acute sorrow had filled me as I stared at Lena and Andre's mystery talisman. A disjointed feeling of being there, but not there, had returned. But, unlike the incident with Evie in the mall, this time I tried to remain in the past.

It was not to be. Eric's words pulled me back, propelled by rage as he explained that my necklace was just another Cathar trinket that could be bought in every gift shop in Carcassonne.

Stunned, I had pleaded a headache and returned to my room. As we packed to leave in the morning, I spoke as little as possible. Andre and Lena seemed disappointed at my forgoing any *petit dejeuner* but, believing my headache story, nodded and pressed a couple of headache tablets on me. Thanking them, I asked permission to take photos of their property and hurried away at their agreement.

My emotions churned as I walked through the rooms, shooting two rolls of film before hurrying outside. Once in the courtyard, I felt the energies as more perplexing than sorrowful. As I peered through the lens I felt confounded by the house's relationship to its surroundings. I looked up when Eric neared.

Lena and Andre accompanied him, extending their business card as they bid us farewell. Eric exchanged cards, assured them he'd remain in touch and, throwing our luggage inside, ushered

159

me into the car. His testiness had been thinly veiled as he gave a smart salute to our hosts, got behind the wheel and drove away.

Precariously poised, I warred between offering an explanation for my jumbled emotions and hanging on to them. As I stared out the window, I let myself return to that brief second when Andre and Lena's *mystere* was revealed. Incipient tears warned me away. Anger I could handle, but not the sorrow it covered. I sat up straighter, squared my shoulders and turned to Eric.

"So—every gift shop in Carcassonne hawks my necklace!" Eric remained silent as he turned, his look bleak. Shocked, a suspicion dawned that his light response last night may have taken an effort of incredible will. I remembered his strangeness when my eyes met his the instant after I saw the matching seals. Acute emotion filled them, but whether anguish or excitement, I couldn't say, having so swiftly retreated to the past.

He began to speak. "I was shocked that you wore it, and wanted to make light of their response. But, now that we've put some distance behind us, I must admit I'm thrown by it all. It's either a *folie à deux* or…" Eric's voice faded as he turned away.

"I'm not sure." Suddenly I felt drained by emotions too heavy to bear. "I need some space to…"

"To examine it." He nodded his head. "My thoughts precisely. The sight of the hair twined together, the seal on the cloth…" His choking cough took a minute to bring under control before he continued. "Suffice it to say, it got to me. That's why I drove straight through Mirepoix." He looked perplexed. "I'm not sure how far we've gone or what that village is up ahead. It can't be Fanjeaux." He watched as I picked up our map, saying, "Never mind—there's a sign up ahead—"Vals.""

I found it on the map. "We really do need a breather. We've taken a wrong turn, away from Fanjeaux."

Eric pulled over and studied the map. "I'll head back."

"No, don't. Maybe Vals is the perfect place to take a break."

He looked pessimistic as we drove through the village. Nary a solitary soul huddled in the few doorways. We'd nearly left it behind when I spotted an impressive stone building up ahead.

"It looks like a quiet spot to regroup." He seemed unconvinced at my words as he looked out at an open field with a few sleepy cows. But, having caught sight of a gravel drive leading to the church, we parked and got out. Ours was the only car.

The air seemed hushed as we neared the unusual church. It had been built within, upon, and out of, a massive natural rock foundation. We stepped into a hushed interior, groping our way into darkness. Eric fumbled for a light switch.

I stared, awestruck, as a cobwebby light illuminated the interior. Exquisite frescoes covered the ancient church's rounded crypt. Although religious in nature, the figures embedded in the natural rock were more primitive and organic than any church frescoes I'd ever seen.

We proceeded reverently, conscious of the layers of religious mysticism enveloping us. A narrow, rock-walled passage led down into a subterranean area that gradually sloped upwards and ended in another space thick with darkness. I blinked as Eric found another light switch, illuminating a large area, architecturally very different from that which we'd left.

"Let's sit awhile," I said, moving toward a wooden pew. Seeking to return to some semblance of normalcy, I pulled out my guidebook. "I want to read about this curious place." Eric's gaze circled the room as I read aloud. "Vals was a former Celtic *oppidium,* which they define as a sizeable village. Evidence reveals that the Celts long had a settlement in Vals." As to this church, I read, "The Rupestrian church, partly buried in the soft rock, is arranged on two levels. The lower is richly decorated with twelfth century Roman frescoes of Byzantine inspiration." I looked around. "The upper level dates from the Romanesque era, with its bell-tower turret decorated with a stone discoid grave-marker."

"Hmmm." Eric looked over my shoulder at the illustration in the guidebook. "My curiosity is not only not slaked, but decidedly heightened. For example—what's meant by a Rupestrian Church?"

"It doesn't say." I frowned. "If I remember correctly, Rupestrian is connected with troglodyte—buildings built underground—like the mounds in Cappodocia, Turkey. The use of natural structures to contain dwellings, even churches, within." I closed the guidebook, stood up and stared, feeling an expanded sense of mystery at this amazing structure. "A sign indicated a dig in progress behind the church. Maybe we can learn more."

"Right, but let's not rush off." Eric drew me over to a nearby pew and sat beside me. He scanned the entire space before saying, "This seems a perfect opportunity to examine last night's events."

I looked around. "Granted, if we were perched on the other side of the moon, we couldn't be as removed as here." I tried to force a light note. "But, as a setting for objectively examining 'woo-woo' stuff—no way. I say we go outside."

"Agreed," he said as we retraced our steps, turning out the lights as we went.

"How incredible that we were able to explore such a place entirely on our own." Even though we were outside, with not a soul around, I spoke softly.

"Strange. Like Buckingham Palace without guards." Eric gave a wry grin as he led the way around the structure. "Maybe we'll run into someone at the dig."

No such luck. The site had plenty of signs everywhere, their diagrams showing a series of archaeological digs undergoing painstaking work. Very few were walled off, but we contented ourselves with admiring them from a distance. I resumed my reading of the English translations. "Archeological and anthropological studies continue of remains dating back to the fourth century BC." I looked up at Eric. "Lots of information on the dig but no mention of who is sponsoring it."

"Right you are." He grinned, a heightened echo of irony coloring his comment, "Thereby revealing unquestionably that it couldn't be our immodest Benjamin Taylor." I laughed as I pointed to another sign.

"Look here. Seems Vals has a *Musée Archeologique.* Maybe we should check it out." I was surprised to find Eric had strolled some distance away.

His upturned gaze was focused on the discoid grave-marker high on the bell-tower. Ancient and weatherworn, a cross was enclosed within a circle, bearing not a little resemblance to my necklace. "Oh," I said as I touched my naked neck, remembering that I had returned my necklace to an empty film container.

"'Oh' is right, but not a strange coincidence." Eric swung around, staring at my expression. "So don't go spacey on me, Ms. Palmer. It's my turn to share of bit of research." He spoke in mendacious tones. "Although commonly referred to as Cathar crosses, it seems certain that the Greek crosses within a circle, or the circular Occitan crosses, have been wrongly attributed to the Cathars."

"What a relief. Then I'm sure to run into them everywhere." I said as he stared at my neck.

"I trust you have hidden your necklace well, so we don't have a repeat of last night's debacle."

"I put it in a film can." I let out a sigh. "But I feel naked without it."

"Naked or not, from the response it caused, better you should err on the part of caution. I suggest a safer place for it would be in my briefcase." Eric nodded toward the car. "Its secret compartment would do your CIA proud."

"Maybe. I'll decide when we reach Benjamin's." As I glanced up at the large cross Eric let out a sigh.

"Well then, that decided, let's sit on that rock and continue our talk."

Eric's serious tone prompted me to stay with a matter of fact approach. I began with Coustaussa, describing the incident of the horse and rider and the man crying out the name "Clotilde." Without pause, I recounted how such strangeness had heightened when we reached the "Auberge Mystère." From the moment we drove in I had felt consumed with a mixture of wild joy and deep sorrow.

I remained objective until the words, "When the silk-wrapped stone, with its seal of Jean and Clotilde" brought tears.

"Clotilde" again. No wonder you looked like someone had hit you with a hammer." Eric tilted my head into the curve of his shoulder. "Let them flow."

I'd heard the expression, "to cry as if your heart would break" but I'd never experienced it before then—not even when breaking up with Alex. Deep sorrow rolled through me like waves on the ocean—rising, crashing, leveling out, only to be followed by another. Feeling the last set was spent I turned to Eric.

Staring into the distance, his expression was that of a volcano about to explode. He remained riveted by his interior landscape for what seemed ages before he turned as I spoke his name. "Eric."

"Dana." He spoke hesitantly, as though testing a strange name on his lips. "Dana." He let out a deep sigh. "Earlier I used the phrase '*folie à deux*'—not inappropriately. I've had moments recently of not only sensing strange images but unquestionably feeling them." He stared at me. "I definitely felt the mood of the auberge and tried to drown my emotions with drink. When I saw that packet of hair, I was filled with rage, but more..." His voice trailed off.

"More." Mine was so soft as to doubt it was spoken.

"Give me a minute to describe it." He shook his head as he continued. "It felt like..." He hesitated, as if testing the right emotion. "Urgency, haste, some must-do imperative, like..." His words faded with a shrug as he stood. "Probably just the old can-do male need for action rearing its head," he said, giving a dismissive chuckle.

"Maybe, but it doesn't explain what it all means." I waited.

"All we can know are the facts. Something is happening, here in France and to both of us. As to why and how, our difficulty lies in trying to use reason to understand it. As one of my fellow countrymen said, 'There are more things 'neath heaven and earth, Horatio, than man has dreamed of.'" Eric held out his hand. "For the moment, let's reserve judgement and see where it leads."

"To the funny-farm." My response matched his note of lightness.

"Maybe. But for now, I'd recommend to lunch." His look took in the church, its cross and the archaeological digs. "This place seems to have lightened my mood."

"And the talking helped," I said as we drove away, the church's spell remaining. "Let's go find something to eat."

"*D'accord,* Mademoiselle Palmer." His imitation of me made me smile. "However this thing unfolds, it'll come easier on a full stomach." We soon arrived at an intersection marked "Fanjeaux-two kilometers."

Eric smiled. "Now that we're on the right track, let's watch for a restaurant."

I glanced down at my watch. "Restaurants don't open for lunch until noon."

"Right you are, so let's park and walk around Fanjeaux, maybe even find a market and buy a picnic lunch." I watched as Eric ran that idea through his thoughts.

"If we do that, we can be on the road sooner." I said. "The closer we get to Toulouse the more excited I am at seeing Evie."

"It's Benjamin Taylor that draws me. So, a picnic it is. Watch for a place to stop for a loaf of bread, a jug a wine and…" Eric hesitated.

"And cheese and fig jam and maybe *gateau au chocolat* and…"

"You really are hungry." Eric laughed.

Enough to keep a close watch for a market, I thought as we approached the main avenue leading to the town square.

"There's always the old city of Fanjeaux up on the hill," Eric said as he drove up the steep road that led to it. "We should have luck there."

"Right." I said as I spotted a sign saying, *Huit à Huit—one kilometre à gauche.*' "Turn left." I shouted. "That sign means a market open from eight to eight."

It was open and stocked most of what we wanted. Replete, we finished the last of our lunch high up on a hill that overlooked the Laurangais plain below and the Montaigne Noire in the distance. "To Fanjeaux," Eric said as he touched his plastic glass against mine and finished his wine. I began to pack away the remains of our lunch when Eric asked what the brochure said about Fanjeaux.

I glanced down long enough to relay the highlights. "The village is famous for its connection to St. Dominic, as well as for being a stronghold of Catharism. There's a mini-map of the old town, most of which we can see on our way back to the car."

Ancient homes lining narrow cobbled walks winding along our way. A sign pointed out the house of St. Dominic. A nun stood at the door. With my smattering of French, we learned that St. Dominic's residence was actually located in a little community called Prouille. She pointed into the distance, indicating Prouille and the landmark building that dominated it. We thanked her and walked off.

"The brochure mentioned Prouille. It said that Dominic chose Prouille after he had a vision of a fireball striking the Fanjeaux area."

Eric let out a low chuckle. "He was quite the pyromaniac, it seems. I read about a famous debate where he claimed that when the Cathar bishop threw Dominic's arguments into the fire, the parchment leapt up and scorched the ceiling."

My smile turned to a frown. "And soon after, he and his Dominicans were put in charge of the Inquisition's endless fires." I moved faster. "Let's get underway."

As we left Fanjeaux and entered open countryside, the roadsides of the Ariege district were vivid with green grass and red poppies. "Next stop, Toulouse." Eric's voice broke my stare as he glanced at the dashboard clock. "One-thirty. Maybe we should take the toll road. The entrance is up ahead in about seven kilometers."

"I'm game," I said. "Enough of blood-drenched towns."

"Except that Toulouse was the source of the bloodletting—the most important city in all of France at that time." Eric reached over and gave me a little pat to soften his remark. "Because of its importance, I'd wager my eagerness to get to Toulouse matches your own."

"I'm anxious for you to meet Evie." As I spoke, a sign appeared saying, *toll road-one kilometre*. I watched for the direction to Toulouse. "That way," I said, waving my arm as we neared the roundabout.

Eric steered our little car into the heavy flow headed toward Toulouse as I began to organize a stash of coins for our toll when we exited. "Toulouse is fifty-four kilometers head," Eric said as he asked, "What time are we expected?"

"Late afternoon sometime." I looked out at fast moving lanes of traffic. "But we'll need to stop somewhere and call for directions. I'll watch for a rest stop." I began a scrutiny of every sign that appeared, nearly missing the most obvious. "There— *Petrole-8 Kilometres*.' It has gas, phone, restrooms and food."

"The first three we can use," Eric said as he sped up.

I sat back, straining to read the sign saying, "Chateaus-Pays de Cathare," or "Eglise." Some showed little piles of boulders beneath, indicating ruins. I felt pleasure at the efforts to revive the lost land of Occitania, mixed with sadness that a culture so rich had been extinguished. I shared these thoughts with Eric.

He listened thoughtfully before responding. "I read that the Renaissance would have begun two hundred years earlier had the Occitan culture endured."

"So sad," I replied as I spotted another ruined castle on a distant hill. "According to the 'Chanson de la Croisade' and many troubadour's ballads, the culture was remarkably inclusive. Jews, gypsies, Moors and Cathars—all were embraced as part of the rich tapestry of the area."

"True, but with little love for the papacy," Eric said. "According to the troubadour's *sirventes*.'" Eric kept his eye on the road, his grin undisguised as I fell silent. "No ready response, dear colleague?"

"I give up. Tell me what sirventes are."

"A popular means of song and story-telling as a vehicle to attack politics, religious, moral or military rivalries. Certain troubadours became polished practitioners of the genre, including Bertran de Born, Guilhem…"

"I get it." I smiled in acknowledgement of his research.

"But you don't really get it until you've read some of them." Eric pursed his eyebrows, his expression solemn. "I couldn't believe how full of fury they were. They railed, but ever so cleverly, against the venality, debauchery, hypocrisy and avarice of the Church—particularly the local prelates."

"Your fellow brothers." I regretted my comment as a look of shame washed over Eric's face. My shouting and pointing erased it. "Look, a phone-stop."

As Eric filled our car with petrol, I headed for the ladies room where I spotted a phone. I reviewed my phone card instructions and dialed. A man answered.

"*Allo. C'est Benjamin Carter l'appareil.*"

"Hello. This is Dana Palmer speaking."

"Dana, where are you?"

"About forty-five kilometers from Toulouse, going west on the toll road."

"Very good. You should be here in no time." The voice in the background was easy to identify. "Your friend, Evie, is wrestling me for the phone, but first let me give you directions. It's easy to get confused when you reach Toulouse." I wrote down his directions and repeated them back to him. "Correct. Rue de Perigord, near the cathedral of St. Sernin. You can't miss it if you follow the signs saying 'Route de St. Sernin.' It should take about forty minutes. Now to pass you over to Evie."

"Dana!" Evie's excitement exploded through the receiver. "I'm so glad you'll be here soon." Lowering her voice, she added, "Is Eric with you?"

"Yes, of course. Can Benjamin put us both up?"

I drew the receiver a little distance away as she laughed. "Benjamin could run an auberge from this place." Evie halted, listening to background comments from Benjamin. "He says to make that a *château,* and of course it has room for all. I say, hurry up. We've got a lot of ground to cover."

I hung up, warmed by Evie's enthusiasm. She could make a trip to the dentist feel like an adventure, I thought, as I walked back. Eric was lounging against the car, drinking a large bottle of mineral water. "Looks like you made contact." He said.

"I did, and they are ready, willing and more than able to put us up." I held out the lengthy directions.

"The route looks likes a labyrinth." He smiled as he passed me some water and got in the car. "I'll depend on you to navigate when we exit into Toulouse."

Our remaining kilometers passed swiftly, our smug complacency shattered as we reached the exit for 'Toulouse-Centre Ville.' The city was large, sprawling, traffic-filled and rife with confusing signs tempting us to turn, as we did, into bottlenecked arteries. At one point we found ourselves paralleling the Canal du Midi. Frustrated, Eric suggested we park alongside the tree-lined waterway and review our route. We glanced at the barges going by, studied the directions, pinpointed our location, and, re-oriented, drove on.

Eric remained calm as my fretfulness grew. Finally—I saw a sign saying, *St. Sernin.* "Turn left and follow the signs to the church."

"Rue de Perigord" appeared as a lane alongside St. Sernin. We parked and began a stroll down a street lined with chestnut trees and regal, ancient buildings. "At the size of these buildings, I'd say they were residences for the bishops," Eric said, admiring the iron gates and railings that protected their graceful façades. We walked slowly until we reached our address. If anything, it was even more elaborate than its neighbors were—and yet somehow heavier. Its formidable impression caused a ripple of reluctance as I rang the bell on the gate.

A rousing cry reached our ears. "Bonjour. Bonjour!" Evie was out the door, through the gate and grabbing me before the echo faded. "Dana. You look marvelous!" She said, breaking as I introduced Eric. "Dana didn't tell me just how dishy you are." Wrapping her arm in his, she steered Eric into the house and, with no sign of our host, promptly began a guided tour.

It was hard to take it all in. High ceilings of embossed metal, baroquely garlanded at every corner with cherubs and flower filigree, Russian icons on the walls, exquisite furnishings, all massive yet elegant. "Louis the Fourteenth, my dear." Evie said as she pointed to a large armoire and then to the floor. "Aubusson." She whirled through several rooms until we reached a wood-paneled library where a man sat, back turned, deep in animated conversation. One look and I knew that I wouldn't want to be on the other end of the phone. Icy vituperation rang throughout the room.

"That's not good enough. I must have the actual items before Friday." Benjamin turned, his eyes flashing irritation. He uttered a few more words sotto voce, replaced the receiver, stood up and approached us. The metamorphosis was swift and total, his look instantaneously warm and welcoming. Not a trace of darkness remained. "Dana. Delighted you're here." He bestowed two swift kisses before turning to Eric. As they shook hands, I studied Benjamin.

My first impression at Carcassonne had been of a younger man. That image wavered, in spite of his casual gray slacks, cashmere sweater and tennis shoes. It was the eyes, I decided, that negated any youthfulness.

In the intimate setting of his home, little distracted my up-close observation. Benjamin's dark hair fell casually toward midnight-black irises that dominated their sockets, leaving only the merest hint of white. Hypnotic, I found it hard to break my focus as he caught my stare. His smile was disarming, completely submerging any earlier impressions in the gleam of his white toothed, full-lipped charm.

"Dana, my dear, you look lovelier even than I remembered. Eric tells me you've had lunch, a picnic—how charming." He took my arm, his subtle, but intoxicating, cologne leading the way. "Come then, let us adjourn to the terrace."

The terrace was equally seductive, I decided as Benjamin eased me into a chintz-covered lounge. Eric caught my eye and gave a furtive wink before Benjamin turned to him and asked, "Now then, whiskey straight if I remember correctly." At Eric's nod, Benjamin motioned to a servant who had unobtrusively entered, took each request, departed and returned swiftly with our drinks.

Evie smiled appreciatively at she sipped. "Whatever you've ordered, you simply must try this." She raised her glass to extend a toast. "To old friends." She smiled widely at Benjamin and Eric. "And to new."

I grinned as she turned and winked at me. "Thank you, Evie. By the way, you are looking radiant," I said, taking a minute to study her impact. Tailored and sophisticated, her ensemble reeked of money, from the Cartier gold pin to the Piaget watch, to the Bally shoes. Pale cream, her suit was accented by a leaf-green silk scarf with a contrasting russet *fleur de lys* pattern. The green brought out her eyes, the scarf highlighting her blond hair whose wild curls had been tamed by her chignon.

"I've been shopping, darling." She twirled for her audience, laughing as she turned to Benjamin and poured him a glass of wine. "I insisted we stop at Dior enroute from the airport."

"Dior and three other couturiers. I've never seen a more committed shopper, nor one more generous with her credit card," Benjamin said as he drew Evie down beside him on a chaise lounge. "They loved you, as do I, my dear." He held her eyes for one brief second, his look belying his words. "And always will, but only if you never serve me wine. I drink *only* single malt whiskey."

I watched to see if Eric had picked up on this, but he had moved to open the door for the maid as she entered carrying a tray laden with food. More cheeses than Wisconsin, I thought, eyeing them alongside an assortment of olives and breads. Centered on the tray was a large crystal decanter of single malt whiskey.

"Very good." Benjamin sat his glass of wine aside as he began to pour.

Eric smiled. "It seems your British schooling predisposed you to Scotland's pleasures over the vines of France."

"Just so," Benjamin said as he touched his glass to Eric's. "Along with my old school tie, my love of great whiskey is a legacy of seventeen years in Britain."

"Your family is British?" Eric asked.

"French, but with only an aging uncle, I spent most of my years in boarding schools. Except for school holidays spent in France. When he passed away, the family estate was left to me." He looked a bit bored, I thought, as he turned to Eric. "Rather traditionally dull, I'm afraid. Your background is British, of course, and Oxford, I presume." Benjamin waited.

"Cambridge, with a year at Edinburgh."

"Ah, that's what fooled me." Benjamin turned to me and smiled. "Quite a bastardization, that accent of his. But now to you, dear Dana, I thought I detected some French heritage." He surveyed me with the look one would give a painting at Sotheby's auction house. "Legs too long, skin a bit pale, hair dark enough to suggest an Italian heritage, and yet…" He rose from the chaise and stared. My hand instinctively went to my throat. "There's something that says French." He turned to the others. "Am I right?"

"Yes," I said in time enough to halt Evie from what I feared would be a full account of, not only my ancestry but also my life. "On both sides of the family."

"But you didn't grow up speaking the language?"

"Only the curses my mother used."

"Dana's mother is pure angel. I'll vouch for that." Evie turned to Benjamin. "In spite of being French." I grinned at the subtle *touché* in her delivery and waited to see what Benjamin's response would be. He reached for the decanter.

"Tell us more about your discoveries, Benjamin," Eric said, as Benjamin, still standing, decanter in hand, looked from Eric to me.

"Later. For now I'd like to hear more of your adventures these past few days." Benjamin replied, giving Evie a glassy smile. "Our dear Evie has told me something of what led you here." He positioned his chair facing Eric and me.

Evie promptly added, "Not all," giving me a reassuring look.

Eric attempted to bridge the unease that threatened. "Good, you know of our work on a series about the Cathars. Since we last spoke in Carcassonne, we have been visiting some of the sites." Eric grinned at Benjamin. "Where your name came up several times." Eric reached for a bit of cheese. "That's it for us, your turn."

"Very well." A touch of the pedantic colored Benjamin's account. "I am a Director of the Museum's team of archeologists and anthropologists. There are twenty-seven in my department. Our focus, as you know from my lecture in Carcassonne, is on the Cathar period. So, it is no coincidence that as you tour Montsegur, Montaillou and other Cathar sites..." He held open his hands. "Virtually all recovered remains from that era are the province of my department."

"Seems the ghost of the *bonshommes* must have guided us to you." Eric looked over at the library. "I'd love to read what you've written on the topic."

"I've written four books covering each major dig. But most are in French. I'd be happy to lend you the one that has been translated into English."

"Thank you. It should prove invaluable." Eric said, adding, "Given that I intend to earmark the next few days for research."

Benjamin looked at his watch. "Good, four thirty-five, a perfect time and a perfect place to begin your research with a tour of my department." He extended his hand, giving me an irresistible smile.

In that moment, if he'd offered me a tour of an abattoir, I'd have responded the same. "I'd love to see it."

"Count me in." Eric said, asking, "Do we drive or walk?"

"Walk." Benjamin gave a Gaelic shrug. "In Toulouse we make better time walking." He led me to the entrance.

I looked askance. "I need to get extra film for my camera."

Evie chimed in loudly. "Count me out, Benjamin. You know I'm not one for walking." She noticed my frown. "Don't fret, sweetie. We'll have plenty of time later. I need to make a phone call, maybe take a nap. Still jet-lagged, I fear."

The maid showed Eric and me to our rooms. Situated alongside one another, their doors stood open revealing large balconies, big beds, a fireplace and views onto a garden. I nodded agreement at Eric's soft, "Wow" and said I'd be down soon.

Not five minutes later, I rushed downstairs, balancing two cameras and a film bag on my shoulders. Benjamin stood at the entrance door, looking impatient as Eric walked up. "So it's off we go." Benjamin turned to Evie. "I've told cook to prepare dinner for seven PM in honor of Mr. Taylor's commitment to research. Expect us to return in time for cocktails. Adieu."

Evie waved as we hurried away. As we reached an intersection, I looked over at the spires of St. Sernin. "I'd love to take a few shots of the cathedral."

"A splendid idea." Benjamin's remark surprised me. "I shall introduce you to my colleagues—one man and a woman, both archeologists and researchers."

"Perfect. I'll take plenty of photos." I said as I reached for film and shook my head. "Drat, seems I brought the film I've already shot."

"I'll run back and fetch it," Eric said as he turned.

"No, Eric," I said. "It's too confusing to tell you which and where."

"No problem, Eric old chap." Benjamin linked arms with Eric. "Dana's got a straight shot back to the church. We'll go on ahead and she can join us." He turned to me. "As you enter the church, head for the far left corner and a sign saying, "Musee Toulouse Annexe." Someone will direct you if you get turned around."

"Take these." I thrust my camera bags at Eric. "I should make it back in ten minutes." As I turned, Benjamin thrust his hand in front of me.

"You'll need the key to the terrace door. It works easier."

I reached the house, walked around the side and entered the terrace. About to call for Evie, I stopped as I remembered her nap comment. Treading softly up the stairway, I stopped at the landing where I heard subdued sounds of conversation. I was about to let her know I was there when Evie burst into laughter. "Alex, don't be silly. Dana doesn't suspect a thing. She's out anyway, gone with Benjamin and her writer friend to the Museum." Silence, then, "I know it's the middle of the night in Georgia, lover. But I just had to hear your voice."

My heart beat fast, my mind reeling at the word, "lover." No, no, no, it silently screamed, not Evie and Alex!

SIXTEEN

Toulouse, France- May, Present

My throat constricted so tightly I could hardly breathe. My body couldn't move. My mind grasped at denial, seeking the more bearable hope that I'd really gone over the edge and imagined the unimaginable. But continued phrases, seductively soft and low, refuted and replaced logic with rage and pain. A silent scream of "How could you?" filled every fiber of my being. I longed to bash through the door, scream the question into Evie's face and Alex's eardrum.

I couldn't bear it, even after having closed the chapter on Alex and accepting the reality that he must have someone else. A nameless, faceless someone else was enough to enrage and sadden me–but Evie? How long and how could she—and how could he— have done such a thing to me? Dazed, I moved back down the stairs and out the terrace doorway, suddenly aware of the strange absence of tears. Entering the garden, I found a maze of tall hedges—its labyrinthine design a perfect sanctuary.

Secluded within a natural cloister, I sat down on a cool cement bench and stared. The total otherworldliness of being there, of having heard what I heard, of feeling what I was feeling, overcame me. Suddenly, out of the deep silence came a bizarre sensation of not really feeling anything. Some part of me had gone deep inside, as though to the bottom of a well. I knew where I, or at least, my body, was. I was aware that I could see and touch and walk, even speak if I had to, and yet "I" had gone away. Maybe this is what "shell shock" or "soul-retrieval" means, I thought.

Whatever it was, I was grateful for its gift of anesthesia. In numbed neutral, I made my way back to the house. Moving quietly up the stairs, I glanced into Evie's room as I passed. She was sound asleep, softly snoring. I went to my room, found the film, walked down the stairs and out the door.

As I quick-stepped it toward St. Sernin, I felt surprise that an automaton could move so efficiently and recall information so clearly. As I reached the corner, I stopped and stared at the church. Its basilica rose in dominant splendor, a semi-circular apse crowned in a tiered wedding-cake-style, capped by a five-story bell tower. I marveled that a structure begun in 1080 still retained such power. As I approached the main door I remembered to look at the carvings on the doorway.

As I looked, I cringed. Mary and the Christ child on one side of the ornate doorway and an Inquisitor slaying Cathars directly opposite. Even within my cocoon I could register the audacity of its grisly testimony.

I hurried through St. Sernin's vast interior, scarcely pausing to look at the frescoes on the transept as I headed for Benjamin's department.

"You got lost," Eric said before Benjamin could comment. As he walked up to me, Eric's look of faint censure turned to puzzlement. "Are you all right?" Where did I get lost is the question, I thought, as I fumbled for an answer.

"I know exactly where she got lost—with Evie. That woman can talk the ear off a statue." Benjamin's remark was delivered with one of his high wattage smiles as he approached me. "Odds are I'm right."

"Not exactly. Evie was asleep. I couldn't find the film I needed and..." I gave him what I could of a charming, helpless female imitation-smile. "I took a little detour to buy film and got sidetracked."

"Fortunately we've been deep in discussion." Benjamin took me by the arm, steering me past Eric and to a door marked, 'Laboratorie Prive.' "I want you to meet Veronique. Her colleague is out at a dig, but she's the brains behind the team, anyway." He pushed the door open to a large room that resembled my high school biology lab. A woman working in a nearby cubicle turned as we approached.

"Veronique, I'd like you to meet Dana Palmer."

She stood up, revealing a modern blend of student-woman. Her short-cropped blond hair framed piercing blue eyes that held a trace of formality as she held out her hand. I took it and stared. Every contour of her clean, firm face suggested a reserve of vast intelligence.

"It is my pleasure, Mademoiselle Palmer."

"And for me, Veronique." I turned to Eric who had walked up. "I'm sure my colleague has already quizzed you on your work, but I'd like to ask you a few questions." Her smile revealed a shadow of wit held in check as she replied.

"Of course. These two are eager to visit the church's oldest relics. While they are away, we can talk." Veronique drew out the chair alongside her desk.

"Looks as though we've been given our hall pass," Benjamin said to Eric. "So off we go. First stop the *enfeu,* where the church's oldest relics await."

"It's the tombs of Counts Raymond VI and VII that intrigue me," Eric said.

Benjamin laughed. "Well, you won't find them, neither in fact nor mentioned in any brochure. I'll explain enroute."

Eric looked puzzled, but Benjamin gave a brisk turn, opened the door and glared impatiently. "You're in good hands, I'm sure," Eric said as he gave a quick smile and nodded to Veronique. "Mind she doesn't run off to any camera stores."

Benjamin stuck his head, and watch, around the closing door. "We'll return for you in exactly thirty minutes."

I nodded, still cocooned in my one-dimensional state. I hope such vacancy isn't visible, I thought, as I turned back to Veronique. "That doesn't give us much time together, especially since I want to take some photos. Unless we can combine a few questions with my taking of photos in our thirty minutes."

"But of course. We'll talk as we go." She locked the door as we left, moving swiftly up the stairway. "First stop the inside of the church." I nodded as she added, "The frescoes date from the Romanesque period." She sensed my hesitancy. "You may take photographs. Monsieur Carter arranged for it."

I made haste taking my interior shots, wishing I'd brought along a tripod for the special lighting requirements. As I finished one role of film I turned to Veronique. "Every corner surprises."

"True." Veronique replied. I returned my attention to the soaring transepts, gilt emblazoned altars, polychrome statues and marble floors. "But it is the crypt that holds some of the oldest

175

artifacts—the marble sarcophagus of Guillaume III, 'Taillefer' as he was known. He was the Count of Toulouse who died in 1037. If you have enough photographs of the interior, we should, in our time, see it."

I smiled my readiness and matching her long strides, we moved out and around the southeast transept to the subterranean depths of the crypt area. Surprised at how well illuminated it was, I wasted no time. I was so absorbed in photographing Guillaume's tomb and a sarcophagus belonging to a subsequent count, Raimond-Bertrand, who died in 1050, that I hadn't noticed Veronique's absence.

"I'm sorry to abandon you, but I went to see if your colleague was nearby with Benjamin. They had gone. Is there more you would wish to photograph here—the relics of the saints, perhaps?"

"Yes, of course. But I am curious about the burial places of the Counts Raymond VI and VII," I said as I followed Veronique to a lighted display.

Veronique sighed as I snapped a few shots of the relics of saints. "The counts were excommunicated and thus forbidden a church burial. As we return, I shall try to explain. I'm afraid that is all we have time for now."

"I understand. Fortunately we are staying with Dr. Carter, so I can take additional photos of the exterior," I said, shouldering my camera gear as Veronique led the way back through the main foyer of the church.

She sounded a bit anxious as we neared. "You are staying with Monsieur Carter?" Veronique's look seemed to hold more of the question than her words.

"Why, yes," I replied. He's a friend of a friend and has been very generous to us, given that we have only just met. Have you worked together long?"

"Three years now, since the project on Montsegur and now with the preliminary work on Usson and Coustaussa. I understand that…" She hesitated, stopping at the bottom of the stairs before going down. "You visited Coustaussa."

"Yes, but how did you know?" I stared, bewildered.

"I assumed that Mr. Taylor told Professor Carter. He discussed it with me." Her stare made me nervous, her next comment fraught with emphasis. "Professor Carter was very interested." She lowered her voice as we approached the lab. "How much information have you exchanged with Professor Carter?"

"Very little, certainly nothing about Coustaussa."

"Ah yes, well," She paused at the lab door. "Perhaps, if time allows, we can meet again. I will give you my card."

"I would like that," I said.

Suddenly the lab door flew open. Benjamin glared. "I looked for you. You are eleven minutes late, Veronique." His obsidian eyes deepened as he waited.

"I am sorry, Professor, but—"

"Benjamin, blame it on me again." I interjected my words and myself between him and Veronique. "Veronique kindly agreed to assist me in getting the best shots of St. Sernin. It was I who detained her."

He did a swift about face. "Enough said. Let's get underway." Benjamin turned to Eric, whose look waffled between dismay and resistance.

I opened my camera case and said, "I'm ready, or will be as soon as I stash film. You two head on up and I'll join you in five minutes."

Eric grinned as Benjamin turned away. "Come Eric, bloody females." I finished with the film and buckled my camera bag. Veronique watched me, a strange look on her face as she extended her business card.

"I have included my home phone. It would be best if you call me there." She gave me a light farewell kiss on each cheek. "I feel we are as friends." I was caught by the strange stare that accompanied her words.

"I feel it as well, Veronique. Thank you. And I will call you—soon."

"Hurry, you mustn't keep Professor Carter waiting."

Benjamin was talking with Eric as I approached. But Eric turned as I neared, his glance lingering. "What an incredible introduction to Toulouse Benjamin has given me." He turned back to Benjamin. "Thank you."

"Only an appetizer, as you shall see." Benjamin took me by the arm. "*If* we step up the pace a bit."

We fairly raced down the streets leading to the Place du Capitole. I did my best to match their strides while looking everywhere. "Toulouse is incredible."

My remark prompted Benjamin's running commentary: "Toulouse, ah Toulouse, 'For all the towns, it is the flower and the rose,' so claimed Guillaume de Tudele, the author of "Chanson de la Croisade," the song of the crusade. Toulouse has been a capital since Gallo-Roman times, during the Visigoths and after the acquitaine War in the eighth century. As the capitol of Occitania, it stretched from the Agen region to Avignon. Toulouse was the major crossroad on the road to Compostella and as such became one of the richest and largest cities in the Western world." He paused at a busy intersection.

Eric took the opportunity to comment. "Benjamin was filling me in on the concept we were referring to earlier. It goes by the term '*Paratge.*'" Eric looked from me to Benjamin as I repeated, "*Paratge.*" My raised eyebrow prompted Benjamin to resume his lecture.

"Toulouse was a free city, governed by the Capitouls, what Rome called consuls, and later overseen by the benevolent Counts of Toulouse. The concept of *paratge*, meaning honor and tolerance, was a generations-old legacy of the people of the Languedoc. Toulouse in the twelfth century was the finest example of medieval society. The city sparkled with ideas, cultural expansion, the music of the troubadours, courtly honor, and equality for women." Benjamin halted and looked up. "Architecturally, as you can see, such beauty and grace was captured as well." He motioned toward the magnificent buildings lining the central square as he named them, "Les Jacobins, the Hotel de Ville, the Capitole Theater and the Toulouse Museum." He pointed to an ornate building and turned to Eric. "That is the Hotel Saint Jean, the one I referred to in discussing the Counts Raymond VI and VII."

I waited—genuinely expectant. "Do go on."

"As Cathar supporters, the two Raymonds were excommunicated. A document was unearthed that suggests that the Pope, Urban II, ultimately authorized them to be buried in the cemetery of another church called "La Daurade." But there is no proof that such occurred." Benjamin motioned back toward the Hotel Saint Jean. "This is the place where the *Chevaliers de l'Ordre de Saint Jean de Jerusalem*, now known as the Templars, lived during the twelfth and thirteenth centuries—until, that is, the Inquisition decimated them as well. There was a church here at that time. There is speculation that one of the sarcophagi found here is Raymond VII's. When he died, he was still excommunicated and thus, forbidden to have a sepulchre in St. Sernin. Since he was known to be very close to the *Chavaliers de Saint Jean*, we have reason to believe they gave their poor count a place to lie in secret for eternity." Benjamin stared at Eric who was scribbling notes as he spoke.

"Have the authorities verified this?" Eric's question hung in the air.

Benjamin frowned before answering. "I volunteered to do the analysis for them, but they chose another group of archeologists to study the remains. They'll come up with the results, but how..." He shrugged. "Suffice it to say, not as accurate as my team would have provided."

I turned away, letting my gaze roam along the buildings that comprised the square. Stately sentinels of the past, their exquisite façades overlooked a modern maelstrom of sidewalk cafés, musicians and street vendors. Cautious tourists dodged the teeming masses of Toulousians racing for the many streets and alleyways leading off the square. I reached for my camera.

Benjamin grabbed my arm. "Look now and take photos later." He flashed a stern look as he propelled us across the square. "That is, if you're serious about viewing genuine Cathar treasures." As we neared one of the stately buildings, he steered us into its surprisingly modern lobby. A guard and a receptionist were at the ready, both all but bowing as Benjamin walked up. "Of course, Mr. Carter" was the only phrase I could make out due to its repetition. Benjamin led us through impressive double doors and into a large corner office. "Be seated. I'll have someone bring coffee," he said as he led us toward the most massive executive chair I'd ever seen. Black leather, calfskin undoubtedly, with a high back. It actually had a control panel for a built-in massage. His six-foot frame disappeared into its accommodating depths as he reached for the phone.

"Clarice, coffee please."

Clarice and the coffee appeared as swiftly as though she had been waiting outside, steaming pot in hand. I raised my cup and erased my smile as I looked at Eric. He stood at the window, drinking in the view of the town square.

"Now, where were we?" Benjamin asked, causing Clarice's hand to shake as she poured the steamed milk into his coffee. "That will be all, Clarice" prompted her to vanish instantaneously, like a wraith that dematerialized on command.

Eric walked over, politely declining Benjamin's proffered cup of coffee. "We are more anxious to see your finds."

"And so you shall." Benjamin pointed to the sofa. "But first, do sit down. Given you have not yet read my books, I will attempt to put you in the picture prior to my Albi announcement." We both fell silent as Benjamin stood and smiled down at his captive audience. His cat that swallowed the canary smile was barely repressed as he said, "Dear Dana, I have extended an invitation to Eric, and in turn shall offer it to you." He drew a deep breath. "I am providing the keynote address to an illustrious gathering in Albi tomorrow. My compatriots will attend, well-fueled by curiosity over news that I intend to reveal a *very special* Cathar relic." His emphasis lingered as he ran his tongue over his lips, savoring what he expected we would find irresistible. "You will attend, I trust. The drive to Albi will take a little less than an hour, but we must leave promptly by ten."

I hesitated long enough for Eric to chime in. "Dana must be torn by your offer, Benjamin." He turned to me. "I'd venture to say you and Evie have planned a day together." He smiled as he waited for my response.

"Actually…" I turned to Benjamin, whose tight-lip look eased at my words, "I wouldn't miss such an opportunity." Evie had destroyed any such option.

Benjamin smiled. "Very good."

Eric gave me a quizzical look as Benjamin opened his desk drawer and removed a large portfolio of drawings. He spread them carefully along the desktop. "These are the photographs of our latest digs at Montsegur, Coustaussa and Usson." We stared at the precise drawings, covered with dates, depths, levels and time periods. It was those of Montsequr that held me. I squinted at markings in French that indicated the garrison quarters, keep, barbicans, well, areas for worship and, lastly, areas for living quarters. Feelings pried at my shell. I subsumed them by fixing my attention on a sheaf of pages showing the design of a village below Montsegur.

Eric broke the silence. "Even with my scant understanding of French, I can appreciate your thoroughness, Benjamin." He pointed to the plans of Coustaussa. "I'm puzzled, however, by your interest in Coustaussa."

"Coustaussa castle was at a critical intersection of the route the Cathars took after they escaped with the treasure," Benjamin replied. "And, the area surrounding Coustaussa provided a honeycomb of caves in which to hide both the treasure and themselves." His tone took on added gravity as he unlocked a console behind his desk and withdrew a large box. I stared, intrigued by the unusual design of its divided enclosure. Each half was labeled, describing the contents. I translated it as, "The discoveries at Usson and Montsegur."

As Benjamin removed them, Eric peered closely at an engraving that repeated on several of the items. "That appears to be the figure of a dove."

"Most probably," Benjamin responded. "You must be familiar with the dove symbol." Without waiting for Eric's reply, he turned to me. "Are you not, Mademoiselle Dana?" His silence was weighted with tension that remained as he continued. "Surely you have noticed crosses with similar markings." Benjamin's stare, like two burning coals, moved from my face down to my neck scarf. I curbed an instinct to move my hand to my throat, my silence prompting him to add, "The dove, thought to have been connected to the Cathars, prompted shopkeepers to incorporate them in jewelry." He waited.

With what I hoped was credible curiosity, I nodded, "Now that you mention it, I believe I read something about it in the guide books." Disappointment colored Benjamin's expression as he turned from my throat back to the contents of the box.

"These contain only a few dove images, but they do expand our awareness of the everyday life of the Cathars. I'm especially pleased with that which we've unearthed from our digs at Montsegur and Usson." Benjamin ran his hand across a large assortment of belt buckles, keys, arrows, candleholders, spurs and what seemed to be fragments of weapons. "Each article illumines the Cathar's world."

Eric examined them as closely as possible without actually handling them. He turned back with a look of respect, but gave a slight shake of his head as he said, "They shed light on the world of that time surely, but as to being definitively Cathar, I can imagine what a challenge that presents."

"The challenge is yours." Benjamin's response was icy. I gave a start at the wrath in his tone, but more at the red flush of his face. Benjamin let out a slow rush of air before resuming his professorial approach. "You are excused for your ignorance of the provenance of these treasures." He swiftly returned the box to the credenza. "Tomorrow, after you have read my book and heard my speech in Albi, you will understand." His smile, restored by smugness, widened. "That which I shall unveil in Albi is unquestionably *the* Cathar treasure." He pointed to the locked drawer. "Without my efforts, even the items you have seen here would never have been retrieved." His tongue licked his lower lip before he continued. "I am proud of them, of course. But tomorrow's announcement will stun the world."

181

I was hooked. One glance at Eric revealed his curiosity. Benjamin's smugness aside, it was obvious he intended to unveil more than belt-buckles. "We look forward to attending," Eric said, moving to the edge of his chair. "Tell me, in light of your Cathar discoveries, what opinion do you hold of them as a people?"

"I don't deal in conjecture, only tangibles." A dismissive superiority edged his words. "The Cathars were heretics. The church eliminated them. I search for relics of that time as a scientist who produces hard and fast evidence." Benjamin gave a snort of contempt. "Others, whose names I shall protect, approach them with ideas about poetry, magic, mysticism, even despair over their eradication." His look cautioned us not to join their ranks. "I've given you a preview of what awaits you in Albi. Tonight I look forward to an equally candid account of your discoveries."

Our journey back had been grim, I thought, as I dressed for dinner. Benjamin resumed our mad-dash-tour through the city, continuing his didactic account of Toulouse, much of which would have been more interesting if I'd had time to absorb it. I'd so wanted just to look, not hear, to stroll, not run, maybe even to sit at a sidewalk café, sip a glass of wine and absorb the city gently. I dreaded returning to the house and seeing Evie. Like a patient under novocaine, I feared the point at which my numbness would wear off and the pain return.

So far, so good, I thought as we entered an empty house. "Dr. Arnstein went shopping," Beatrice responded to Benjamin's question. He gave a wry grin of exasperation as he entered his library with a reminder that dinner would be promptly at seven. I sighed in relief and headed upstairs.

Eric followed me, stopping as we reached my room. "We need to talk. I'll plead the demands of a deadline and try to get us off the hook early tonight." He stared as I opened my door. "But we'll need a quiet corner."

"I'm all in favor of bowing out early," I replied, "if we keep the focus on work."

"If you say so." Eric hesitated before continuing, "As to work space, I doubt Benjamin would give us free rein of his library. But I could ask."

"And invite his scrutiny of everything we do." I gave a slight shudder. "That reminds me, did you make mention of our visit to Coustaussa?"

"Of course not. I can't believe you would ask."

"I'll tell you why later, after we've found a quiet place to work." I followed his stare still fixed on my balcony. "Since our balconies are connected, we could work out there—if it's not too cool."

"It could work. If we put the tables together it should be big enough for your photos and my manuscript." Eric lowered his voice at the sound of voices. "I'll lead the charge to escape early if you promise not to get sidetracked by Evie."

"Not a chance," I said as footsteps neared. "Until dinner." I closed the door, turned the key in the lock and headed for the bathroom, turning the tub faucets full force. It almost drowned out Evie's loud call, "Dana—are you in there?"

I sank under the bubbles as emotions threatened to surface. Only by forcing my thoughts on the events in Mirepoix and Coustaussa did I silence them.

Just let me get through dinner with Evie, I prayed as I dried off and reached for my black skirt and camisole. I stared at my image in the mirror, examining my face for clues that betrayed that I was somewhere else. The externals looked the same, except for my hair having gone curly from the bath and an almost invisible tremor lurking at the corner of one eye.

As I stepped into the corridor, I nearly ran Eric over. "You look great," he said, his focus solemn. "Whatever's going on, I trust you to hold your own." He tucked my arm under his, the silky smooth warmth as reassuring as his words. "If not, give me a nod and I'll run interference."

We entered the terrace, talking animatedly about Toulouse. "I knew you'd love it!" Evie said, rushing over with outstretched arms. I sidestepped her reach, as she lamely added, "Benjamin is the perfect guide to Toulouse." She looked puzzled as she turned to Benjamin, who was absorbed in a heated phone conversation. He covered his mobile phone and said, "Take your seats, all. I'll join you soon."

Evie drew close and whispered, "What's wrong, Dana?"

"Deceit, my faithless friend." My response threatened to unleash an avalanche of anger. I spun away, facing Benjamin, who had just hung up the phone. He seemed oblivious to any drama as he took my hand and planted a kiss on it. "*Magnifique*, Dana. You look lovely. Do come sit beside me."

"Then *you* must sit by me," Evie said, her look pained as she took Eric's arm. "Perhaps I shall have better luck communicating with you."

I flinched, struck by an Evie who seemed to have deflated on the spot. She moved as though her legs didn't work. Eric gave me a perplexed look as he helped her settle into the chaise lounge alongside him.

Her words drifted back to me. "Thank you, Eric. From the little Dana has told me, I look forward to knowing you better."

Scarcely aware of Benjamin's attentions, my stomach lurched at Eric's response. "And I you. How happy Dana was to hear you had arrived."

Benjamin handed me a glass of champagne and whispered, "Seems Eric has corralled Evie—or vice versa. All well and good, that leaves us time to talk." He pointed to a divan. "Come sit by me, my dear." His look seemed the sort prompted by too much whiskey, but something warned me to proceed with caution.

I focused on the sequence of events leading up to my coming to France. "The Cathar assignment was a godsend," I began. "I'd been feeling limited within my career and wanted to move beyond photographing 'Gone With the Wind' days."

Benjamin laughed, responding with a Southern drawl, "I declare, Dana. Disappointed enough to 'think about it tomorrow,' I expect."

I laughed. "Your accent is perfect. Did your family live in the Deep South?"

"Actually, my grandmother did." Benjamin studied my reaction. "I'm a blend of French-Canadian. One branch of our family settled in the bayous of Louisiana, while the shrewder of them remained in Paris." Benjamin reached for the tray that the maid had placed beside us. As he refilled my champagne, he said, "But enough of me. Tell me of your experience in Mirepoix and Coustaussa."

I stumbled over an appropriate response and fell silent. Benjamin seemed amused as he lifted his glass to mine. "To be continued over dinner." His declaration coincided with the announcement that dinner was served.

Dinner began better than expected, with no further mention of Eric and my adventures in Coustaussa and Mirepoix. Thanks to Evie dominating the conversation. She babbled on with intensity beyond her usual loquacity. Her voice, more deadened than I'd ever heard, told me that her litany was just that, words filling the space needed to wall away emotion. Tales of her hassles with French bureaucracy in the sale of her Biarritz property went on and on. Benjamin was the only one who remained intent on her tale of a search for title documents. He stopped her long enough to provide advice as to the best way to handle French notaries. As coffee appeared, I turned to Eric, signaling my desire for him to begin our exit conversation soon. Evie, who'd caught my glance, looked desolate.

"It's been a great evening, Benjamin," Eric said. "But Dana and I have a lot of work to do, so we'll pass on coffee." Benjamin's eyes narrowed as Eric added, "I want to read your book before we leave for Albi tomorrow."

Benjamin drew my chair back. "By all means, away with you." Evie's silence caught his attention. "Evie, are you joining us in Albi?"

"Impossible. I have to leave for Biarritz early in the morning." Evie turned to me. "I'd hoped we could drive down together, Dana. Any chance?"

"None." I heard the ice in my voice. So did Evie. I turned away from the expression on her face to smile up at Benjamin. "I wouldn't miss your talk."

Benjamin looked pleased as he turned back to Evie. "Evie, darling, perhaps you could loan Dana some jewelry to wear." Benjamin's strange request stunned the room. Even Evie looked startled out of her stunned state.

"Yes, of course." She looked perplexed as she stared at my neck and turned back to Benjamin. "Dana always brings her necklace with..."

My look was as sharp as my words. "We'll leave it at that, Evie." Taking Evie's arm, I added, "If Eric's ever to get at Benjamin's book." I gave Evie a certain stare that we had established long ago, our "keep your mouth shut" look. Back when I trusted her.

SEVENTEEN

Montsegur, France-January, 1244

Clotilde shivered as she ran through an icy dawn. She'd given her last woolen cloak to one of the injured. From the looks of the growing numbers of sick, injured and elderly, not all her remaining clothing could help. She sighed as she reached for the makeshift sling bearing the body of yet another of the dying. Taking care to move the feeble old man as gently as possible, she headed for her quarters where space had been given over as a shelter for those awaiting the consolamentum.

Crowds of people, young and old, jammed her route. The steady barrage of the stone-guns, merciless in their constant onslaught, filled the air with noise and dust and the fearful sounds of the crumbling outer wall under fire. As she arrived at her destination, she paused and gently set her burden down.

"Clotilde, I have searched everywhere for you." Blanche stood in the entry, anxiety coloring her look as she stared at the man. "Oh no, not another one." Clotilde, too weary to respond, gently edged the makeshift stretcher over the ledge.

"You'll never let up on trying to save the hopeless, I fear," Blanche said as she watched Clotilde's efforts to move the man into the room. "There's no space near the fire." Blanche stared at the shivering form. "Who is he?"

"The father of the Parfaite, Raymonde d'Alba. His daughter was all to him. Since her death, well..." Clotilde turned to the man who, at the sound of his daughter's name, began to make a small sound and move his hand. Clotilde leaned over him, a wave of compassion filling her as tears formed in his rheumy eyes.

"How may I help you?"

"A Parfait—consolamentum."

"Yes, of course. Rest now. Today he will come." The old man's mouth eased into a slight smile as he closed his eyes. Clotilde turned to Blanche. "Go and find Bishop Marty. I saw him earlier. He was attending to one of the Parfaites who had fallen and wished healing."

"It'll take more than his healing powers to help…" Blanche halted, her hand sweeping the room in despair. "I'm not like you. From the first I laid eyes on you, so much younger and yet so strong, so self-contained, I prayed such fearlessness might rub off on me." Panic iced her next words. "Don't leave me."

"Put such thoughts away, dear Blanche. Go and sit by the fire. I'll go find Bishop Marty." Clotilde glanced down at the ailing man, wondering whether his smile of peace was from anticipation or from having already departed. "I must hurry. Not only this man, but many of the others await him."

Blanche covered her ears as she moved closer to the fire. "Do hurry. The noise frightens me so." The noise, Clotilde thought, as she moved back into the chaos, was a small part of her concerns. The ear-splitting barrage had become, like the icy winds, a constant background. She'd adjusted to it, the unbearable shortage of space, the shivering masses and the endless days of winter's cruelty. For herself, she could handle any circumstance. She'd learned long ago to not only endure the unendurable, but to call on her resourcefulness to outwit it. For herself that is—but as to Jean, her inability to provide his safety focused all her fears onto one target, the unthinkable loss of him. Jean, who dared make one more trip, "In order to find a sanctuary for the Church leaders, should…," he'd explained before turning away from the silent question in her eyes. As long as it was still possible to get in and out of the fortress, he must, he said, help others.

She knew what he said was true, or, at least as long as the sympathy and support of most of the villagers at the base of the mountain continued. Enough pockets of support still existed, motivated if not by compassion then by their greed for gold. Increasingly it required ever more gold to assure them of looking the other way or of acting as guides. To reassure her, Jean reminded her that Deacon Clamens and three other Parfaits had recently made it down safely, traveling as far as Carcassonne.

She'd responded, "Why do our church's leaders place themselves in such jeopardy?"

"To bring spiritual support." Jean spoke with great deliberation, his words carefully formed as he broached a subject never before discussed. "But, increasingly, to seek trustworthy guardianship for the Church's treasures."

She felt shock at his reply. "I don't understand what treasure could be of greater value than the safety of the Bishops themselves."

"Of that I am pledged not to reveal—not even to you." Jean's words and his inviolable vow, although obscured by her hectic days, haunted her nights. She looked for him in every grime-smeared face, peering at every litter carried past. It had been nearly a week now with no word of him. Fearing his ability to outwit his foes and scale the sheer mountain pass to safety, she looked for someone with whom to discuss the odds. For, in spite of the unflagging efforts of their defenders, Clotilde knew full well that Montsegur's situation was worsening.

Suddenly, out of the dusty bedlam of the forecourt, a man appeared as though called up from her thoughts. William de Plaigne, a knight of the Montsegur garrison, pushed through the dispersing crowd to reach her side. "Madame Clotilde, you must not remain here. The wall is under siege and may collapse at any moment." He wrapped his cloak around her as he moved her to the shelter of an interior wall. "What brings you here?"

"I'm searching for Bishop Marty."

"Surely you passed him." He peered through the teeming throngs rushing an endless supply of boulders to the catapults. "I don't wonder you didn't recognize him in this maelstrom. The Bishop was about his task, offering the consolamentum to those whose time had come." William gave Clotilde a solemn look as he turned. "Now I must return to my task, and you to yours."

"Hold, brave William. I shall do as you say, but allow me one question." Clotilde spoke before losing her courage. "Jean has not returned. Tell me true, the chances of his making it safely back to Montsegur."

"Good, at least to the village below. As to making it up the mountain, it is more dangerous than ever before."

"Jean climbs like a mountain goat, no matter how sheer the precipice."

"Perhaps, but the French army has signed on a detachment of Basque mercenaries, the hardiest of mountaineers, to guard all passes up the mountain."

Clotilde turned away, wincing in wordless anguish.

"Forgive me, dear lady. Your husband is a brave man, and doubtless supplied with enough gold to satisfy any who would block his return." William swung around at the arrival of one of his men-at-arms. "I must depart. Keep heart."

Clotilde moved in a daze deep enough to obscure the nightmarish scene around her. Only the sound of her name penetrated. "Clotilde, Clotilde, my child." Fabrisse's face was atop hers before she recognized her and began a quick adoratio.

Fabrisse motioned her action away. "We have reduced such practices." She seemed impatient to depart. "Esclarmonde is administering the consolamentum to several departing souls. I am called to aid Bishop Marty. Please accompany me."

"It is the Bishop I seek. He is also needed in my quarters."

Fabrisse took Clotilde's hand. "He is at your quarters even now."

Clotilde and Fabrisse moved as one to reach their destination. Stepping over the dying as they entered, they noticed that Bishop Marty had already prepared the white cloth and the New Testament. At their adoratios, he mumbled a hasty response. "May God bless you, make you a good Christian and lead you to a good end." Before his blessing ended, he turned back to the dying. "We must hasten to administer the sacrament. Have these souls made their *convenza?*"

"Yes, Father. All have reaffirmed the *convenza* within the past few days. The vow, 'Even if I have lost the use of words, but provided I still have a breath of life in me, I desire the consolamentum,' daily echoes from every corner."

The Bishop nodded as Clotilde helped with preparations. She glanced briefly at Blanche, whose eyes remained fixed, not on the holy ones, but on Clotilde. As changed as Blanche had become, she yet was family, Clotilde thought, a rush of sadness descending at her awareness that no family remained to honor the seven departing souls. The sound of Bishop Marty's hasty recitation of the consolomentum filled the air. She recognized the abridged Benedicites, Adoremus, Paters and the reading of Saint John's Gospel, each followed by his silent touching of the book. Bishop Marty was ill, she thought, wincing as the hoarseness in his voice deepened with each repetition of the ritual. The one constant,

Clotilde observed, was the serenity on the faces of the bonshommes as they received their blessing.

Although it was likely that four would not open their eyes again in this world, the remaining three smiled their gratitude at the bishop's presence. As he gave his final blessing and turned, Clotilde whispered, "Do have some cabbage soup."

"Soup sounds lovely, my dear," the bishop said as he glanced at the motionless four. "They have left for the feast of eternity." As Clotilde turned to prepare the soup, the bishop stepped carefully around the other three. At the entry to the kitchen area, he glanced back. Those who were able softly mouthed prayers.

"I have arranged an area where we won't disturb them." Clotilde whispered, as she guided Bishop Marty to the remaining space that allowed privacy. "Do sit here, Bishop." She pointed to a small table with benches. "And you here, dear Fabrisse."

Blanche quietly placed two large bowls of soup on the table. "The mead is ready. I'll return with it soon. And you, Clotilde, will you sup?" As Clotilde shook her head in denial, Blanche frowned. "She scarcely eats, you know." Her voice held despair as she spoke to Fabrisse.

"You must keep your energy up, my dear," Fabrisse said as she began to eat. Bishop Marty took Clotilde's hand in his. The sensation was comforting, with a strength beyond that provided by food.

"Sister Fabrisse has told me how much progress you are showing in your studies. She describes you as being hungry to know God." Revived by the soup, his voice seemed less hoarse.

Clotilde replied, "Montsegur has expanded my desire to know and to serve God." She turned to Fabrisse. "But as this holy lady knows, my questions are many and my faith often shaken."

"Nevertheless, my dear, such questioning shows deep consideration." Fabrisse added her hand atop Bishop Marty's.

"Remain steadfast, my dear," the Bishop said. "Fabrisse is one of God's great messengers." He smiled at each in turn. "Sadly, I cannot join your studies today, but Esclarmonde hopes to attend."

Clotilde noticed distress in Bishop Marty's voice as the last few words left his lips. His look of distress betrayed his concern over the dissolution of the paired socios and socias. Fabrisse's words offered compassion. "I shall accompany you."

"It is more important that your spiritual teachings continue." His gaze moved to Clotilde. "I know your heart grieves greatly for word of Jean, my child. You must have faith." With that he turned and made his way across the crowds.

The Bishop's departure seemed to enliven Blanche. She loved the lesson period. More for their captured time together than any spiritual benefit, Clotilde suspected, as she watched Blanche pull two boxes forward. *"Voilà!* Our schoolroom is ready. Will Bernadette join us?" Blanche asked. Clotilde glanced at Fabrisse, each waiting for the other to respond.

"Dear Blanche," Clotilde drew her near. "Bernadette has taken ill."

A slowly rising moan accompanied Blanche's look of disbelief. "No!" She wrenched away from Clotilde's embrace and slumped heavily onto the bench, her words bitter. "It's tending to the sick and working in the freezing cold that has done Bernadette in. As it will do us all in, I fear." Blanche buried her head in her hands.

"Dear Blanche, I know just what would help." Clotilde responded. "You could take some of this lovely soup to Bernadette."

Blanche jumped up and went to the kitchen area. "Yes, I'll take her some soup, that's what I'll do."

"She would like that, dear Blanche," Fabrisse said, watching Blanche fill a goatskin with the cabbage soup. "Go to her. You serve God there as much as with your studies."

Clotilde nodded. "Seeing you will be a tonic for Bernadette. Give her my love and tell her I shall come by in the morning."

"A tonic, yes. I must take herbs." Blanche flung the cupboard open. "Dandelion, where is it?"

Clotilde shook her head. "Gone, I fear. We have used all our stores of herbs for those taken ill."

Blanche's despair returned, filling not only her features but also her movements. She brushed away Clotilde's embrace and hurried away.

Fabrisse took Clotilde's hand. "My dear child, it is hard to be a soul trapped in a physical form. That is our lesson for today. May it bring you some peace." She drew out a well-worn manuscript. "Esclarmonde is delayed, but let us begin."

Fabrisse settled herself alongside Clotilde. "I know how difficult you find it to comprehend one of the core teachings of the Cathar Church—the idea that there are two opposing creator-principles, God and Satan, Light and Dark, Soul and Flesh. It is of these we shall speak today."

Clotilde fixed her attention on Fabrisse, aware of the contrast in appearance between Fabrisse and Blanche. Where Blanche had withered from a woman not much past youth into an old, embittered shell of her former self, Fabrisse was radiantly ageless. Her whole being, from the bloom in her cheeks to the strength in her step, exuded joy in her faith. It was this quality Clotilde sought with her dedication to her studies—that deep inner knowing, the gnosis that bridged doubt.

"When you look around this room you see only frail bodies and you sorrow. That is the time for you to remember your teachings." Fabrisse raised her eyes to Clotilde's. "We are not this cage of flesh. We are pure soul, a particle of divine substance that has been exiled into illusion. Do you understand?"

Clotilde nodded, "I've learned that it is as if the soul has been imprisoned in matter and time and forced to forget its true essence. What I don't know is why the good God would do that, exile his divine sparks into the horrors of..." Clotilde surveyed the dead and dying, her raised hand falling limply back onto her skirt.

"God is all Good. He does not create conditions that allow Evil to exist. Evil happens separate from God. Evil, known as Satan or the Prince of Darkness, is not created but is co-eternal with the good God. But Satan is not a true God. He is the negative, destructive principle, never the Creator in the real sense."

"I don't understand."

"Satan's creations, including his seduction of Spirit with flesh, must be understood, dear Clotilde, as the everlasting attempt at the destruction of the Good Creation of God. Faced with the beauty of the Spirit, Satan designs Matter, convinced it would deceive and make the Spirit fall. Faced with Eternity, he comes up with the cruel illusion of time, so that his flesh-encased creatures become fearful of death."

"But that makes Satan seem equal to God."

"No my dear. God's Goodness is eternal and omnipotent against Satan's force, which is one of annihilation. Such energy is opposite to God and Spirit, almost the reverse, but never the equal of God. Neither in import, affect, or even in Being, is Satan equal to God." Fabrisse studied Clotilde's look of introspection.

Clotilde held up her hand, scratching at her palm with a fingernail. "I feel, I hurt, I fear, I die. That is very powerful magic."

"That is our lesson for today and every day, to resist the seduction of the flesh, turn from Satan's physical temptations and honor the Spirit within. What is the Cathar doctrine that tells us how we do that, dear Clotilde?"

Clotilde paused as she reviewed their last session. "We honor the Spirit by not killing, not even so much as the ant, since within even the smallest of God's creations, resides God's spirit. We avoid the eating of flesh, since it corrupts our bodies with greater physicality. We fast so as to digest the presence of Spirit without the distraction of physical digestion. We meditate to enter the presence of God."

Clotilde halted, mentally reviewing her list as she noticed Fabrisse's hushed wait. "Very good, Clotilde, but how else do we resist our fleshly prisons?"

"Through simplicity and service. The way of the bonshommes is to seek not for worldly goods, but to learn and teach and help one's fellow man." Clotilde paused, her mind blank as Fabrisse continued to wait expectantly.

"There is one area, going back to abjuring the flesh, dear Clotilde," Fabrisse said, as Clotilde's color rose.

Clotilde hung her head, her response muted. "Cathar teachings instruct us toward celibacy—the total avoidance of the act of procreation."

"And why is that?" Fabrisse's voice was so gentle as to scarcely be heard.

"The act propagates further physicality, thereby deepening Satan's powerful hold." Clotilde's words faded away.

"Dear Clotilde, I understand your emotions regarding this teaching." Fabrisse took Clotilde's hand. "Youth makes it especially difficult to incorporate this concept fully. That is why the church only mandates it for Parfaits and Parfaites, and not for Believers." Fabrisse smiled. "Which is why so many wait to become Parfaits and Parfaites until they leave their childbearing years."

"Thank you for understanding," Clotilde said, tears welling in her eyes. "I love Jean so much that it has blocked that area of understanding." Clotilde drew a deep breath, blinked away tears and turned to Fabrisse. "There yet remains one more area which perplexes me." Fabrisse nodded and Clotilde continued.

"I need your help in understanding something which lately consumes me. Each day I look down on the ant-like spread of soldiers below..." Clotilde shuddered at the image, unable to voice her fears. Fabrisse remained silent until Clotilde's voice grew stronger and she continued. "I know our faith says souls are eternal, always returning to Spirit, but often returning to Earth to continue growing."

"Very often."

"My question has to do with Jean and me. I could not bear for death to part us..." she hesitated, "Or even rebirth to part us." Clotilde looked at Fabrisse.

"You and Jean came together in this lifetime to work on important issues. Although Jean desired to become a Parfait, what his soul needed was to join with yours in order to experience other crucial lessons—love and commitment chief among them." Fabrisse's gaze met Clotilde's so deeply that Clotilde felt touched at the soul level. "And you needed him. The two of you have not completed your souls' mission. You will continue together."

Clotilde grew nervous as Fabrisse stared silently into the distance. "Dear Fabrisse, pray tell what it is you see."

Fabrisse hesitated before responding. "I can assure you that Spirit never dies, that love endures. You and Jean will be of great importance to the Cathar faith. Now..." She lowered her voice "and in years to come."

Clotilde's face shone with joy. "We have years remaining!" She halted, doubt filtering through. "But, my dear Fabrisse— how?"

Fabrisse embraced Clotilde, cradling her head against her own heart. "This is a lesson not yet touched on, dear child." She stroked Clotilde's hair as she whispered. "Those years are yet ahead of you, but not in this lifetime."

Clotilde wrenched her face up, horror deepening her already pale features. "*Not* in this lifetime?"

"Put fear aside, my dear." Fabrisse formed each word with care. "Remember one thing only, your Spirits are eternal. You and Jean have agreed, as part of your joint goals in this lifetime, to undertake an important mission. Do you understand?"

Images returned. "It has to do with that which you and Jean are protecting."

"Yes. Soon you shall learn more of your role in that mission."

Clotilde clutched her heart. "But with Jean?"

"With Jean, yes. Now..." Fabrisse deliberated before she added, "And until world's end."

"World's end." Clotilde swallowed heavily, fearing the import of those words and of revealing that she'd heard them before. "Dear Fabrisse, please forgive me." She spoke carefully, neither adding nor subtracting from her tale of overhearing them from her cave on the mountain. "You spoke those words then. What do they mean?"

"We've talked about Satan's physical world, of greed, venality, concupiscence and self-satisfaction. It is this world which shall, how shall I describe it—be destroyed." Fabrisse hesitated, seeming to listen for guidance within. "No, not completely destroyed, but very much changed. In the time to come, God's Spirit shall infuse many with greater Light, providing a time of awakening to love and service, and the dying away of greed and destruction. At that time, when the world most needs it, you and Jean will complete your mission and unveil our treasure."

Clotilde sighed. "My head spins with trying to understand." She turned her face to Fabrisse. "But my heart feels joy at knowing Jean and I shall be together."

Fabrisse held Clotilde's face as though it were made of crystal. "Mind you guard such knowing." Her voice wavered. "Speak of it to no one."

"You have my word." Clotilde drew herself into her full height, her lanky litheness assuming a stance of rooted integrity.

Fabrisse held her gaze. "Not *even* to Jean." Each word was formed separately, their resonance etched as acid dripping on flesh.

"*Not* to Jean?" Clotilde's jaw sank as her mouth fell open, matching the desolation in her words.

"No one. Not even Jean." Fabrisse watched as the unequivocal firmness of her response imbedded itself into Clotilde. Clotilde's stance solidified, as unwavering as a soldier awaiting his commander's orders.

"Jean knows much and will, as the time nears, reveal much regarding the role you two shall play here at Montsegur. But his information must be focused on what he needs to know now. Your telling him that which I've revealed to you, that which is only yours to know…" Fabrisse paused to look directly into Clotilde's eyes. "You must remember one thing: To reveal such could change the course of, not only your own soul's destiny, but also that of the world's." Fabrisse, instead of reaching out as Clotilde's rigid posture began to waver, added firmness to her next words.

"*Never* forget your own strength, dear Clotilde. It is the power of your heart, not reason, which will enable you to hear and follow God's wisdom."

Clotilde nodded and reached for Fabrisse's hand. "Your words comfort me. Not, as you say, through my mind's understanding, but deep within my heart." Clotilde released a long sigh. "Dear Fabrisse, say you will be there to guide me."

"We are all part of one another, dear one, reflections of the One Spirit. In that regard, I shall appear whenever my soul can contribute to mutual growth."

"Clotilde!" Blanche's cry, more animal scream than human call, burst their solemnity as she entered. "Come quickly. Bernadette is dying."

Clotilde and Fabrisse moved swiftly around the ailing. Many had opened their eyes at Blanche's scream, anticipating their own death. Blanche tried to keep pace with Clotilde, rising panic in her cry. "Clotilde, Clotilde—don't leave me behind!"

Nita Hughes

EIGHTEEN

Albi, France-Present

"Ah, you are coming awake." Eric's words stirred my reluctant consciousness as I squirmed deeper into the makeshift pillow I'd wedged against the car window. "I thought you would want to know that we're nearly in Albi."

I mumbled "yes," but kept my eyes closed. My sleepless night had been filled with painful images of Evie and Alex. Hesitantly, I lifted one eyelid and peered out into a soft rain. "That looks like Benjamin's Jaguar up ahead."

"Right you are. We've kept pace so far." A flicker of concern flashed as he turned back to his driving. "I thought you might feel like talking."

"Not yet." My mind returned to images of dinner last night. As bad as it was, it could have been worse, if Eric hadn't swept us away as coffee arrived, asking that Beatrice bring a full pot to his room later. We were in our rooms before I could examine my bitter exchange with Evie. Eric tried to get me to talk then, but backed off at my curt, "No. Let's get to work."

Work was exactly what I needed. We turned to as though driven, going over each chapter, assigning photos as we went, Eric taking notes of where his story needed more research, clarity or expansion. It was two o'clock A.M. before we called it a night. We both felt pleased with the volume of catch-up we had accomplished. "Brilliant, partner. A night well spent." Eric said as he left for his room.

A night well spent, I thought, but only the part focused on work. Alone, the night was filled with images as painful as razor cuts. Still awake, I rose at five o c'lock A.M., anxious to return to work. I organized my film and cameras and, stealthily escaping the house, walked back to St. Sernin. After capturing the incredible dawn as it bathed its exterior, I used my remaining film to honor the early-morning mood of Toulouse. My visual sense was on overload until another sense was activated. Yeasty aromas of baking drew me to a café about to open. I downed three cups of strong coffee, sopped up with a just baked croissant.

Super-charged with caffeine, I'd done a brisk power walk back to the house before Benjamin's deadline of eight o'clock. I froze at the sight of Evie backing her car out the drive, my heart racing, until I remembered her saying she had to depart early for her meeting in Biarritz. She seemed oblivious to all but departing. As the car shot away, I walked in, nearly tripping over Benjamin's briefcase. As I rushed up the stairs, I met Eric coming down. I told him I'd need every one of the fifteen minutes remaining. Eric nodded, saying he'd put everything in the car and stall if necessary. I tossed me into a cold shower and everything else into a suitcase. We departed on schedule, Benjamin leading the way, Eric wary, and me exhausted.

I still feel that way, I thought, irrespective of a nap. I looked over to find Eric patiently waiting for a further explanation. "I'm not ready to talk. Not really."

"You'd feel better if you did."

"Maybe so, but you wouldn't."

"I'll chance it. I told you before how good a listener I am." His deprecating grin appeared. "Not just *good,* remember, but trained."

"All right, but don't look at me or ask any questions."

"Agreed. Eyes on the road and lips sealed."

I retreated to a neutral tone. "When I returned for film yesterday, I walked in quietly so as not to wake Evie." I felt my heart squeeze in my chest. I let out a sigh and continued. "As I reached the top of the stairs, I heard her on the phone. She was talking to Alex."

"Your fiancé." Eric's words were gentle.

"Ex-fiancé. We'd broken our engagement shortly before I left for this assignment." Eric nodded and waited. "The usual 'there must be someone else in the picture' reasons," I added, swallowing hard before continuing. "A 'someone else' who I felt I'd never have cause to meet—let alone know." My throat ached.

It took a moment to even breathe, let alone speak. "I heard Evie say, 'No, Alex, Dana doesn't suspect a thing. She's not here. I needed to hear your voice, my love.'"

Eric touched my hand, returning it to the steering wheel as I flinched. His grip tightened as he peered into the rain. I rushed on. "Somehow I made my way down the stairs and into the garden. I sat on a bench and tried to absorb it." I looked away, straining to see through the raindrops. "And my feelings went away." I could hear the deadness in my voice. "They vanished as though they'd gone deep into a cave, leaving a separate part of me to function." I turned back to look at Eric. "I was so grateful. That must have been what you sensed—that I wasn't there."

Eric neither confirmed nor denied. "Go on."

"If I could, I'd chose to remain in that condition. But it's coming back." I squeezed my eyes tightly shut, clamping down on tears. "Alex and Evie. It hurts so much." Eyes still shut, I felt Eric's fingers brush the wetness off my cheek. The pain in my throat, so unbearable a second ago, was suddenly replaced by a strange sensation. The touch of his hand brought a tactile memory, indefinable and yet somehow suffused with familiarity and deep consolation.

"Are you all right?"

"I don't know when I've ever felt so not all right." I reached for the little pillow, hugging it closely up against my chest. "How could they?" I heard the anguish in my voice. "I know such things happen, but my love and my friend, I…"

"It hurts, I know."

"So much." I studied Eric's profile, confused by the memory of his touch.

His focus remained on the road, his expression a blend of anger and compassion as he spoke. "I read somewhere that we all have boulders to remove in each lifetime. Mine seems to be centered on shame. Yours, perhaps, betrayal. It is by dealing with these issues that we grow." He glanced over at me. "I know you're going to make it, but take it from me, it is OK to howl—'who put this bloody thing in my way? How could they? It's so big and so hard,' should do for a start."

"Boulders, huh." My mind played with the image. "I'd love to order up an avalanche for the two of them right now." I started to smile, feeling something shift. "Pretty vengeful, I suppose you are thinking."

"Vengeance is mine sayeth the Lord." Eric looked over and smiled. "I've had to remind myself of that a time or two."

"How did you work it through?"

"I left my church. I left my marriage. I howled long and loud…" He paused. "Enraged at a God I'd felt had abandoned me." Eric kept his eyes on the road, his words suddenly tentative, as though they came from a place too tender to examine. "I turned to writing, using words to put my universe in order again." His eyes narrowed. "Seems I keep returning to the issue of what it takes to follow through on a commitment that doesn't end in disaster."

"Obviously these boulders don't easily move."

"My experience suggests forgiveness as the lever. But easy— no."

"You seem very hard on yourself."

"I was hard on others as well. I did my share of railing against reality." Eric's tone lightened. "Very therapeutic it was. I recommend you try it."

"Just what you need in a colleague, a banshee howling through the night." I hesitated, squelching an image that surfaced—"or the centuries."

"What I need in a colleague is a navigator." Eric said, peering into the rain.

"Right you are. That's Albi up ahead." I opened the guidebook.

"Well, be quick telling me what we need to know about it."

"The obvious, that it gave its name to the bonshommes. 'Albigensians' was the term used long before 'Cathar.'" I read on. "Albi wasn't the home of the Cathars. The city of Albi was faithful to the Pope, giving its full allegiance to the Crusaders, even though Albi belonged to the Trencavals. Albi's bishop, Guillaume Peyre, had an iron grip on the town, and would broach no intrusion in what he considered his territory. Since Albi wasn't invaded, it retains much that is eleventh century." I gasped. "Like that incredible bridge up ahead."

"We must be crossing the River Tarn. It's quite the bridge, but nothing compared to the church up ahead." Eric rolled down his window. "Incredible!"

"St. Cecilia's." I looked out at the imposing structure ahead. "We'll have to explore it after the conference."

Eric slowed the car as we neared the town square. "I wish we had more time to explore. Albi seems very much the proud town." He held his palm out the window. "Now that's ecclesiastical magic—the rain stopped the minute we entered Albi."

I smiled but kept a close watch on Benjamin's car as it slowed and made a turn alongside the cathedral. "Where did Benjamin say his meeting was?"

"In the Toulouse Lautrec Museum, next to the cathedral."

"Oh no." I shivered and repeated what I had just read. "The museum was the former Archbishop's Palace. In 1286 and 1287 it was used by inquisitors to try more than four hundred Cathar Believers. Most were put to the stake."

"Benjamin's trying to tell us something," Eric said as he stuck his head out to listen to Benjamin's instructions for us to park in the square.

Eric nodded and parked alongside the Jaguar. As we got out, I stared up at the cathedral, its soaring structure decidedly intimidating.

"I can see the Pope having built this thing as a 'look how powerful we are' message," I said. "It still has a 'don't mess with me' look about it."

"So does Benjamin." Eric lowered his voice, adding, "He looks as though we're about to make him two minutes late." As we joined him, Eric grinned and glanced around, saying, "Quite the city, Benjamin. I'm impressed."

"Albi isn't half the city of Toulouse, but it does have its entrenched bourgeoisie and they don't like to be kept waiting." Benjamin scowled and did an about-face as he headed for the museum.

I held back, trying to take in Albi. The shops lining the square, seductively displaying art, tablecloths, clothing and antiques; the cathedral imposing reverence; the museum, gaily emblazoned with posters of the current featured artists; the cobbled streets leading to the eleventh century bridge; all were seductively inviting.

"Dana, hurry along," Benjamin called out, his frown expanding until a woman approached. In an instant it metamorphosed into a winning smile.

She held out her hand to Benjamin as we neared. "Monsieur Carter, I wouldn't miss your presentation." Her Parisian accent matched her soigné appearance. She glanced at me. "*Americain,* I presume."

"Yes, Yvonne. They are doing a series on the Cathars." Benjamin made the introductions. "Yvonne, Eric Taylor and Dana Palmer, Yvonne Delecroix."

"How fortunate for you to be able to hear Dr. Carter," she said.

"Fortunate, but only if the expert gets to his podium right now. Do excuse me." Benjamin doubled his stride toward the museum's entrance, hurrying through the door and up the stairs.

Eric and I followed Benjamin into a large conference room at the end of the corridor. "Quite a large turnout, but I think I see two seats in the center," Eric said as we headed for them. Benjamin had already reached the dais and was orchestrating the materials for his presentation. "I wonder what's in store." Eric lowered his voice to a whisper. "I confess I barely opened his book last night."

Animated conversations fell to a hush as Benjamin opened a large case, took out an item enshrouded in paper and placed it on the table behind him. My curiosity piqued, I whispered, "Let's try to get up front. I want a closer look at this treasure of his." I peered toward the item on the table. "If that is what it is."

"Probably, but I don't see any closer seats. Wait, there may be two in the second row. I'll check it out and give you the high sign if so."

Eric's high sign was accompanied by a pleased look. I walked up, saying, "Great, We're near enough for me to take photos of his find."

As I sat, Eric lowered his head and whispered, "Carefully turn. End row, near the center—Andre and Lena Villeneuve."

I glanced quickly, puzzled as I said, "I wonder if it's Andre and Lena's *mystère* that he intends to unveil as his special treasure."

"I'm not sure what to think." Eric spoke softly, his head nodding toward the front row. "Looks like the press is out in full force."

A hush fell over the room as Benjamin stood. "Ladies and gentlemen, honored guests and esteemed members of the press, let us begin." Benjamin's voice was made for a lectern, his confident manner resonating. Eric pulled out a pen and tablet and handed them to me. "His speech is in French."

I kept at my note taking, straining over every phrase as I did a rough translation. It helped that Benjamin used an overhead projector, with slides to dramatize his key points, or to show the sites where the artifacts were retrieved. His emphasis soon turned to his recent success at an unnamed dig.

His enthusiasm surged with the applause. His smile betrayed a look of 'you ain't seen nothing yet.' His slides concluded with a focus on his newest digs at Usson and Coustaussa Castles. I made out the phrase, 'Usson provided support and shelter for the escaped Cathars with their treasure.'

Benjamin missed his calling, I thought. His pauses, the transparencies, and the way he held them for an extra beat before he displayed them—all had his audience enthralled, the tension heightened. "Although Usson Castle was destroyed in the thirteenth century, it was subsequently rebuilt, thereby undergoing much scrutiny as to any treasure or important signs that may lead to treasure." He stopped to take a slow drink of water before returning to his rapt audience. I glanced at Eric to see how he was reacting to our host's presentation. Oblivious to my look, he kept at his task, making quick drawings of the slides Benjamin was showing, slides showing mounds of raked dirt, their layers labeled and dated, along with photos of artifacts—belt buckles, candle holders and goblets.

Benjamin completed his explanation of the slides. With a dramatic raising of one eyebrow and a glance at the mysterious item in the background, he seemed to salivate as he lowered his voice. "Now let us return to the Cathar treasure. Did it exist, and if so, what was it and where was it?" I heard much shifting as people moved to the edge of their seats. "In all our excavations, we've turned up little in the way of coin. Does this mean that the Cathars had no wealth? Quite the contrary. Despite the emphasis placed on the Cathars' abjuring wealth, we know that they were supplied with gold and silver." The comment triggered a flurry of discussion in the audience.

Benjamin continued. "While it is true that the Cathars lived ascetic lives and asked no tithes or contributions from their Believers, they did require money for their Houses. These Houses were established as places of worship and as schools to train Parfaits and Parfaites. For this, the Church required financial support. Much aid came from the lords of the Languedoc, many having close relatives who were Parfaits and Parfaites. So, surely the Cathars had wealth, if not to use for themselves, to use in support of their growing church and, during Montsegur's siege, to pay guards, sentries and escorts providing safe passage on and off the mountain. To go where and do what?" Benjamin took another sip of water before continuing.

"Surely, in the early days at Montsegur, it was to go down to their flock to preach and teach in the caves and forests of the region, as well as to visit lords receptive to them. As the siege intensified, however, their focus changed. It became necessary to plan for the safety of their deacons and bishops. But, as the end seemed imminent, their most important task didn't involve people." Benjamin turned to motion to someone just offstage. "Please prepare to dim the lights on my signal."

"Their most crucial task was to remove their secret treasure. Not the treasure of coins which had been moved over the prior months." Benjamin paused, letting the silence in the room build before he continued. "But their true treasure—the Inquisition's primary focus—was referred to as '*pecuniam infinitam.*'"

I did a rough translation from my Latin. Scribbling down the words on my tablet and underscoring "unlimited treasure" or "endless wealth," I angled it over to Eric. He nodded, but remained fixed on Benjamin's hushed tones. "A treasure much more priceless and of keen interest to the Pope." He looked out at the audience, taking a satisfied breath at their rapt attention. "So valuable as to necessitate the formation and ferocity of the Inquisition."

The lights dimmed. A spotlight illuminated the still-covered object on the table. "Many are the tales of what that treasure was. Legion are the zealots who have searched for it." Benjamin smiled as he looked out over the audience. "How fortunate that I have always disregarded the endless fantasy tales. Using a strictly scientific approach, I can now announce that I have solved the riddle and retrieved the treasure." Benjamin made a magician-like turn and, with a sweeping motion, slid the silky covering off as he backed away and pointed to a richly gleaming object. "The Cathar's treasure—The Holy Grail!"

The room burst into a frenzy of shouts, questions and activity. Some tried to reach the stage. A flashbulb went off. "No photos are allowed." At Benjamin's stern words, a guard rushed to retrieve the camera. "Please be seated. I will only take questions when it is calm and orderly." Benjamin's imperious tone was accompanied by a smug smile that beamed more radiantly than did the vessel. Although painstakingly polished, it was so humble in its unadorned design as to belie the fantasies long ascribed to it. Nevertheless, it compelled an avalanche of questions.

"In order, please. We shall start with the gentlemen of the press. You, sir." Benjamin pointed to the elderly gentleman in the front row. "Your question."

"The obvious—as a reporter: 'Who, what, where, when and how'—beginning with *who* verified its authenticity, *what* proved it to be the Grail, *where* had it been hidden all these years, *when* did its location make itself known, and *how* do you know it is *the* Cathar treasure?"

"Well, that about covers it, esteemed sir. But, since I can see that you are also a man of thoroughness, I shall reply in kind." Benjamin made a small motion to center his cravat before answering. "Who verified its authenticity? The Museum of Toulouse did a thorough testing, using modern carbon dating methods. What has proved it to be the Grail? The care with which it was hidden and the value placed upon it by the Catholic Church. Where had it been hidden? I am not at liberty to say at the moment. You can understand why when I remind you that the site would be overrun and destroyed. When did it make itself known, and how did I know it was the Cathar treasure? My thorough study of the Cathar sites, the Cathar history, their rituals and the records of the Inquisition, as well as the *Chanson de la Croisade*. All led me to trace the most logical route taken and the sites most likely to have been used by the Cathars to conceal their treasure. The 'how did I know' part of your question had to do with the site dating, coupled with other objects found with it." As the old gentlemen pursed his lips, preparing for a rejoinder, Benjamin pointed to a young man who had stood up. "You, sir. Another member of the press, I take it."

"*Paris Match*." It was said with an air of quiet condescension. "As you must know, the Holy Grail has been discovered several times." He paused to look around. "One as near as Valencia. None has proven, incontrovertibly, to be the real thing. Can you release enough substantive evidence to authenticate your claim?"

Benjamin drew himself to his full height, his dark eyes widening, his response bristling with contempt. "My dear sir, I am a scientist, not a 'paparazzi.' Certainly I can prove my claims." The crowd tittered. "My research is impeccable, and it shall be made available to the scientific community for scrutiny." Benjamin pointed to a conservative looking man sitting toward the back. "You, sir."

"From all that is known about the Cathars, theirs was a faith which did not build churches, a faith which rejected sacraments, disdained holy relics and repudiated all that was physical. A group unlikely to have an interest in such an object." He paused, looking around the assembled group. "Even given that the chalice from which Christ drank still existed in the thirteenth century, I'd find it highly doubtful that the Cathars would seek it out, or, as a scientist, that you'd be so gullible as to support the plausibility of such an item being the Cathar treasure."

I thought Benjamin would come down off the dais. His face reddened with full-blown rage, his contemptuous stare at a level of malevolence that would intimidate the strongest. I turned around to observe its target and found the gentleman, who looked like a professor or a statesman, calmly unruffled. By the time I turned back to Benjamin, his color had gone down a notch as he sipped from a glass of water. He set the glass down, took a deep breath and addressed his questioner with disdain. "The facts will prove me out, sir." A dozen hands flew up around the room.

"That is all—no more questions for today." Benjamin's brisk dismissal, for one brief moment, threatened to bring the audience en masse to the podium. "Thank you for coming. You may follow my studies in the scientific journals."

The audience seemed to waver between borderline bedlam and stunned resignation. Their questions and energy had nowhere to go. They took their cue from the more sophisticated among them, who shrugged and began solid applause. Benjamin's acknowledgement seemed a bit restrained as he bowed solemnly and quickly exited the stage, clutching the controversial treasure to his chest.

Eric took my hand and began to thread us through the crowds in the direction of a side exit. "My best guess is that this exit might lead us to Benjamin." He said. "Move nonchalantly so the parade doesn't follow us through."

We held back, letting the masses pass. Just as we were about to slip through the doorway, Andre and Lena Villeneuve walked up. "Mademoiselle Palmer, Monsieur Taylor, how fortunate we meet again." They extended a hand to Eric and kisses to me. "Professor Carter's announcement was *extraodinaire!*"

"Very interesting, I would agree." Eric's words were agreeable but his look impatient as he returned his hand to the doorknob. "We hope to interview him."

Andre responded, "Yes, but of course. The Professor is intrigued to interview you as well." He stared at my neck. "Mademoiselle Dana's necklace—that is, when we discussed with him its matching exactly the seal on our own treasure, he became very excited." He glanced again at my neck, a look of understanding slowly dawning. "Of course. The Professor seemed alarmed at your wearing such a treasure and doubtless cautioned you."

Eric nodded vigorously. "He is eager to continue the discussion. We have exactly five minutes to spend with him now, so if you'll excuse us, it was good to have seen you again." Eric's words trailed behind as he steered me through the exit and up a stairway that ended at a closed door.

"Who is it?" Benjamin answered our knock. At our names, he slowly opened the door. "Close the door." His face flushed as he peered around to make certain no one followed. "I now know what a film star feels like. They were going to swarm over me like bees on honey." He reached for a tissue and wiped his brow. "You wanted a treasure to end your series with—you got one." His eyes went back to the door. "But you'd better hurry if you want to claim first rights to the story. Those journalists will try to ambush me any minute now."

"Now may not be the best time to talk," Eric replied.

"Very true," Benjamin said, squaring his shoulders. "I'll need to put off these vulture newsmen, assuredly. I have guards to protect the treasure, and me, from any importunate advances." Benjamin pursed his lips as he looked from me to Eric. "You mentioned you were going to Montsegur soon."

"The day after tomorrow," Eric confirmed.

"Good. A perfect time and place for me to fill you in for your series." He leaned closer, staring at me. "And to put together the pieces that led me to the treasure." He did a swift about-face, his manner as he turned to Eric almost erasing the challenge implied. "The press is sure to break the news of today's meeting, old chap, but I stand by my offer of an exclusive."

"We appreciate such an opportunity. Montsegur should work for us." Eric turned to me. Curiosity won out.

"Yes, it should work. We need to finish a few things." I wanted to stall for time until we could discuss our strategy. Eric understood. He gave me a complicitous look before turning back to Benjamin.

"We'll call you to confirm," Eric said, with a Benjamin-like look at his watch.

"Of course. I shall return to Toulouse today and will remain there during the weekend." Benjamin extended his business card.

"Leave a message if I happen to be out." He turned to me with a bemused look. "Knowing your friend, Evie, she's apt to have made plans." His restraint in not staring at my neckline was transparent. "I assume I can't persuade you to return to Toulouse to join Evie and myself."

Eric cut in quickly. "Impossible, old chap. Dana and I are here on business, as you can appreciate." His tone left no room for debate. "As to our meeting in Montsegur, we shall get back to you with a confirmation by Sunday."

A loud knock rang out as we neared the door. An anxious voice said, "Monsieur Carter. The journalists are waiting."

"As you can see, my fans await." Benjamin assumed a haughty demeanor as he opened the door, dismissing us with a hasty "Bon jour."

We retraced our route through the auditorium, Eric running interference, dodging reporters. My focus was on avoiding Andre and Lena. Unnoticed, we reached the entrance of the museum. "Let's get out of here," Eric said, pointing to St. Cecilia's. "A quiet cathedral should do it."

"Sounds good to me. If there's a phone, I'll call Veronique. She seemed eager to talk." Misty sunshine seeped through rain-clouds as we walked.

"Very good," Eric said. "After our tour of the cathedral, I'd say a dashed good lunch is in order."

"You're on," I said as we crossed the threshold of St. Cecilia's and entered another world. We echoed each other's hushed awe as we looked around.

The interior reinforced the cathedral's overwhelming power, wealth and drama. Its soaring Gothic pillars were rich with carvings, gleaming with gilt and an overpowering abundance of intricate architectural designs. An ornate screen dominated the chancel area up ahead. It was covered with what looked like fairy tale illustrations. I hurried up front to have a closer look. Monsters and demons, deranged and bloodied humans, all writhed too realistically in a vast section dedicated to the horrors of Hell. Cauldrons of naked men and women compelled attention to tormented sinners screaming for pity as grotesque monsters breathed flames of fire and prodded them with lances.

I jumped in surprise as Eric touched my shoulder. "That would throw the fear of God into anyone not in lock-step with the Church. Heretics beware."

"Such detail," I said as Eric leaned in for a closer look. "It's like a demonic comic book." A parishioner stepped past us and slid into a pew to pray as I opened a brochure on the cathedral and read about the religious art in the rear of the church. "Let's have a look."

Eric grimaced. "Hopefully it's not in this same vein." He grinned. "I'm game, but I want to study the pipe organ on the way." Eric pointed to a soaring marvel of rococo carving and gilt pipes.

"It beats the carousel at Coney Island," I said, thinking that the beauty of the organ almost redeemed the horrors of the monsters. After a few minutes, we headed off for the back section of the cathedral.

What met our eyes were endless aisles lush with icons and carvings and hushed with reverence. It seemed combination of art museum and church, Stations of the Cross and polychromatic saints of all descriptions filling our path. Luxuriously bathed in rich woods and gleaming gilt, the overall impact was that of a haunting strain of music from the twelfth century. Eric whispered, "Not Cathar-like."

I nodded, frowning as I said, "Such excess compared to their simplicity."

A few more aisles of saints and Eric took my arm, saying, "I'm ready to go if you are." I nodded as we headed for a side door and out into bright sunshine.

I looked around the square. "Let's find a restaurant. There's bound to be a phone nearby," I said as we crossed the main square into an alley which led behind the storefronts, a quieter lane of shaded cobbles and delicious smells.

Eric pointed to a sign up ahead. "Lautrec's, how does that sound?"

"Perfect and there's a public phone outside. I'll call Veronique. And Madeline, we'll need to give her an idea of the timing for our return." I looked up at Eric. "Any thoughts as to going straight to our *gite*, or..."

"If you say so." He spoke hesitantly. "But I can't get the twelfth century Cistercian monastery out of my thoughts." He laughed. "I guess it's my priest persona. We don't have to stop if you'd rather not."

"We'd kick ourselves if we passed it by. I'll tell Madeline we'll return to our *gite* tomorrow afternoon—and why. She'll love our taking her recommendation."

"Good. You do the phoning and I'll see to lunch." Eric slipped behind the café's glass doors, releasing a heavenly scent to tease my hunger.

I returned quickly, pleased at having reached both Madeline and Veronique with no problems. Eric was sitting at a corner banquette, studying the label on a bottle of wine he was holding. I watched him reach for the reading glasses poised on the end of his nose, his hair tousled as he leaned over, his attention etched in solemn study of the label. It took a moment before I noticed the bouquet of lilacs in the center of the table. I felt a frisson of pleasure as Eric looked up.

His gaze hypnotized me, although it seemed he was equally transfixed. I felt a welcoming sense of peace as I walked over and said, "Hello."

"You're here." His voice was so intense as to rivet his simple words with a level of meaning beyond my brief absence.

"I said I wouldn't be long." I slid into the banquette, closer to him than any space requirements dictated.

"I'm glad." He fumbled at an explanation, a boyish grin of confusion overcoming him. "I mean, it's good to see you." Eric nervously reached for the lilacs. "You always loved them."

"Always." I touched his hand, wary at the emotions that filled me.

"You are celebrating a special occasion, Madame and Monsieur?" The tiny brunette waitress asked, her smile wide as she added, "An anniversary perhaps?"

Yes, we are." Eric said. "Please bring us a bottle of an excellent local red wine, with *foie gras* and bread to accompany it."

The waitress nodded. "*Bon.* Our *vin de pays d'Oc* is very good. You will enjoy." She smiled as she hurried away.

"What's happening, Eric? I'm feeling such a peculiar sense of..."

"Of reunion." Eric studied my face as though only now seeing me. "It's like your description of your soul going away, except that I felt mine return from some far off place when you walked in." Eric held my hand like a father's grip on a lost child.

"I know." I sighed. "It feels like reuniting with family, a where have you been, how did I forget and, and..."

"And thank God you're here!" Eric looked up. "As is our wine and paté."

212

We toasted and drank and ate every morsel. Eric drank surprisingly little wine, causing me to notice other differences in him. He seemed a different man. Gone were the deep furrows, the constant cigarettes, the anxious anticipation of a drink and the cynicism that had coated his humor. He still joked, but with a lightheartedness that was absent before. A sense of ease and strength, a deep peace settled over us, erasing any thought of my phone calls until we'd nearly finished.

"I forgot to tell you what Madeline and Veronique had to say."

"Good news from the looks of you." He smiled. "And I'll be looking at you as much as I can."

My tone rose as I said, "Madeline was so happy when I told her we would be staying at her friend's abbey. She warned me of a surprise waiting for us."

Eric laughed out loud. "I'm not surprised. And what about Veronique?"

"Veronique was delighted that we'd be staying at the abbey. She lives less than six kilometers away, in the village of Montolieu." I studied Eric's reaction as I added, "She insists we stop in Montolieu. It's a town created around books—old, new, manuscripts, ancient papers, books in English, and…"

"Perfect—more books," Eric said, as the cheese tray appeared. "The only thing writers love more than writing is reading. Anything else?"

"She invited us to dinner." I spoke slowly, torn at being with strangers. "She has something important to discuss concerning Benjamin's treasure."

Eric handed me a slice of brie and poured the last of the wine into our glasses. "Then of course we must go." He held his glass high. "A toast to our good fortune in the synchronicity of such meetings—and to being together." Our glasses touched and remained, as if warding off anything but good portents.

Nita Hughes

NINETEEN

Montolieu, France-May-Present

Our approach to Montolieu was a gentle roller coaster sweep past green fields, small villages, and roadsides dotted with wildflowers. I half-stared at the fields, the streams and the flowers, when I wasn't looking at Eric. Having him beside me felt so peaceful that I nodded off. The sound of tires braking on gravel woke me.

"Sleep well?" Eric asked as he turned off the engine and took the map.

"Yes, very." I glanced out at a road sign. *Mazamet—6 kilometres*. We must be close to Montolieu."

"Not far, but I needed to check our turnoff." He did a rough calculation and held the map out for me. "At Mazamet we take D118 saying 'Carcassonne.' Ten kilometers on we should see a sign saying 'Montolieu.'"

I studied the map as we pulled away. "Seems we'll be crossing some mountainous country. It could slow us down a bit." I said, watching as he frowned. "But beautifully scenic. If you want to stop, get out and stretch, just say so."

"I'd rather just get there. I'm getting anxious about the availability of rooms in the abbey." He grinned. "I know Fontfroide Abbey left me unmoved, but sleeping in a twelfth century abbey is a different story."

"We'll call when we reach Montolieu. Somehow I think they'll have a room for us," I said, smiling as I spotted a sign ahead. "D118, right on schedule."

Montolieu was magic, a book-lover's dream. Not only did it have books of all descriptions in every language, it had art and sculpture and cozy sidewalk cafés. We parked, got out and meandered along curving cobbled byways as we peered into boxes of books, windows of books and a shop saying, "The English Bookstore."

"Let's go." Eric took my hand. We dodged a motorcycle careening around the corner, crossed the street and headed for the shop. As we entered, Eric greeted a smiling woman behind the counter. "We're looking for books in English on Cathars."

"You've come to the right place." The woman led him to an alcove. "Look to your heart's content. If there is anything I can do, please let me know."

"Why yes, there just may be," Eric said as he followed her back to the desk. "Before we get lost in books, we need to reserve a room for the night. A friend told us about an abbey nearby." She flashed a confident smile as we both waited.

"Ah yes, the *Abbaye de St. Marie de Villelongue*." She raised her ribbon-trimmed pince-nez glasses and looked in her Rolodex. "I'll be happy to call for you."

Eric stood close to the counter, straining at the French words as he studied the woman's expressions while she carried on a voluble conversation. She halted, covered the receiver, and spoke to us. "He rents only two rooms, one is reserved for tonight, the other is actually the most enchanting. It was the Abbot's room."

Eric turned to me, waiting until I said, "What are the accommodations like?" I asked. "I mean, in terms of bath or shower, is breakfast included…" Eric's forceful clearing of his throat prompted what I hoped was a tone of French *savoir faire*. "Is it two beds or one?"

She spoke briefly and turned to us. "Two beds, double size, a very large bathroom, but shower only. And a wonderful French breakfast." She held her hand over the phone. "The abbey is famous for its jams. Be sure to comment on them. It will please him so much." She hesitated, looking from me to Eric. "Would you like to see it before committing to the room?"

"No. We'll take it," we both said.

"Good." She smiled, spoke briefly and hung up. "All is settled. I'll give you directions. It's only six kilometers from here."

Twenty minutes later, loaded down with a bounty of eight books and great expectations, we took our receipt and directions and headed off.

A short distance from the shop, Eric turned the car off onto a country road that led to the abbey. I felt as though we were entering another reality as we drove past green hills, sheep and cattle scattered on their slopes with spring flowers at their feet. We crossed little bridges over rushing streams, caught sight of ruins on distant hilltops, but saw no sign of civilization—no people, no villages, nor anything that showed our connection to the twenty-first century. I began to wonder at our directions when we rounded a curve and suddenly came upon a large rock wall surrounding an ancient abbey. We let out a subdued cheer at the sight of a man making broad gestures for us to pull into a parking area. A large red lab trailed him, wagging his tail in agreement with his master's welcome.

"Bonjour!" No cassock-enshrouded mystic, although the man's hearty welcome told us he was in charge. He looked like every-man—fortyish, comfortably dressed in corduroy slacks, a deep blue sweater that picked up the blue of his eyes, and sturdy boots. He seemed completely at ease with a life center-stage in a setting out of the past. We shook hands and introduced ourselves. He spoke English fairly well, but seemed more comfortable in his own language. With my limited French, lots of gestures, and more tail wagging from *le chien,* we were registered and taken outside to follow the route to our room.

As we exited his all-purpose lounge-dining room-office, the grounds drew my attention. Definitely not a manicured abbey for tourists, but a wild and free refuge, it awaited only the special few. As we walked past a catch-your-breath assortment of antiquities, I spotted sculptured figures, urns and shards lying wherever they had fallen. It would take months, I thought, perhaps years, to examine everything. A wisteria-covered cloister, its marbled gothic columns lining our enchanted passage, led us to another wing. As we neared, I stared at a small ovoid stone resembling a weatherworn fertility figure. It lay casually on the ground, among a tumble of assorted stone artifacts that would have a museum curator salivating. My photographer's heart beat faster.

Our host's voice brought me back as we reached a door. "You enter through here. Please turn on the switch for lights and turn off as you leave each area."

Eric nodded, asking a question as the owner turned to go. "One more favor, monsieur," he said. "Mademoiselle wishes to take a few photos."

"Yes, of course, as you wish. With the exception of my living quarters in the front section of the property, you may film freely."

I echoed Eric's 'thank you,' my grin widening in response.

"If you wish a reservation for dinner, please let me know."

"Thank you, Monsieur," I replied. "That won't be necessary. We are having dinner with a friend in Montolieu. May we use your phone to confirm later?"

"Certainly. Whenever you wish." He pointed up ahead. "Your room is at the end of this hall." He gave Eric a large key, turned and left.

I stepped gingerly as I followed Eric, breathing air that seemed to have hung in the hallway since creation, as did the furniture, tapestries and art objects that lined our path. A doorway stood partly open midway along the corridor. I peered inside as we passed, half expecting to find novitiates on their knees. The room was empty.

"Here we are." Eric inserted the old-fashioned key into the keyhole of the massive door at the end of the corridor. The door opened onto two solid wooden beds, rising high off the ground, depressions in the rippled green coverlets betraying the mattresses' age. As I entered, I did a double take. A wall-sized mirror, trimmed in rococo gilt, reflected my surprise.

"Come look at this," Eric said from across the room. I was surprised to find him crouching alongside the furthest bed. As I neared I saw that he was kneeling on a strange set of stone stairs just to the left of the bed. They led to an opening that was paned, as if it were a window, but obviously it once was not. I stared out at very worn and winding stone steps that circled down into the interior of the ruined twelfth century church. Wide-eyed, our attention moved from barreled arches forming coved ceilings to spectacular ruins of walls soaring into an empty sky, their vacant windows looking onto riotous wisteria blooms. I gasped and drew back. Impish faces stared down, mystical carved figures tucked high among the corners of the gothic pillars. Their ancient visages stared back, enigmatic smiles in place.

"This must be what our host was trying to tell us. I wasn't sure of the French translation." I rose from my kneeling position on the step and turned to Eric. "He said that the Abbot's Room had a secret exit used to enter the church and pray."

"That's probably the surprise Madeline mentioned," Eric said as he rose to check out the rest of our room. "Definitely beats the Abbey Fontfroide." He smiled as he walked over to another doorway, saying, "That must be the loo."

As he went to check it out, I noticed the window he passed. Large panes of old glass, deeply recessed, created a window seat of solid rock. I hopped up onto the expansive ledge, my outstretched legs unable to touch the other side. As I pushed the antique glass open, my hand reached out to touch an opulent cluster of purple wisteria. I sighed with contentment, wanting to stay forever.

"Me too." Eric whispered as he took my hand and kissed it softly.

"Me too, what?"

"Me too' whatever is in your eyes, your thoughts, your heart and your soul. Your deepest desires are mine." He slid his arms under me, lifting me close against him as he turned and gently placed me on the bed. "I've searched such a long time."

Our lovemaking was slow, like the gentle surging, enveloping sweep of ocean waves, powerful, deep and endlessly joyous at reaching land. His kisses were all over me as mine were on him, each ravenously hungry to explore one another, an exploration that seemed at once both new and yet very familiar. A feeling of coming home, with all the poignancy of almost not making it back, caused a chill to pierce me. It expanded, exploding into escalating heights of ecstasy that rose and crashed, taking me deep into almost unbearable feelings of joyous release. I cried and laughed as we rode our bodies and souls throughout all time, coming together in endless waves of rapture whose ebbing left us shattered and rejoined as one. We slept.

I opened my eyes to find him watching me. Our faces, but not quite *our* faces, were reflected back by the massive mirror. "Hello, my love." His soft words were offered like a gift, with confidence and delight in being able to speak them.

"My love." I whispered back, tasting the words on my tongue, tracing them to my heart, feeling a surety with them and with him that I'd never felt with Alex.

"Those will do for now. There are many words, taking a few more lifetimes I expect, but those will do for now." Eric rolled over to admire the deepening shades of soft blue-grays. "Feel up for dinner in Montolieu?" He asked.

"I'm famished. I not only feel up to it, but as though I could fly there." I ran my finger gently over his face, feeling sorrow at missing the years it took to form those creases, but great happiness in being here now. He smiled.

"As long as all flying is done together. Up you go." He held out his hands and lifted me to a slightly swoony tilt. "Let me feast my eyes on your naked bum as it waltzes to the loo." He laughed as I danced away.

* * *

I remember calling Veronique, getting directions, and taking photos of the abbey grounds just before the last light left the sky. I remember it, but like someone enveloped in a magic sheen of delight that heightened everything with a sharp patina of extreme acuity while at the same time enveloping all in gauzy unreality.

On the drive to Montolieu, Eric said, "You look like I feel, totally besotted."

A silly smile floated on my lips. "Besotted, hmm. So that's how it feels."

"That's how it feels." He traced my grin before returning his hand to the steering wheel as we turned into a cul-de-sac just beyond Montolieu's church.

"We're here"

"Yes, we are." He said as he opened the door, tilted my chin up and gave me a lingering kiss that ended in a breathless, "Really here."

"If I continue to stare into space, give me some sort of sign," I said as we walked down an ancient alleyway to a bright blue door.

"I promise," he said as he reached for the golden knocker, giving one quick kiss just before the door opened.

"*Bonsoir, mon ami's!*"

"*Bonsoir*, Veronique."

"Please come in. Do excuse the boxes. We've recently moved in."

"Of course." I ignored the boxes, focusing instead on the sense of comfort and style the Spartan décor suggested. Like their owner, it was understated, classic and rich with hidden depths. I smiled as I walked over to examine a large vessel, its pointed end securely resting in its cradling stand. "How lovely."

"It is very old, a Roman amphora once used to store wine," Veronique said.

I turned and took her hand. "We are so delighted that you invited us."

"I felt immediately such a strong sense of *sympathique*." She fixed her vivid green eyes on me, causing vague memories to stir. Giving an almost imperceptible nod, she turned to Eric, who stood beside a beautiful grand piano across the room. "And with you also, Monsieur Taylor."

"Thank you, Veronique." Eric gently touched the piano. "Do you play?"

"Sad to say, no. It is my partner's piano. Claudia is a doctor. She is on call at the hospital today, but will try to arrive by nine to join us."

"We look forward to meeting her," Eric said, turning to me. "In the meantime, Dana and I would be happy to help with dinner."

"I would not think of it. Anyway, dinner is simple and will prepare itself while we talk." Veronique walked over to a sideboard, removed trays and placed them on the coffee table in front of the fireplace. "Please have some olives and cheese." She held out a small bowl of each, pointing to the centerpiece crock of *foie gras*. "You must try this. A little grandmother on a farm outside the village made it. As a connoisseur, I can assure you that its taste shall live on your tongue forever."

I spread a little on a square of bread, savoring the buttery richness of every silken swallow. Every scent, taste, touch and sight was destined to be indelible. Veronique quietly refilled our glasses with champagne as the conversation flowed.

"You were saying that your archaeological finds were sometimes spectacular. I assumed you meant the chalice that Professor Carter exhibited in Albi this morning." Eric's reference was as pointed as his stare. Veronique returned an olive pit to her plate, her expression suddenly solemn as she replied.

"Understand that I intend to speak the truth, but I must insist you forget where it came from." Her green eyes flashed a warning that she'd not utter another word without our agreement to keep it secret.

"We would never betray your confidence," Eric said. I rushed to agree.

"Never, Veronique. It is obviously something of great sensitivity."

"Very. Enough to lose me my job—certainly to lose Benjamin his." She began a nervous twisting of her napkin. "I fear I cannot go to the press, nor to the museum committee, until I have evidence to outweigh his fabrications."

We waited through a long silence, doubting whether Veronique would continue. It was Eric who spoke. "And you think we might be able to help you?"

"Or, at least, not help that monstrous man." She drew a deep breath before going on. "You must realize his intent is to use you to add validity to his claims."

"Via our series. That explains his 'I'll give the exclusive to you.'" Eric said.

"But of course. He intends your series to affirm his discovery of the Holy Grail as definitively *the* Cathar treasure." Veronique looked scornful.

Champagne splashed as Eric sat his glass down abruptly. "He can't believe that we'd ever agree to such a thing."

"Certainement."

Eric turned away in disgust. "Tell us more about his treasure, Veronique," I asked, the image of Benjamin's smug unveiling of The Grail spoiling my *foie gras*.

"It is certainly *not* the Grail that he exhibited." Veronique stood up, nervously pacing the room until she stopped at the fireplace. "That he would pass it off as Cathar is abominable." She stabbed at a log, sending sparks up the chimney.

"What is it, if not Cathar?" I asked.

"A chalice taken from a dig near the Chateau Coustaussa, very near to a little village called Rennes le Chateau."

"Rennes!" Eric stared at Veronique. "Then it's Sauniere's treasure."

"Quite possibly. Professor Taylor has long been obsessed with discovering the source of Sauniere's sudden wealth." Eric walked over to help her add a large log to the fire. "It seems you have heard of it," she said, wiping soot off her palms.

"Yes, we passed near to it." Eric said as he turned to me. "And we picked up a book about Rennes at the English Bookstore."

I nodded. "As for me, I learned of it in my obsessive reading about the Cathars and the Cathar treasure. Rennes was mentioned as a possible hiding place."

Veronique and Eric walked back to where I sat. "The story is compelling." The room resonated with mystery as Veronique continued. "A poor priest, with a small stipend, suddenly began building villas, ordering expensive statues and paintings and completely restoring his church." She paused. "Surely Sauniere had found a treasure. But it was not Cathar." As her words hung in the air, Veronique paused to pour us each another glass of champagne. "Take your glass with you to the dining table. We shall continue our conversation over dinner." A worried look came over her as she glanced at the time. "Claudia must have been detained."

The phone rang as soon as we sat down. Veronique rushed to answer. "*Allo.* Ah, Claudia." She listened solemnly, nodding and saying '*D'accord*' several times before replacing the receiver. "A bus of sixty students was in a very bad accident." She looked at us. "Claudia must remain to treat them. It is so very sad."

"I am so sorry, Veronique," I said. "Claudia must be a very good doctor."

"A very good doctor and a very good human being." Veronique looked away, a film of moisture coating her eyes. "She works too hard, but she loves her profession." As she sat down, her tone brightened. "Well then, you two must do justice to the bouillabaisse. I have prepared so much."

We did justice to it as well as the crème caramel. Replete, we adjourned to chairs in front of the fireplace, glasses of Armagnac in our hands. Eric settled into a wing chair and turned to Veronique. "Now. Back to this so-called Holy Grail of Benjamin's and its connection to Sauniere's treasure."

"More likely it and Sauniere's wealth are both from the same source—Visigoth treasure, not Cathar." Veronique stared into the fire as she sipped slowly at her drink. "Rennes was a major Visigoth center, and before that, a Roman *oppidium.*"

"An *oppidium*?" Eric scribbled on his note tablet.

"A stronghold where people could take refuge in case of danger. Something like the walled forts along the Silk Route." Veronique replied. "Its history and use is why Professor Carter does endless research in digs around the area. Coustaussa provides fertile ground in his search for Cathar relics, as well as Visigoth treasure."

Eric's voice rose. "In finding the latter, he means to pass it off as the former."

Veronique nodded. "Professor Carter's great confidence grew massive when he found the remains of a burial site, an extremely difficult site at that." We listened intently as Veronique continued. "The Visigoth kings had an intricate means of burial. They diverted rivers, creating burial chambers for the kings and their

223

wealth. Restoring the river's channel covered all traces and frustrated any recovery."

I leaned in toward Veronique. "Was it the grave of King Dagobert II?"

"That is the strongest rumor." Veronique's gaze held respect that I should know of him. "Another says his grave is in a crypt beneath Sauniere's church."

Eric looked up from his rapid note taking. "So, whether a diverted river burial chamber or a vault beneath the church, what was found seems to be the identical treasure that Sauniere and Benjamin claimed."

"Quite likely one and the same." Veronique motioned to refill our glasses of Armagnac. Eric and I declined, too intoxicated by her discussion. "Doubtless more remains will be revealed, depending on the circumstances of the weather and the persistence of Professor Carter. His lust knows no bounds in seeking Sauniere's treasure." Her grin was bitter. "Everyone thought those boulders Sauniere brought up for his rock garden were just boulders, not fortification stones from a gravesite."

"Back to the goblet." Eric's hands lit a cigarette, stared at it and snuffed it out before putting it to his lips. "Benjamin swears it dates back to Christ."

"Perhaps there is some credibility in his statement," Veronique said, her scientist's penchant for accuracy counterbalancing her desire to denounce Benjamin. "History claims that Titus of Rome sacked Solomon's treasure of Zion in the Holy Land and removed it to Rome."

"But you're implying that it may be just a rumor." I listened intently.

"No, not a rumor," Veronique replied. "Part of the treasure trove is shown on Titus' triumphal arch in Rome. Nothing of the treasure remained, however, after Alaric the Visigoth raided Rome in AD 410." Veronique halted as Eric paced.

"Taking it back with him to Rennes. So it *could* be the Holy Grail?" Eric's eyes lit up as he swung around to face Veronique.

"Which Holy Grail, Monsieur?" Veronique asked. "The one whose legend began with the Celtic oral tales of a magical vessel of unlimited powers? Or the one mentioned in Cretien's, 'Le Conte del Graal,' the grail of Arthurian romantic lore? Or the cup from which Jesus drank at the Last Supper and which was used to collect his blood as he died on the cross? Perhaps the one rumored to have been brought to Glastonbury by Joseph of Arimathea?"

"I'd not considered even one a reality, let alone several," I said, suddenly aware of why the French consider their American counterparts unsophisticated. "And the one Benjamin unveiled this morning?"

"Not likely any of them. From the carbon dating and the character of the goblet it is more likely—" She held up her glass. "Part of a royal set of goblets, but created no earlier than AD 300."

Eric frowned. "But Benjamin wouldn't expose himself to ridicule."

"Nor will he expose himself, or it, to close scrutiny." Veronique's eyes sparked in anger. "Except, of course, by his cronies who are willing to attest to the dating being 'perhaps off by a century or more.'" She pursed her lips, her brow furrowed as she added, "It isn't the provenance of the Grail that concerns me, it is his insistence on connecting it so blatantly to the Cathars."

"How absurd! The Cathars didn't venerate objects." I tried to moderate my outburst. "They treasured only Christ's teachings of love, service and Spirit, certainly nothing physical."

"Exactly. That, along with the intense focus of the Inquisition, would eliminate any tangible item, let alone the Holy Grail, as the Cathar treasure." Veronique's expression grew more solemn as she gazed off into space.

I remained deep in thought, surprised when my voice broke the silence. "There is another definition of the Grail, not as a goblet but as a transformational outpouring of Christ's teachings, the truth behind creation. I'm convinced the treasure might be..." I fell silent.

Eric smiled. "Continue. You are onto something, my love."

"It could be something locked within those teachings." I spoke slowly, drawing on the feelings that surfaced after I had finished reading the Gospel of St. John and Revelations. "What the Cathars revered was the wisdom of the Gospel of St. John, along with the esoteric writings in the lost books of the Bible." I sighed as I turned to Veronique. "Teachings, writings, a manuscript conveying Christ's power, that would be a more formidable fit, one accounting for the Inquisition's fearful definition—a treasure with the power to change the world.'"

"True, Mademoiselle Dana." Veronique placed her hand on mine. "A profound and powerful treasure yet awaits. But that it lies within this goblet of Benjamin's, or any golden artifact—most assuredly it does not."

"I agree with you, Veronique." Eric replied. "Your description of where and how Benjamin's goblet was found would seem to rule out its being anything but Visigoth. Is there anyone who could validate your claims?"

"Yes." She seemed to weigh any mention of the name before she replied. "There is one man. His name is Monsieur de Lahille from Arques."

"Pierre!" I gave a little clap. "I knew it. He had that look of wisdom that..."

"You know him?" Veronique interjected, looking astonished.

Eric smiled. "Yes. We had an interesting meeting with him in Arques. He encouraged us to go to Coustaussa and forego Rennes until later." He turned to me. "I'd say we call on Sunday to arrange a visit with Monsieur de Lahille."

"The sooner the better." I said, turning to Veronique. "From the moment we met, I knew that he *knew,* certainly enough to caution us not to mention our visit to Coustaussa to Benjamin. But even much more."

"Pierre knows more than all the Benjamins in the world." Veronique gave a firm nod of her head. "As to the real Cathar treasure, he of all men would know what and where it might be." Veronique glanced down at her watch. "Forgive me for keeping you so very late. But this evening has been so enjoyable." She hesitated. "I'd like to offer a suggestion."

"Of course." Eric smiled as he added, "You've saved us from journalistic disaster, as well as providing a delightful, provocative evening. So let's hear it."

"I would be happy to call Pierre and arrange for your meeting."

"Perhaps you could join us," I added.

She hesitated. "Perhaps, if Pierre deems it appropriate. And it will all depend on Claudia's return." She sighed. "But it could only be on Sunday. I must return for work on Monday."

"To listen to Benjamin gloat," I said, my distaste transparent. "The, the..."

"The perjurer, for one." Veronique laughed.

"He will regret trying to use us." Eric's words were as emphatic as his handshake as we rose to leave. "To be continued Sunday in Arques, I trust. Call us after you reach Pierre." He gave Veronique our *gite's* number.

"I shall." She smiled conspiratorially. "Together we will defend the Cathars."

The drive back was uneventful. But our night in the abbey, although beginning with delight, ended with terror. Eric's scream brought me wide-awake. It was the same cry, holding the same anguish I heard in Coustaussa.

"Clotilde!" Eric sat up, frozen in horror as he stared at me in the dim light. He grabbed me and held me close to his chest.

"Dearest Clotilde." His grip grew tighter until I moaned and he held me away and stared. "Dana?"

"Yes. You called me Clotilde."

"You were in my dream, only you were called 'Clotilde.' Montsegur was under siege and I was leaving. They called me 'Jean.' It was terrifying."

"Did we escape?"

He shuddered. "I did. It was dangerous. You were to join me later, guided by..." Eric shook his head as he sat up and switched on a lamp. "My brother?" Confusion warred in his expression. "It seemed so real." He jumped up and stared at the mysterious staircase. "The scent of incense woke me. You must have smelled it." I shook my head no. "It was so distinct, exactly as if priests were wafting old censers while praying in the abbey." He sat on the bed and pulled me close.

I began a slow, gentle massage of his tense shoulders, but suddenly my hands halted as a memory surfaced. "'Clotilde' and 'Jean' were the names of the Cathars at the Auberge Mystere in Mirepoix." I whispered.

"That explains it." Eric shook his head. "My subconscious must have focussed so keenly on that incident that I dreamt of them."

"Maybe." I hesitated. "If it weren't for the fact that 'Clotilde' was the name I heard at Coustaussa." I sighed at the memory. "Called out in the same voice."

Eric rubbed his chin. "What is going on here, Dana? Either I've caught—I refuse to call it 'woo woo' –this past memory thing, or..."

"Or?" I looked up at him, my defenses quietly marshalling.

"Or there is such a thing as reincarnation." Eric spoke slowly. "If—and I emphasize if—we were Jean and Clotilde—I know it sounds absurd—but it would explain a lot of things."

"My necklace matching the mystery packet at the auberge for one." I let out my breath in relief. "It would also explain my experiencing so many images and emotions connected to the

Cathar period." I looked away, mulling over something that had nudged at the edges of memory. "Even Veronique."

"Veronique?"

"I swear I've known her. It's something in her eyes."

Eric hesitated before replying. "I'm not convinced. But I'm willing to reserve judgement for now. In the meantime, we should consider all the players we've come in contact with in France." Eric grabbed his note tablet and pencil. "But for now, I want to get down everything I can remember of my dream."

He leaned back and began to write. I walked to the window seat, stretched and took a deep breath—no scent of incense. Eric glanced up. "You look better."

I smiled, the answer coming spontaneously. "I am, at that. I find it comforting that we might be connected on a soul level. Whether it is reincarnation or whatever, it feels more purposeful."

"Purposeful in what sense?" He asked. Seeing my hesitation, he added, "Go on. It might help me capture the you of the thirteenth century."

I tried to put it into words. "In the sense that we know what we're here for. Not just you and I, but all of us—at least at some level."

"All of us—Even Benjamin?" He grinned.

"Even Benjamin." I gazed out the window as an almost full moon spotlit our room. "But not as an ally. Anyway, it's all so vague at this point. Continue writing; I'm going down to take some pre-dawn photos of the abbey grounds." I rummaged around, picking the best lenses for moonlight.

Eric smiled as I walked by. "I trust you're not going out in the altogether."

I laughed, grabbed a pair of jeans, tee shirt, and shoes and put them on. I stopped at the door, blew him a kiss and, fighting the urge to linger, scurried away.

Anticipation counterbalanced reluctance as I stepped into the cloister. I love early morning shoots, I thought, shivering not from the cool morning mist but from pure pleasure. The magical atmosphere was somehow heightened by the focus of the lens. My shutter winked softly as it captured the full moon scudding behind a mound of wine-red clouds. The sepulchral walls of the ruined church glowed faintly, their ghostly images teasing me with evanescent echoes of the past. I smiled at the knowledge that their unearthly beauty, traced by gray shadows of wisteria, would be captured perfectly on black and white film. How strange, I thought, that although a Catholic abbey, I felt no fear or repulsion. Wouldn't I have if I had been Clotilde? The carved faces in the corners stared down. "We did not subscribe to our brother's bloodlust," they seemed to respond. Shaking my head, I decided that I would do some research on this particular Cistercian abbey.

After shooting two more rolls of film, I caught a whiff of the aroma of baking. It was daybreak. I gathered up my gear and returned to the room. Showered and dressed, Eric looked surprisingly bright-eyed as I entered. "I watched you from the window-ledge—my dream lover in the moonlight."

"And my name is?"

"Dana. But whatever your name, you are mine."

"True." I said as I wrapped my arms around him and inhaled the scent of soap and love. "I need a shower."

"If you say so." He held me at a little distance, a look of longing mixed with humor flickering through his expression. "If I'm going to resist the temptation, I'd better head for the dining area and drown my libido in strong French coffee."

I laughed as he walked out the door. "I'll be right down."

Ten minutes later, fresh and famished, I walked into the dining room to find Eric fixing a warm croissant slathered with jam. He extended it as I sat down. "Umm" I said, turning to the proprietor. "What is the magic ingredient in the jam?"

"Wild peaches, oranges, and a touch of vervain." He smiled as I scooped up another large spoonful. "I understand you are leaving us today."

"Yes, as much as we would love to remain," I replied. "We are expecting a call, but we'd like to take one last turn around your marvelous abbey."

"But of course. If you wish, I could escort you."

I hesitated, but one look at Eric confirmed my response. "Thank you so very much, Monsieur. But we would like to explore it with fresh eyes and ask you questions later." I had a bumbling time trying to translate my feelings, but his soft murmur of "newly weds," told me he understood. He smiled as we walked out.

Our lone adventure included walking, looking, touching and inhaling every aspect as we tried to emblazon the abbey in our memories. Although I thought I had captured it all on film earlier, Eric pointed out aspects unseen by my camera.

Just as we reached the wing where our room was, our host ran up. "Pardon, you had a message. Mademoiselle Veronique called to say that Sunday in Arques with Pierre and herself is arranged for ten o'clock A.M." Looking us up and down, he broke into a broad grin. "Honeymooners, you say in English. Correct?"

"Correct." Eric said, pulling me into an embrace. "We thank you."

" Oh, yes. Your abbey has given us memories that are, are…" I stuttered.

"Timeless." His perfect English word brought a smile as he added, "I am pleased that you have enjoyed your stay."

We thanked him again before heading for our room. We packed hastily, took one long look around, blessed our refuge, sighed and closed the door behind us.

Luggage secured, we settled into our car. As we drove off, we waved to our host and his dog until they vanished from our rear-view mirror. "I think this place is like Brigadoon, destined to return every hundred years." I said, blinking away tears.

"Like us," he replied.

TWENTY

Montsegur, France-January, 1244

The situation was growing more desperate. Clotilde slept fitfully, her senses more keenly alert with each passing hour. The roar of the siege engines drove her thoughts into an endless review of their situation. Morale among the defenders of Montsegur continued to remain high in spite of the bitter winter. Aiming to exhaust their assailant's patience, each time the defenders checked another assault, hopes had risen. Clotilde prayed Montsegur would prove impregnable.

She fed her belief with increasing rumors that Raymond VII had indeed made plans to support them. Optimism had grown when, immediately after the Bishop of Albi had an advanced and very effective siege-engine built to attack Montsegur, certain unidentified Cathar supporters provided an excellent engineer who, gaining entry to Montsegur, built and mounted a similar machine on the eastern barbican. It performed valiantly, answering the defender's prayers each time it repelled the attacker's fire. Encouraged, Clotilde yet explored the realities of their situation.

The inability of the Cathar defenders to get sufficient replacement troops up to the fortress had begun to takes its toll. Occasionally two or three would make it through, but they were insignificant as the number of defenders fell to scarcely one hundred versus the King's thousands. In spite of the overwhelming disproportion, as long as the fortress remained impregnable, morale held. The booming clamor of the endless hail of boulders, shattering nerves if not walls, sounded increasingly stronger.

Its fierceness recalled the morning, a week ago, when she knew that the tide was inexorably turning. A bitter cold had kept her awake all night. She shivered in the dusty dark of pre-dawn. A loud crash announced that the barrage had definitely increased in intensity. Clotilde had jumped up, her heart racing, as Jean sprang out of bed, alert to whatever action was required.

"That last attack shocked me," Clotilde said, lowering herself back down onto the bed. "I'm sorry to have woken you." Jean mumbled as he returned to their bed and drew her close. Snuggling into his protruding ribs, Clotilde felt worried at the toll his ceaseless effort was taking. She knew he kept a strong front for her, but she couldn't help voicing her fear. "Surely such relentless attacks demoralize our troops."

"True. Morale is waning, my love. The troops are exhausted. Even Pierre-Roger de Mirepoix has confessed his doubts," Jean whispered as he doubled over their coverlet and pulled it over her.

Clotilde rushed forward a question, seeking true warmth in the answer. "Pray tell me that the messages from the Count remain encouraging."

Jean's tone of voice vanquished her hopes. "We must consider the level of truth in such accounts, my love. Such assurances come, not from the Count, but from people *presumed* to be in contact with him. Always their message is the same, 'plans are prospering.' Increasingly, Pierre-Roger doubts the accuracy of such information."

"But Pierre-Roger is such a valiant leader, and his troops..." Clotilde's look begged for an avenue of optimism.

"Are zealous in their commitment to the Cathar's defense. True—but the reality is that it is becoming a futile endeavor." Jean sat up, shaking his head. "Pierre-Roger had an incident today which fed such futility." His expression filled with shock. "I've never seen him so enraged. He took me into his confidence, revealing that his second-in-command had actually arranged for a personal interview with the commander of the Crusader's army— to discuss surrender!" He shook his head. "Pierre-Roger tore the armor from his disloyal aide."

Clotilde gripped his hand, her voice sounding much calmer then she felt. "It would seem the troops hope to end the siege at any price."

"And not unreasonably. Without reinforcements, they cannot prevail much longer. The Cathar leaders are aware of this. There is discussion among some of the Cathar Believers as to whether they could assure victory by taking up arms." Clotilde's sudden sharp intake of breath prompted Jean to reassure her. "As great a crisis of conscience as this has caused, they cannot abrogate their beliefs against the taking of life. They have intensified efforts in every other way but to join the troops in battle." Jean's expression betrayed his misery and confusion. "I struggle with my beliefs, feeling deep shame when our noble defenders fall and I cannot lift a hand."

"Dear Jean. You do lift a hand, ceaselessly." Clotilde heard the anger in her voice as she saw how downcast Jean felt. "You've risked your life many times with the dangerous missions you've undertaken. Now that those are no longer possible, you replenish ammunition, monitor supplies, treat the wounded, and, and…"

"As do you, my love, in tending to the children and those ailing." Jean shook his head. "And aid the Parfaites and look after me and Bernard and Blanche."

"Blanche." The name rekindled despair in Clotilde's eyes. "She clings to me like a crazed animal since Bernadette died. My only respite is when Fabrisse takes her for lessons and prayers."

Seeking movement as an antidote, Clotilde rose to prepare a kettle of tea. Jean pulled on his doublet and joined her, stirring vigorously at the embers in the fireplace. "As for Blanche, we must pray her faith will see her through."

Clotilde looked up. "Blanche has rekindled her faith of late. She actually welcomes the flames as her entry to heaven." Turning away from Jean's look of shock, she grasped the bubbling kettle. She took a deep inhalation of the steaming warmth before extending hot cider and a bit of bread to Jean. "Something to fortify you, my love," Clotilde said, shivering as she looked over the rim of her tankard at the feeble light of dawn, knowing it to be the harbinger of Jean's departure. When he stood, she held out her hand. "Do linger a moment." A long look passed between them as he slowly sat back down. As she poured a second cup, she looked up at him. "What is to become of us, my love?" Before he could answer, a Parfait rushed in, calling for Jean. Clotilde watched them go, knowing Blanche would soon awake.

It had been more than a week since that pivotal morning. The constant barrage of attacks, the cries of children and the moans of injured numbed Clotilde's awareness to the fact that she'd not seen Fabrisse for some time. She looked up from the ailing woman she was tending, her gaze moving past the sick and dying to where Blanche sat rocking a fretful child.

"Blanche, you've been at prayers this week. Have you seen Fabrisse?" Clotilde was shocked as Blanche rose abruptly, letting the child slip to the ground.

Blanche rushed over to Clotilde, asking, "Is it time?"

"Time?" Clotilde gripped Blanche's shoulders and spoke slowly. "No Blanche, it isn't about time. It is about Fabrisse. Have you seen her?"

"She is ill and has taken to her quarters." A strange look spread over Blanche's face. "Surely she has chosen the *endura.*" Her eyes held a crazed glee as she stared back at the woman picking up the now-crying child.

"That can't be so, Blanche. I must go to her." Clotilde turned, heading blindly for the quarters of the Parfaites. A wailing Blanche ran behind her. The icy courtyard teemed with defenders readying their early dawn assaults, children running about and exhausted families huddled together, soothing their ailing elderly. Clotilde blocked out all images and thoughts except those of Fabrisse. It cannot be true. No Parfaite would put an end to her life through the *endura*—a fast until death came. She'd heard rumors of it being a means of ending one's life, but it was Fabrisse herself who countered them. She explained that, even though disdaining the physical world, Cathars had such respect for all life that martyrdom was unthinkable. Clotilde had evidence of such bravery these past few months, not from any indifference to living, but due to a deep-seated confidence in the teachings of their faith. "It simply cannot be true," Clotilde said as she reached Fabrisse's quarters.

"Fabrisse," she whispered.

"Fabrisse!" Blanche's shrill voice made Clotilde turn and place her hand gently over Blanche's mouth. "Quiet, dear sister. Those here are ill."

"Yes. But not very, dear Clotilde." A thin form approached and placed a bony hand on Clotilde's. "As you can see, I am not ready to be laid out as yet."

Clotilde led a shaky Fabrisse back to her bed. "I'll prepare a tisane of herbs."

Fabrisse shook her head slowly as Clotilde reached for the kettle hanging from a hook over the fire. She soon returned with a mix of weak wine and hot water. Blanche clutched at her skirts. Rage welled up. "Blanche, leave loose of me."

"Do sit beside us, dear Blanche." Fabrisse's weakened tones seemed to soothe Blanche. She released her hold on Clotilde's skirt and sank slowly to a sitting position on the floor, docilely gazing from Clotilde to Fabrisse.

"Blanche sorely feels the loss of Bernadette," Fabrisse said, her words consumed in a cough. Clotilde held a cup to her lips as blood spewed into it.

"Dear Fabrisse," Clotilde said as Fabrisse closed her eyes and let out a sigh. "Rest now." Clotilde fought to curtail her panic as she stared at Fabrisse's withered face. So superhuman had she been, so wise, so kind and with strength for all. That's the problem, Clotilde thought, Fabrisse has given herself away to all that beg help. Clotilde looked at Blanche, knowing the drain she'd placed on Fabrisse's strength.

In a burst of impatience, she said, "Blanche, go to the supply area and bring as many vegetables as you can find." Blanche stared in alarm, rooted to the spot. "Go now and come back immediately with them." Clotilde's tone caused Fabrisse's eyelids to open. Blanche, to Clotilde's surprise, rose and ran out the door. Clotilde soaked a cloth in cool water and began stroking Fabrisse's forehead. "Thank you, child." Fabrisse sighed. "I can feel God's healing energies in your hands." She resumed her wracking cough.

"Don't speak. Rest, and when Blanche returns I shall make soup."

Blanche returned with a handful of limp carrots, onions and one wilted head of cabbage. Clotilde put every morsel in a large cauldron. When cooked, she gently spooned the broth between Fabrisse's lips, persisting until Fabrisse had managed to keep down nearly a cupful. Blanche downed one cup of soup and then another.

Clotilde remained with Fabrisse through the long night. Before dawn, Jean arrived. Assured of Clotilde's whereabouts and Fabrisse's condition, he declined any food and departed. Clotilde returned to her relentless staring at Fabrisse's chest. All through the night, it had heaved with ragged breaths. Soon after daybreak Fabrisse's breathing leveled out and her sleep deepened. When she awoke late into the morning, Clotilde smiled at the return of light to her deep green eyes. Although subdued, it nevertheless held a feeble radiance lacking the night before. Her voice showed spirit as well. "Thank you, dear Clotilde. But go now, you look exhausted."

Clotilde wandered off into a nightmare, Blanche stumbling behind as they made their way back to their quarters. No warmth of Jean remained under their coverlet when Clotilde fell into her empty bed. She thrashed through a fitful slumber, aware of Blanche's moans.

* * *

"Dear God!" An avalanche of noise shook Clotilde out of a fitful dream. She was at the door in an instant, squinting through a rain of dust toward a familiar form. As Jean neared, his face blackened with soot, his eyes flashed relief at the sight of her.

"Thank God you are safe," Jean said as he grabbed and held her.

"And we are together." Clotilde shuddered, her words lost in the roar of another explosion. "Everything shakes so. I feared the wall had been breached."

"Let us go back inside." His words drowned away in the cacophony of noise enveloping them. As they entered, fearful eyes sought news. "Rest, my friends. We are all right." Too ill to move, they quieted at the firmness in his voice.

Jean led Clotilde through the crowd and into their private area. "And now tell me the truth," Clotilde whispered.

"The Crusaders have breached the eastern barbican."

"Just as I feared. But how?" She shook her head. "That tower was considered impossible to storm."

Anger suffused Jean's features as he paced their confined quarters. "They cut a trail out of the rock face to allow the army to climb up and bombard it during the night. Our eastern defenses were taken completely by surprise." A groan escaped him. "They were downed before anyone knew what had happened."

"No! Then the Crusaders have entered the fortress." Clotilde sprang forward in anticipation of breaking doors, her fists clenched, poised to do battle.

"No, my warrior queen," Jean said, as he sat her down. "Not yet. The space between the castle and the tower protected the defenders who had rushed to the support of the forward troops." Jean slammed his fist against the table, sending a candleholder to the floor. "It was treachery! Entry was gained by guides we trusted."

Clotilde shook her head. "The Crusaders must have bribed them dearly."

"Enough for them to betray friends." Bishop Bertrand's voice filled the room as he walked in, his face lined with deep compassion as he took the proffered place at the table and resumed speaking. "Do not despair. Our troops have things under control for the moment." He leaned in to Jean. "We must gather a meeting."

"When?" Jean squared his shoulders in wait.

"My quarters at eight PM." He stood to go. "I must inform others."

As Bishop Bertrand left, Blanche ran up to Clotilde. "I am frightened." The volume of emotion in her voice seemed to exhaust her as she turned and slumped down on Clotilde' bed. The sight of Blanche's crumpled form, so childlike in its curled posture, stirred a rush of compassion in Clotilde.

"Fear is taking a heavy toll." She said to Jean, staring at the scarcely recognizable person she once called sister, mother, and friend.

"Yes, my love." Jean drew her close. "But we must keep strong, for them and for one another." He released her and turned. "I must go find Bernard. With his hot head, he may have joined the battle this morning."

"Be quick to bring word of him." Jean was nearly through the main door when she added, "And of Fabrisse and the others."

"I shall." He hesitated, his gaze taking her measure. Stance tall, shoulders squared, she gave the image of endless courage and resourcefulness. He departed.

As she returned to the kitchen area, Clotilde felt a nagging pain. Impatient at its persistence, she remembered she'd not eaten in two days. She downed a cup of soup when a trio of men entered, carrying two wounded defenders. "We need help."

One look and Clotilde's stomach threatened to return the food she'd eaten. "Of course." Peering closer, Clotilde recognized two of Montsegur's most stalwart defenders. She drew forth a large basin of water and began to clean their wounds. Their painful cries were mixed with sporadic babbling of needing to return to battle. But soon their eyes closed.

Clotilde winced at the depth of their wounds, her heart filled with anger and sorrow. She'd no herbs for a poultice, not even feverfew for pain. All she could do was bandage their wounds

237

with remnants of cloth and pray for healing as she held her hands over the man most grievously afflicted.

Esclarmonde entered and with one glance at the severity of the men's afflictions, began preparations for the consolamentum. After Esclarmonde completed the hasty phrases of the consolamentum for both of the wounded, she began adding her healer's energy with a laying on of hands—one over the wounded stomach, the other on the top of his spine. Clotilde pressed a cloth soaked in water into the fast-graying lips of the man whose wounds were the most profound. As it dribbled down his chin, he let out a sigh, gave a slight smile and was gone.

"Can you do without me?" Esclarmonde asked, staring at his still living colleague as she waited for Clotilde's response.

"Of course. There are others in need of the consolamentum."

After Esclarmonde departed, Clotilde turned her vigilance and prayers to the other man. "Dear God, help him." Her hands trembled when she heard a response.

"Water." The man spoke, his voice weak and his eyes closed as Clotilde rushed a wet cloth to his lips. He exhausted himself in swallowing the cool drips of water that Clotilde squeezed from the cloth. His eyes closed in sleep.

Keeping a watch on him, she returned to cutting the remaining vegetables. The injured would need sustenance to recover, she thought. Sounds of bedlam filled her with an urge to rush to assist those outside. And yet, she must remain to aid those brought to their quarters—now a makeshift hospital. She glanced over at her charge. His breath continued. Blanche murmured and resumed her sleep.

"Clotilde." A soft call of her name accompanied a begrimed man's entry.

"Bernard!" Clotilde clasped him in an embrace. "Jean went to find you."

"I saw him. He remained to help with the injured." Bernard moved around the injured man as he went into the kitchen area. Lowering his brusque tones to a raw whisper he said, "I've come to fetch an extra basin and more rags."

"I'm so relieved that you are safe, brother," Clotilde said as she began gathering fabric. She placed the remnants in a large basin. "Have you eaten?"

"A piece of bread." He touched his mouth, brushing at his scraggly beard.

Clotilde added bread, figs and a wizened apple atop the rags in the basin. "Insist on Jean eating," she urged.

"It's been a long while since my little brother has taken his big brother's advice." Bernard's tone held anguish.

"If you'd seen his fear for your safety, you would know how important you are to him," Clotilde said as she held out the overflowing basin.

"Yes, well—important enough to fetch, anyway." He turned away.

"Bernard, do return. Jean would want you here with him," Clotilde entreated.

"If he's not got more important matters to tend to." The unceasing maelstrom swallowed Bernard's bitter words as he left.

Dark had long settled over Montsegur, ending a day the likes of which Clotilde prayed would not occur again. For those able to take nourishment, she offered water and a bit of soup. In one brief time of silence from the wounded, she recalled Bernard's words. His fears of being considered expendable, she thought, would surely be inflamed if he knew that the meeting Bishop Bertrand had called did not include him. She pushed her fear aside, so consumed was she in care taking all day long and far into the night. As she put the kettle on, she heard her name.

"Clotilde." Jean's face was a mask of deep introspection and concern as he entered their quarters. He scanned the area where Blanche and the injured soldiers lay, and, assured they slept, began a cautious account of his meeting.

"Not only did it not include Bernard, but only myself, Bishop Bertrand, Bishop Marty and three others were there." He drew her near. "All were sworn to secrecy." She pulled back in shock as he murmured to shush her response. "Listen, my love. Listen, accept, and forget what next I tell you."

He took her over to their bed, drawing the coverlet over them, his words barely audible. "Short of a miracle, our days here are numbered. I must help remove some Cathar valuables down the mountain to a safe hiding place." He felt her sharp intake of breath as she stirred in his arms. "Hush now and hear me out. Do not fear for my safety. The route is so dangerous that it hasn't been considered necessary to post guards. But I know every boulder and handhold." He tilted her head back, struck by the bleakness in her mute stare. "It is necessary, my love. Apart from securing the remaining gold, I shall attempt to bring back much needed reinforcements. Only I can see them safely up such a treacherous pass." A heavy sigh escaped. "I must get sleep if all is to go well."

Aware of his complete exhaustion, she held him as he slipped into a deep sleep. Long into early dawn she studied his sleeping face, unwilling to lose sight of him for fear it would be her last.

* * *

The siege continued. Clotilde, working non-stop to aid the wounded, had slept little in the three days since Jean departed. Blanche seemed oblivious to anything except where Clotilde was at every moment. Even the fact that the three soldiers seemed on the path to recovery didn't ease Clotilde's anxiety. Her focus was on Jean, every sense poised for an indication of his return.

Only once did she brighten. Fabrisse walked unaided, thin but steady on her feet, into their quarters. Embracing her, Clotilde felt optimism stir. If Fabrisse returned to her, surely Jean would.

"I come bearing good news," Fabrisse said, taking the cup of cider Clotilde offered. "The Crusade's latest attempt at another surprise attack has failed." Fabrisse took a labored breath before continuing. "Pierre-Roger has set up another siege engine to deter such attacks." Fabrisse studied Clotilde, knowing that no news but that of Jean's safety would fully penetrate. She leaned in and whispered into Clotilde's ears. "Fear not. Jean is as steadfast as a goat. He shall return safely."

"Clotilde." Bernard's entrance startled them. Fabrisse smiled and held out her hand. He made a swift adoratio and turned to Clotilde. "Where is Jean?"

Clotilde recalled what Jean said to use as an explanation. "He is meditating with Bishop Marty. They have undertaken a long fast and cannot be disturbed until they break it themselves."

"So we're reduced to that now." Bernard collapsed heavily onto the bench. Clotilde stared, thinking that the only echo left of his nickname, Bernard the Bull, lingered in the bullish peevishness in his voice.

Just then, the sound of Jean's voice startled them. "Bernard, dear brother. I'd have called upon you to join us, but one of us needs to keep his physical strength intact." Clotilde froze to the spot, scarcely recognizing the tattered figure as Jean. Gaunt, dirt-streaked and red-eyed, he looked even worse than the wounded.

Bernard put his arm under his brother's shoulder and lowered him onto the bed. "Gawd, but it isn't you!" He ran his gaze the length of his Jean's form. "You look like Bishop Marty had you undertake the *endura.*"

"More like a journey through the valley of the shadow death. But worth it."

"Worth it—I suppose God promised angels to repel the accursed Crusaders."

Clotilde moistened a cloth and began wiping Jean's brow as Fabrisse and Blanche entered with soup. Clotilde smiled at the strength in Fabrisse's voice. "Bernard, be a love and don't say another word until Jean has supped." She looked at Blanche and Bernard. "Let's be off and leave them alone for now." With her slight form and strong will, she steered them both out the door.

Clotilde watched anxiously as Jean devoured the soup. "Don't speak until you are stronger, my love."

He reached a limp hand toward her. "I must speak while I can." He raised his finger to her lips and continued in a whisper. "We fulfilled our task, although one almost did not make the arduous climb. It was nothing short of a miracle that we not only got through with a couple of replacement soldiers, but I was able to deliver an important message to Pierre-Roger. The Count of Toulouse wants to know if Montsegur can hold out until Easter. The messenger from Toulouse informs us that the Count is mounting an army to march on Montsegur and raise the siege." With these words, Jean fell into a deep sleep. Clotilde, overcome by exhaustion and relief, slid alongside him and slept. Images of Easter—only two months away—and the joy at their rescue, filled her dreams.

Nita Hughes

TWENTY-ONE

Aude, France- Present

Lost in a haze of silence, Eric looked as surprised as I felt when we drove up to our gite. "I now know what highway hypnosis is," he said as he turned off the ignition key. I grinned and began gathering scattered maps and books.

Madeline's lilting call filled the air as she approached. "How lovely to have you back." She smiled the wide grin of a Cheshire cat. "I have planned a special dinner for you this evening," she said, looking us up and down as we got out of the car. "I would say you are both very happy and very tired."

"Yes to both." I smiled, happy to be back but reluctant to tell her that we'd be leaving tomorrow. I decided to postpone such news until dinnertime.

"I long to hear of your adventures, but after you rest. Dinner is planned for eight o'clock, but please join us at seven thirty for an aperitif."

"With great pleasure," I said as I planted double kisses on Madeline's cheek.

Smiling in delight, she moved away with lithe grace. "Seven thirty then."

Eric began to unload the car. "I'm taking everything in."

I stared at the jumble of cameras, suitcases and miscellaneous. "Right. We'll need to repack it along with the things we left in our rooms."

"*Our* rooms." He grinned. "One room for storage and one for us."

That was the extent of our dialogue until I mumbled, "What…" Dazed, I couldn't open my eyes.

"I said it's a quarter to seven and Madeline expects us at seven thirty." Eric's voice penetrated my fog. I thrashed about in the folds of sheet, feeling drugged with exhaustion, lovemaking and turbulent dreams.

"I have the feeling I talked to you in my sleep," I said, yawning.

"If you did, I wasn't aware of it." Eric planted a kiss on my eyelids. "You'd worn me out too much to register anything until five minutes ago."

"I feel strange," I said, putting my feet over the edge of the bed and onto the floor. "Whatever I dreamt seems to have left a residue of…" I paused. "Fear."

He took my hand and steered me toward the bathroom. "There's nothing to fear now that you and I are together. Whatever it is we're meant to do, we'll do it together." He watched the bathroom mirror reflect my grin.

"Together, hmm. Does that mean in the tub as well?"

"Not if you mean to go to dinner at Madeline's." He laughed as he turned away. "Take your bath. I'll go next door and start packing." As he turned to go I startled him and me with a yell.

"Eric—don't go!" I felt shocked at my words and at the worry on his face. "I remembered my dream. You were leaving and I feared I'd never see you again."

"It's just a dream—of the past, not today." He took my hand. "I'll stay."

"No. I'm okay," I said as I stepped into the tub and blew a handful of bubbles his way. "Go and pack, but bring me my necklace please. I feel naked without it."

"You *are* naked." Eric laughed and turned to go. "Enjoy your bubbles."

Somehow we made it on time. Madeline complimented me on the color in my cheeks, winking slyly at Eric as we walked in. "The abbey worked its magic, I see."

"So much so, that it's hard to come back to the real world," I answered, smiling as she handed me a glass she described as her vineyard's best wine.

"Good. That's exactly the state you shall stay in for the evening. I have a surprise guest." She stared in the direction of the stairwell. "My father arrived from his home in Colours yesterday. He remains in another world as well. As a staunch resident of the lost world of Occitania, his stories are certain to captivate you."

Eric lifted his glass. "To the past. May it unfold its wisdom to the present." As we toasted, a figure appeared in the arched entryway.

"My dear child, you began without me." He shook his mane of white hair as gently as the chiding he gave his daughter, and enfolded her in a warm embrace. Madeline clearly had inherited her willowy frame from her father. Although tall, he had a dancer's slim body, which he turned gracefully toward us.

Madeline beamed as she made the introductions. "Father, please meet Monsieur Eric Taylor and Mademoiselle Dana Palmer. Eric and Dana, my father, Professor William Marty."

We exchanged small pleasantries as we settled into our chairs. The professor seemed eager to further the conversation. "My daughter tells me you are writing of the Cathars," He said, looking solemnly from Eric to me. "I would be interested in knowing what you think of this group's unfortunate extinction."

I could hear passion bleeding through my words. "I think their massacre was a tragedy every bit as horrific as the Holocaust. It destroyed a rich and unique culture." His solemn nod encouraged me to continue. "This area was rich with inclusivity, love, appreciation of the feminine, and a deep reverence for God." I could feel my anger build. "What a tragedy that it should have been destroyed."

Eric squeezed my hand as he added his thoughts. "I can't help but think that had the Viscount Trencaval, the Count of Foix and Count Raymond VII of Toulouse aligned themselves, they could have squelched such horrors as Simon de Montfort and the Inquisition." Eric paused.

Madeline gave her charming laugh as she looked at Eric and smiled. "You don't know what a Pandora's box you've just opened, Eric."

"Exactly my sentiments." Professor Marty said as he took Madeline's hand. His cultured, modulated tones seemed to expand as he continued. "My daughter knows me too well. My fervor at the enormity of that crime only grows through the years." He went on as if it were today's news, accounting for each battle and each rash move. His fists clenched as he came to a resounding wrap-up. "At any stage of the game, Raymond VII held the high cards—if only he had played them right."

"Calm yourself, Papa." Madeline looked worriedly at the high color in his face. Her tones were those of logic and reason, an approach which seemed to calm her father. "I thought you told me that Raymond dared not, as an excommunicated Catholic, show any more resistance to the church without sacrificing all."

"Humph, yes, well…" Professor Marty, although returning to a more professorial approach, seemed reluctant to be reined in. "It doesn't belie the fact that if he'd acted aggressively early on and joined with his fellow lords, he could have changed history." His mouth turned down into a solemn frown. "Their cooperation could have ended the slaughter and maintained the Occitan culture."

"One cannot undo history." Madeline rose and held out her hands to her father. "Dinner awaits, Papa."

Dinner was delicious, but the focus remained on continuing our Cathar dialogue. Our tongues' favorite flavor was the taste of words. "It's not over, Madeline. The betrayals of the past linger to this day." Professor Marty turned to Eric. "You are a man of the world. Do you think history made the right turning?"

"If you mean toward greed, a discounting of the feminine, the promulgation of power in the hands of the few and the extinguishing of life forms at a rate soon to leave a bleak planet for future generations, then my answer is emphatically 'No.'" A pall of pessimism hung in the air as he turned to Professor Marty. "I'd like to know if you think there is any returning to love, service, honor and cooperation."

Professor Marty fell silent. He remained deep in thought before raising his eyes to his daughter. "Have you told them of the documents?"

"No, father." She hesitated. "You wanted to meet them first."

"Yes, of course." He looked at Eric and me, his smile enigmatic. "From what my daughter has told me, it is obvious that you are…" he hesitated, "part of the family." Madeline nodded emphatically at the word "family" as she turned to me.

"Dana, please remove your sweater."

"Remove my… Oh, my necklace." I unbuttoned my sweater, unclasped my necklace and placed it in the outstretched hands of Professor Marty.

He turned my necklace over in his palm before bringing it close to his eyes. As he looked up, I saw they had begun to water as he addressed his daughter. "I don't expect you've shown them…" As if at a signal, Madeline rose from the table and strode off down the hallway.

All fell silent. Professor Marty's stare seemed to pierce my soul with a certainty that I'd known him before. I'd blocked such awareness earlier, deflected by his resemblance to my image of the Man of La Mancha.

Madeline broke our silence as she entered carrying a small box that she handed to her father. He let out a sigh as he gazed from it to us. "I trust you will recognize the item, if not remember it." He handed my necklace back as he opened the box and removed its twin. It was a bit smaller but the dove looked as though it had been chiseled yesterday.

I turned away, overcome by a sudden choking sensation. Eric patted my back until my breath evened out its fierce paroxysm. "What does it mean?" Eric asked.

"On the night the treasure was withdrawn from Montsegur, these were given to each of the four Cathar Parfaits." Professor Marty stared intently at Eric.

Eric took the medallion and turned it slowly in his hand. His comment stunned me. "Three Parfaits and one Believer, who guided them."

Professor Marty beamed. "Exactly, each was given one so as to identify themselves when they rendezvoused." He turned to me and smiled.

I hesitated. "But they would surely know one another."

"Not necessarily, not if the meeting occurred at the turn of the next millennium." Professor Marty turned to Madeline. She nodded and left the room.

I gripped my necklace. "I can't understand how it is, if the four Cathars had possession of these, I would have come by it."

"It is important not to think linearly, my dear. Souls do not necessarily reincarnate in a direct generational line—nor in the same gender." Professor Marty turned to Eric, whose face filled with puzzlement as an 'ah' escaped and he continued in a halting voice.

"I had a strange dream a couple nights ago, at the abbey." Distraught, he looked at me. "I didn't know what to make of it." As he continued, I took his hand. "In it I had the exact talisman but also something much more valuable. But it was stolen." Eric withdrew his hand and clamped his fists tightly against his eyes. His body shook with pain and anger as he looked up.

Professor Marty leavened the atmosphere with a question so straightforward as to deflect Eric's emotions. "*What* did you see?"

Eric responded as though he were watching it take place. "I was entrusted to deliver part of the treasure to a safe hiding place. I failed." Shame filled his eyes as he looked away. "Exactly as I failed in the trust placed in me by..." He turned to face me. "Clotilde." The words, "I couldn't..." were cloaked in pain.

Madeline looked around in confusion as she entered and placed a box in her father's hands. He removed the lid and handed it to Eric. "Is this what was taken from you?" He waited.

"Yes! But..." Eric's shock reverberated through the room. "Is this mine? There were others. Where..." he halted.

"Yes, my boy, you are correct. A total of four, you had one and your three colleagues the others. This is not the one placed in your care. Each is different and each essential to the others. Professor Marty looked on as Eric stared at the contents of the box—his attention held by a fragile parchment manuscript. "They are written in the ancient Langue d'Oc, the language of Occitan. Together they form the true treasure of Montsegur."

"I am totally confused. That really blasts a hole in Benjamin Carter's announcement in Albi. And I must confess, his Grail looked more like a treasure than this." I leaned over for a closer scrutiny of the fragile parchment, as if by staring, understanding would come clear.

"Benjamin Carter knows that which he revealed is not the true treasure." Professor Marty began to pace the room. "And I knew it the minute I read of his grandstand play in Albi." His forehead pursed, his expression moving from deep concentration to fear as he looked up. "He is trying to bait someone to reveal the real treasure." His gaze rested on me as I clutched at my necklace. "It's coming to a head my dear. You must proceed with extreme care."

"Whether Benjamin Carter or someone else, even if a manuscript surfaced, you said the real treasure can't exist without all four of them."

"True. One has no meaning without the others." Professor Marty said as he held up a page. "The initial page states clearly that in order to comprise the treasure, all four must come together." He halted. "At world's end."

Eric's stare fixed on the Professor. "Then my stolen one must materialize."

"Yes, four manuscripts and the four persons necessary to decipher them must come together. And the time is now." Professor Marty's words fell into silence.

"I can't comprehend that now is the time referred to as 'world's end.' It sounds much too ominous." Eric looked agitated as he turned a skeptical gaze on the Professor. "Why rejoin these manuscripts if the outcome is the world's destruction?"

The Professor poured us each a large brandy before he continued. "'World's end' does not mean the destruction of Earth." Inhaling deeply, he took a leisurely draught, staring into the elixir's depths before continuing. "As a professor of history, my focus is on world religions and myths. Many legends corroborate the Asian, Indian and Mayan teachings concerning the beginning and end of various 'worlds.'" He watched Eric's look of perplexity. "Think of them as periods of time when our planet undergoes major changes. Certain scientific theory postulates that changes occur as a result of a natural increase or decrease in the electromagnetic, or light, energy fields. These energies impact all life, including the direction of humanity's cultural and societal evolution. The recorded history of these episodes indicates that soon we shall enter a critical time of planetary changes." He looked at me as I struggled with confusing images.

"What exactly does it mean?"

"Leaving aside the more mystical aspects, science records that our planet has had very advanced civilizations whose demise was sudden, causing chaotic upheaval. Majestic ruins and geological evidence reveal societies that suddenly and mysteriously were abandoned, only to be followed by less developed civilizations. Fortunately, many have left enigmatic records that show a great deal of concurrence. Whether described by the Mayans as the 'sixth world,' or by the Shaiva oracles of India as the 'twilight of the seventh world,' their records conclude that very soon we can expect another period of dramatic Earth changes."

"Caused by global warming or..." I halted.

Professor Marty looked pensive. "Scientists debate as to whether a pole shift or climate change, even our sun's electromagnetic anomalies, triggered such catastrophic events." He took another long swallow of brandy before lifting his head with a grin. "Granted, it can all seem like hocus-pocus, but I ask you to reserve judgement as to the 'how' and look at the what is and what was. Given that the last episode was over ten thousand years ago, there is much we cannot understand." He switched off the lamp beside him. "Who among us doesn't find electricity mysterious? As to electromagnetic influences—wasn't it one of your economists who based a sophisticated analysis of the behavior of the stock markets on periods of unusual variation in sunspots? 'As above, so below.'" He grinned as he switched back on the light.

"But I digress. As to what role the Cathar treasure may reveal..." He pointed to the manuscript. "During the twelfth and thirteenth centuries, cultures were undergoing dramatic change throughout the planet. Prompted by..." He shrugged. "Whatever forces dictate such changes throughout our planet. During the thirteenth century, the mystical and liberating Christianity of Christ's original teachings, the humble joy of the Cathars, feminine equality, the poetry of Rumi and the Sufis—all aspects of enlightenment were present. Such conditions led to fear on the part of the Pope. The Catholic Church promulgated a religion that was dogmatic, moralistic, puritanical and militantly controlling. The Cathar's threat to the Church's doctrines went beyond their gentle teachings into a secret that could destroy the Church. Thus the formation of the Inquisition—to possess that secret or to keep it from surfacing. Hundred of years were spent stamping out any dissention and consolidating power."

Madeline, whose gaze never left her father, tried to diminish his growing rage. "Father, take care you don't give them the satisfaction of raising your blood pressure."

He reached over to take her hand. "Never fear, my dear. I have about reached the end of my discourse. But a glass of water would be welcome." He turned back to Eric and me as she left the room. "Our planet is now at a point where greed and power have reached their apex. But now a seminal change begins to manifest, a longing, even a remembrance of some mystical Camelot, is re-igniting." He held out the manuscript, lovingly looking from it to us. "The reemergence of the Dead Sea Scrolls and the Gnostic gospels, even the increased turmoil in the Middle East, are signs of a new direction ahead." He stared into the glass Madeline handed him as if into a crystal ball.

Eric broke the silence. "I take it another sign would be the return of the Cathar treasure." He gave a nervous chuckle. "Obviously it is not any physical Holy Grail, but certain wisdom teachings of..." He pointed to the manuscript.

"Of what the Cathars described as *lux vivens*, living light. The enlightenment to remember who and what we are—as creators." Professor Marty stood and opened his arms wide. "You have read how Christ manifested abundant loaves and fishes, turned water into wine—even walked on water and raised the dead."

"Yes." Eric's voice rose. "He also said that whatsoever he did, we could do."

"Exactly—and even greater." Professor Marty paused and let his emphasis sink into our awareness. "Just think of it. The ability to create a new direction, a world of cooperation and a return to love and service." He smiled. "Definitely not a Grail whose tempting cornucopia spews forth gold and feeds greed. 'Pecunium infinitum' the Inquisition records said. But unlimited wealth of the Spirit, not Greed."

"Not as straightforward a change, it would seem." My doubt must have been transparent as I stared at Professor Marty.

"True, during the turbulent time of change there will be much upheaval between light and dark, good and evil, love and fear. Many will be impacted as cries for war go forth. But many will rise to counter such insanity."

I looked down at the manuscript. "Your mention of 'light versus dark' reminded me of the Cathar dualism. It would seem to me that such a treasure would be dangerous to possess. That is, if the entrenched faction doesn't want to give way."

"Very dangerous. The danger begins when word is out that the treasure is beginning to come together." Professor Marty reached for his manuscript and dove-engraved medallion, replacing them gently in their boxes. "Of the four that are needed, only three are accounted for—mine, yours and one that is in the hands of one with whom you meet tomorrow." He smiled. "Yes, we know of your meeting."

Eric looked bewildered. "We have three of the medallion talismans. You have one, Dana has one and Pierre de Lahille has one. But I make it only two manuscripts, yours and Pierre's. That leaves one talisman and two manuscripts."

Professor Marty's expression turned dark as he responded. "The remaining talisman, as well as one of the missing manuscripts, you can be sure, are in the hands of a person whose goal was and is—to prevent their discovery."

The entire room fell into gloom. "Whether or not that proves to be the case, that still leaves the fourth missing manuscript."

"Mine!" I was as startled by my response as they were.

"Correct. Yours, my dear Dana." Professor Marty took my hand. "That you are here at this time strongly suggests you shall be led to it." His voice took on a heightened intensity as he stared at me. "Listen carefully. He will stop at nothing to prevent your finding it—and to take possession of the others."

"He?" I spoke in unison with Eric.

"The generic 'he,' but possibly a 'she.'" He pursed his lips. "No, neither is correct. "*They*, those whose mission it was to obstruct change then, must do so now." Professor Marty stood up. "I consider Benjamin Carter a likely member. But Pierre de Lahille will undoubtedly have more to say on that topic."

A stunned silence descended, followed by cold fear. Eric stood. "You knew of our meeting. I take it you will accompany us."

"Of course." Professor Marty turned to Madeline and held out the manuscript. "But not with this. Although all four manuscripts must come together, great danger surfaces when they do." His hands trembled. "For now, return it to its safe place."

"You knew we would be leaving," I said as Madeline turned to leave.

"Yes, but you will return—and I shall return with a message for you."

Her prosaic remark made me feel as though a goose had walked over my grave. I looked over at Professor Marty and Eric. They were locked in a pregnant silence. "Tomorrow, then," the professor said with a nod to Eric as he rose.

"Tomorrow." Eric replied. "Do drive with us."

Professor Marty shook his head. "It's best we remain separate."

Madeline came down the stairway and put an email in my hands.

"Dearest Dana, I am so very sorry. You are the one that matters, not Alex. Can you forgive me? I'll be with Benjamin at Montsegur on Monday. Let's talk. I long to see hope in your eyes. Deepest sorrow, deepest love, Evie."

TWENTY TWO

Montsegur, France-Present

The next morning we packed and were on the road at daybreak. Our route to Arques took us through Villerouge Termenes again. "We won't be stopping there any time soon," I said. "A pity because it is so pertinent to the Cathar's history."

Eric looked smug. "You can forego the guidebook on this one. As I read last night, I came upon a section on Villerouge Termenes and the death of Guillaume Belibaste, the last Cathar." Eric's tone changed. "I even read Benjamin's book."

"I can't believe you read it."

"Well, I did, the whole bloody book. The guy paints an ugly picture of the Cathars." Eric slowed to brake for a turn. "He labels them as heretics whose beliefs were naïve and rigid." He looked incredulous as he continued. "The entire book is a rationale for his claim to have discovered their treasure—the Holy Grail."

"He can't get away with it."

"I'm not so sure. The public will eat it up." Eric frowned. "But as to the scientific community, his Grail claim is guaranteed to cause an enormous stir."

"Give them bread and circuses, with the gleam of gold thrown in for good measure," I said as we passed the debris of the tempest. It matched my mood.

"I nearly put it down midway. But it's a good thing I didn't." Solemnity coated Eric's next words. "At the end, Benjamin refers

253

to a document that will confirm his contention that Cathar beliefs were totally incoherent."

"I'm surprised you didn't mention it to Professor Marty this morning."

"I decided to wait until we're all together."

"Including Veronique. We didn't mention her being there."

"I did. Professor Marty smiled and said he has had her in his class many times." Eric fell silent, his focus straight ahead. I fell into my own reverie, colored with overtones of apprehension. Everything seemed to be happening much too quickly. Until now I could chalk my experiences up to whimsy, something to be handled with a 'let's-see-where-it leads' curiosity. "Suddenly—I stopped.

Eric put a hand on mine. "Suddenly…"

"Suddenly fear rears its head. And made worse because it's not just for us, but for this sixth or seventh world that the professor claims awaits our actions." I heaved a sigh that barely eased how leaden I felt.

"A world that means the end of the society as we know it." Eric smiled. "Good news for us, I'd say."

"Right, but bad news to the 'Powers That Be' folk," I replied—a ripple of paranoia growing. "They won't stand still for anything overturning their power."

"No, they won't, Dana my girl," Eric said. "In reading Benjamin's book, I was left mulling their options over all night long." His look was sober. "Here's what I came up with. They can discredit the Cathars, or locate the real Cathar treasure, the manuscripts, and destroy them." He halted. "Or use them."

My eyes widened. "If, in fact, they do contain the secret of being able to manifest anything…" I gave a shudder. "Imagine that power in the wrong hands."

"Frightening, I'd say." Eric skillfully passed a slow tractor on the road before he continued. "And getting even more so as we come together."

I fell silent as I tried to digest it all. "Professor Marty may be right in suspecting Benjamin," I said,

"The likelihood of his being involved is very strong, I'd say. At least if my antipathy toward the bloke is any indicator." Eric's grip on the steering wheel whitened his knuckles. "It's strange. The volume of my dislike is irrational, going back much farther— as though I knew and hated him then." He glanced in the rear-view mirror to confirm that the professor's car kept pace. "I'm anxious to lay such concerns before the mysterious Pierre."

"Mysterious, but lovable." I laughed as I confessed my image of him. "Pierre reminds me of the 'Yoda' character in 'Star Wars.'"

Eric touched my hand. "I love to hear you laugh. I was afraid you'd fall apart after that email." He studied my reaction.

"I might have fallen apart if it hadn't been for Madeline. She walked over this morning as I was putting my suitcase in the trunk." I hesitated, having held back any mention of it until I'd had time to digest it. "She reminded me of the likelihood of most of today's players being connected in the past. Even Evie."

"Not Evie." Eric looked stunned.

"Madeline apologized for having read Evie's email. Then she went on to suggest that Evie's actions may have been designed to get me away from the wrong man and off to France to join you, and…" I raised an eyebrow. "And complete whatever it is we're meant to do." My throat seized up. "But Evie wouldn't consciously have known that, so…" I stopped as an alternate scenario hit me. "Maybe her role was to get me to find you and lead you to Benjamin."

"Best you stay with Madeline's view of the situation. As for me, I'm grateful for whoever and whatever brought you to me." He touched my down-turned mouth. "I just wish it didn't hurt so."

"I'd like to believe Madeline's version. It would make it easier to forgive Evie." I looked out the window at the greener gorges that led to Arques. "I'll have a hard time seeing her at Montsegur."

"I know how you feel, but Evie could provide a buffer—if you can handle it."

"I'll do my best," I said as we entered Arques.

From the minute I entered Pierre's cozy den, I was enveloped in its rarified atmosphere. Pierre, Veronique and Professor Marty chatted away, referring to people, archaeological digs and scientific gossip. Theirs was obviously a warm relationship.

Pierre smiled at me. "You look happy."

"I am. And I suspect you knew how and why all along."

"I won't admit to that, but your discovery makes our discussion easier." He turned to address everyone. "Let us begin." As they nodded, Pierre crossed to a cabinet and removed a rectangular wooden box. He carried it reverently. "The contents of this box are doubtless no mystery." He stroked the burnished wooden lid.

"Except to me, Monsieur de Lahille," Veronique replied.

"Pierre, please, Veronique," he said, giving a covert look at Professor Marty, who responded with an almost imperceptible nod. Pierre opened the box, allowing for a moment of sighs at the sight of an ancient manuscript resting alongside a familiar talisman. He placed it on the dining table, and began to speak.

After completing the tale of its provenance and reiterating the importance of the three other manuscripts necessary to complete the whole, Pierre turned to Veronique. "I trust you understand the importance of keeping this a secret."

"Of course." Her expression was solemn. "I do understand it—enough to fear it." I was shocked at how pale she became as she spoke. "Unfortunately, I have important information to add to the story. Benjamin has discovered a similar manuscript." A gasp went up. "Not far from the ruins of the castle of Coustaussa. He discovered it deep within the farthest recesses of a cave. It was wrapped tightly in a leather container lying atop a desiccated corpse." Veronique shuddered as she stared at Pierre. "A talisman—identical to yours—was entangled in the bones."

I felt as if a shard of ice had pierced me. I turned to Eric. He looked even worse. Pierre's exclamation broke through our shock. "Another one. It is time."

Pierre and Professor Marty fell into an excited conversation, their words in rapid French, baffling. Puzzled, I watched Veronique strain to follow them. Veronique shrugged. "It is in Occitan, Mademoiselle Dana. Some words I understand—but very few."

Pierre and Professor Marty sat down, looking apologetic. "Forgive our excitement. To hear that each manuscript is coming to light at this time is a monumental discovery. It means that our roles are about to unfold." He turned to Veronique, his demeanor that of one about to enter a minefield. "Mademoiselle, does Professor Taylor know that other manuscripts exist—or who might possess them?"

A hush fell over the room as Veronique replied, "Professor Carter seemed agitated when he returned with the manuscript and attempted an Occitan translation—very agitated. I gathered that it was because the manuscript was totally unintelligible." She looked from Pierre to Professor Marty. "But from what you say, the first page reveals that it cannot be understood without the others." She took a deep breath. "That would explain his increased intensity at the digs." She gave a sardonic laugh. "He'd always been content to let us do the work while he took the glory of any discoveries. But now he is involved in every dig, in every cave, speaking to every person and following up every lead. He is relentless."

"His discovery of the other manuscripts could prove..." Eric hesitated long enough for Veronique to break in, chilling the room with her words.

"Disastrous! *Très diabolique!*"

The full implications of the manuscripts coming together penetrated, and I felt my heart begin to race as I spoke. "So we know the location of one more of the missing manuscripts. But even with his manuscript, that still leaves mine as missing." I drew out my necklace. "How did I come by the medallion without the manuscript?"

"Think back to what your parents said about your necklace." Pierre suggested.

"Only that it was much older than my great-grandparents who had brought it from France." The room fell silent—everyone deep in contemplation.

I suddenly remembered something else. "They gave my brother something, a seal with an engraving. They said it was the crest on our destroyed castle."

"Try to sketch what you remember of it." Pierre walked to a small desk against the wall, returning with a tablet and pen.

"I'm sorry, but I was too young to remember."

"Perhaps they also mentioned a manuscript." Professor Marty held my eyes with a message of "remember" streaming from his.

I shook my head. "I can't. But I can email my brother. He may remember."

"Please do so." As I murmured, "Of course," Pierre turned to Veronique. "Do you know the whereabouts of the manuscript and talisman Professor Carter found?"

Veronique hesitated. "He was so secretive. But I can check certain places."

"Proceed with caution. Benjamin must have no idea of your interest," Pierre said. Professor Marty shook his head vigorously in agreement.

"Yes, certainly. I shall look tomorrow when Benjamin leaves for Montsegur." Her eyes brightened. "He is so anxious to validate his Holy Grail discovery, he may tip his hand on the manuscript in his urge to support it."

I turned to Veronique. "I'd love to know where he would hide it."

"Not in the office vault. That leaves the vaults of the museum or a vault at his home or…" She looked up in horror. "Or he may have sent it to the Vatican."

"Calm yourself, my dear." Professor Marty rose from the table, his eyes fixed upon Pierre's manuscript as he fell into pensive contemplation. Everyone waited. "Benjamin, dear Benjamin of the very dark, very evil eyes, would never let such a treasure out of his control. He would keep it where he could see it, hold it and shelter it from others." He began to pace as his voice raised. "He'd *never* offer it to the Pope—unless he was working under their direction or…"

Veronique interrupted. "Even if he were involved with the Vatican, I know Dr. Carter and, given his hubris, I would say he retains it nearby—in his home."

"Ready for his grandstand play," Eric said, his attention returning to Professor Marty as he continued.

"Exactly! And he hopes to be able to reveal it soon. But he cannot—not without the other three." The Professor hesitated, his mouth down-turned as he looked at Pierre. "I wonder how much he knows of the whereabouts of the others. Or who might be in possession of them."

"Suspects, more than knows. As to the whereabouts, you would be a more likely target of suspicion than I would," Pierre said, as he clasped Professor Marty by the shoulder. "Remember, dear friend, how much attention he devoted to two of the leading Cathar experts, Deodat Roche and Rene Nelli—to no avail. You are next, dear Professor, an expert whose passion for the Cathars exceeds even his own."

Professor Marty frowned. "Others are equally involved in Cathar research."

"No—Pierre is right." Veronique turned from Professor Marty to Pierre. "Benjamin has long suspected Professor Marty of having some secret knowledge. But you, my friend, he has never mentioned."

Pierre rubbed the palms of his hands together. "Very good. That tells us that Professor Marty must not accompany Eric and Dana to Montsegur." Pierre turned, concern filling his eyes. "I shall, however. Independently, of course, and under the guise of seeing my old friend, Giraud, the caretaker of the Montsegur museum." He turned back to Veronique. "Perhaps Professor Carter will ask you to accompany him to Montsegur, Mademoiselle."

"I would have thought so. That he hasn't is very strange." Veronique looked puzzled. "If you feel it important, I could create some plausible reason to go."

Pierre shook his head. "That could tip him off." Deep in thought he began to pace the room, his hands clasped behind his back. He turned suddenly and faced Veronique. "No—best you take the opportunity to search for the manuscript. I shall remain with my friend, Giraud." Pierre stared at Eric and me. "Leaving you alone with Benjamin in what I suspect could become a most dangerous situation."

Eric stood, staring pointedly at Pierre. "How dangerous can it be with tourists all over the mountain?" He waited.

"Very dangerous—irrespective of any tourists." I watched as Pierre's solemn response erased any aura of sanctuary from the room. "Never forget that Benjamin isn't working alone. He is aligned with those whose goal is every bit as urgent as ours is— and much more deadly. As in the past, they must take control of *all* of the other manuscripts." He walked over and took my hand.

"You are the target, dear Dana. The instant he became aware of your medallion necklace, you became the prey. He *must* acquire the manuscript he believes you have." His voice deepened. "They will stop at nothing."

Professor Marty must have seen my fear. He placed his hand on mine as he spoke. "For your own safety, my dear Dana, you must keep uppermost in your mind the awareness that he is not alone in this." He looked over at Pierre. "As to the mention of the Pope earlier, we must consider it likely that the Vatican, just as in the past, still controls all." His forehead furrowed in anger. "Whatever they are up to, it won't stop at scare tactics, as when you were shot at while exploring Coustaussa." Still holding my hand his voice resonated with a familiarity that seemed beyond this moment. "Say you understand." I nodded—my firm "Yes" prompting him to let out a long sigh. "Good, then you'll be wary and not let him know that you suspect him."

As Professor Marty finished, Pierre added, "Benjamin's stated intent for your meeting at Montsegur is to show you what led to his discovery of the Holy Grail. Go along with him on that, but if he mentions manuscripts, keep your response curious but neutral and focus on respect for his work." Pierre looked over at Eric.

Eric shot me a questioning look before he replied. "Keeping a light approach should be made easier with Evie along as a buffer."

"Who is this person, Evie?" Pierre and Professor Marty glanced at one another, apprehension in their look.

"Dr. Evelyn Arnstein. I…" My explanation faded.

"She is a long time friend of Dana's and a friend of Benjamin's." Eric pursed his lips, his expression puzzled as he continued. "The fact that he has invited Evie, not only to stay at his home, but to accompany him to Montsegur, would suggest he's not planning anything." Everyone fell into silence as they contemplated this new information. After whispering with Professor Marty, Pierre spoke.

"Whether or not a long time friend, be careful of anyone in the picture right now. Anyone." Pierre directed his remark to me.

Eric, seeing how stunned I was, responded. "It may not be too late to dissuade Evie from accompanying him." He leaned in to me and spoke sotto voce. "That would get you off the hook."

I took a deep breath before I replied, "Trying to stop her would seem really strange. Trust me, I'll pull off the best act you've ever seen." I frowned. "But such behavior is bound to confound Evie."

Eric, seeing the others puzzled at our interchange, added, "Not if you tell her right away that you've decided to keep the day with Benjamin on a light note."

Pierre's concern at our dialogue prompted him to reiterate his earlier warning. "Nothing is coincidental. You must handle this situation with great care," Pierre said, glancing at the time. "It's nearly two o'clock. I suggest you give yourselves time with Giraud. Besides being museum caretaker, he also has a little *gite* attached to his property. I'll call and book us rooms."

Everyone stood as Pierre walked off to make his phone call. I followed, calling out to him. "I'd like to email my brother before I go."

"Of course." He pointed to a desk with a laptop computer. "I'd appreciate your copying me and asking him to respond to us both." As I sat at the desk, he added, "It's an independent line. I'll call Giraud from the kitchen phone."

I had the message sent in a few minutes. As I disconnected, Pierre walked in and we returned to the others. After a recap of our strategy, we shook hands and prepared to take our leave. Everyone gathered round the cars.

Veronique hesitated at entering her car, turning back to Eric and me, her expression anxious. "Do not take Benjamin for a fool. I know him well. He misses nothing. If I discover anything, I shall call you at Giraud's *gite*."

Pierre smiled at Veronique. "Very good, my dear. Use caution with your search. But it seems the fates are on our side. Giraud has rooms available and no other guests." He held the door as Veronique entered her car. "Use a private phone line if you discover Benjamin's manuscript."

Veronique's words were solemn as she stared at each of us in turn. "You may depend on me."

As she drove out of sight, we threw our things into our car and got in, hesitating as Pierre completed a discussion with the Professor. We heard him mention the email from Dana's brother, adding, "Perhaps I presume too much, my dear friend, but apart from waiting for emails, I trust you'll remain here for security."

"Of course. I'll guard the manuscripts and check the email." Professor Marty's eyes were bright as he leaned into our car, but his words were heavy. "Go with God, my friends."

Pierre added, "Use care. Benjamin and his cohorts surely have something planned." Both heads nodded as Pierre added, "You must outwit them."

"We've come this far. We won't let you down," I said as they handed us a map with directions to Monsieur Giraud's gite.

Eric glanced at it. "I assume Giraud knows nothing of our purpose."

Pierre shook his head. "Not that I am aware of. Divulge only that you are writing your series and would appreciate any advice and information. If he refers to Cathar treasure, act doubtful but interested." He gave a light laugh. "Whether he knows it or not, old Giraud is a Cathar through and through. He claims direct descent from a family burnt on the pyre, and is fierce when it comes to keeping violators away from Montsegur. He is also a hunter by avocation, and a good one at that. And last but not least—he holds Benjamin Carter in contempt." Pierre winked as he and Professor Marty waved us on. "Be off with you now. I'll join you soon."

Professor Marty's last words, before we pulled away, stayed with us throughout our journey. "Your time has come. Be vigilant!"

Nita Hughes

TWENTY-THREE

Montsegur, France-March 1244

The first day of March, with its promise of spring, was to have brought hope of an Easter rescue. It carried neither warmer temperatures nor word of aid. Instead, it brought many more dead and wounded suffered through February's intensifying sieges, which had given no rest, day or night, for its occupants.

Clotilde looked around, her breath heavy in the icy morning air, her ears assaulted by the stone-gun's fierce barrage. She watched exhausted defenders waiting for some letup in the hail of rocks, so that they might be able to erect a defensive fortification on the wall under fire. Clotilde edged her way through a haze of dust, dodging groups of people frantically milling about as they aided the defenders. Those who had lived in makeshift wooden huts on the steep, icy slopes just outside the fortress had sought refuge within.

She avoided eyes that showed a level of fear palpably escalating as she pushed through the crowds, trying to catch sight of Jean. He'd not come back to their quarters through the long night. She had waited until dawn, her heart chilled by their last conversation.

He had drawn her into the farthest corner of their quarters where no one could hear them. "My dearest Clotilde, I wanted to be able to support your hope. Even I had my spirits lift, not at the hollow rumors of Raymond VII's aid, but at the genuine commitment of the Aragonese army's *corps d'élite* to come to our rescue." Jean had shaken his head as if to release its anger and desolation. Strong emotions remained, coating his every word. "Alas. Their Captain Corbario could not break through the French lines. Rumor of his plan to aid us had reached the Crusader's army commander, who strengthened the lines and had them drawn closer than heretofore." Clotilde raised her hand to her face, wet with tears at the memory of Jean's shoulders sinking heavily as he said, "Montsegur has been cut off from any outside assistance."

Even now, Clotilde could only let herself take in his despair, and not their desperate situation. He must have been aware of her state, she thought, as he tried to hold out hope. "Pierre-Roger de Mirepoix has taken counsel with Bishop Bertrand and Montsegur's Lord, Raymond de Pereille. They have agreed that Pierre-Roger will undertake a bold move, to assemble a secret ambush with a sortie of defenders to retake the barbican, kill the Crusaders and destroy their siege engines. It is planned for this very night." He tipped her chin up, holding her gaze with his. "I must help them in whatever way I can." His look hadn't broached any response but agreement. She tried to stifle her fear but it grew through the night—a night filled with terrible screams.

Unable to sleep, at the first ray of dawn she ventured forth. Each step mired her deeper into the maelstrom. A river of wounded and dying lay wherever space would allow. The Parfaits ran from one to the other, oblivious to the tumult of clashing arms and moans of the dying, as they provided each the consolamentum.

Nearly mad with desperation, she suddenly heard Jean's voice call out. "Clotilde, go back!" A dust-covered specter reached her side. Her eyes widened at the sight of blood streaming down his face and a sword hanging from his hands. "The French army has breached our garrisons' defenses and gained a foothold in the forecourt. You must take shelter." He yanked her away, ramming a path through the crowds until they arrived at their quarters.

A piercing yell greeted them. "Clotilde!" Blanche looked insane as she clasped Clotilde's skirts. "You left me!"

"Not now, Blanche. Jean is injured." Clotilde hurried to their room. Once inside she filled a basin with water and gathered cloths to staunch Jean's wounds. Blanche stared in horror. As Clotilde cleared Jean's eyes, she let out a cry of relief. "Thank you, God," she repeated as she peered closer. "It seems to be cuts only, my love—and those not too deep. Can you see?"

"I can, and I must go back." He spoke intently. "Raymond de Pereille's wife, Pierre-Roger's wife—all have all asked for the *convenensa.*" Clotilde's heart skipped a beat at the knowledge of what that meant. The Cathar Church had established the pact of the *convenensa,* which assured the Believer that, even if severely wounded and deprived of the power of speech, the sacrament of the consolamentum would be administered on his deathbed. Jean broke into her thoughts to confirm the worst. "Once granted, they rushed away to fight at their men's side." Clotilde looked so shocked that Jean took her hand. "You are needed to treat the wounded, my love."

Blanche let out a wail. "No. You must not leave me!"

Jean turned with such ferocity that Blanche fled toward her bed, cowering deep into its corner. Jean yanked back the coverlet. "Here me, Blanche! Stay here if you will, or go. But do not restrain Clotilde in her mission." His words rang through the room as he stepped around the injured and vanished.

The area within Clotilde's quarters had more than doubled its injured. She went from one to the other, not stopping to register evening's approach until Blanche lit a candle and held it out to her. "Say you shall never leave me. You are all I have."

"Except for me, dear Blanche." Bernard's words were barely intelligible as he walked up, tunic in tatters, expression exhausted. He gazed out from a mask of dirt.

"Bernard, oh Bernard, you're safe!" Clotilde put her candle down and embraced him as Blanche took his hand. "I was so worried." She looked behind him. "Where is Jean?"

"Last I saw, he was roaring like a bull as he rushed to the aid of Pierre-Roger." He shook his head in bewilderment. "My dear brother was fooling himself that he was meant to be a Parfait. He is a warrior, besting even our valiant leader, Pierre Roger himself. Together they managed to throw back our assailants."

"You mean to say the invaders are no longer inside?" Clotilde sighed with relief as she neared the kitchen area. "Come and sup and tell me more."

"Yes. Stay, Bernard. We must remain together." Blanche's face had replaced its look of despair with one of calm. As she walked over to him, a hint of the old Blanche became evident for just a moment. Had she slipped into the safety of insanity, Clotilde wondered, or had reality shocked her awake?

"Do sit while I bring you some broth, dear Bernard." Blanche said.

"We must not take their retreat as anything more than temporary," Bernard cautioned them as he took the bowl of soup. "Pierre-Roger has surveyed the damage to his garrison and, frankly, can see no recourse but capitulation."

"No!" Clotilde's shout reverberated through the room.

Bernard drained the bowl in one quick swallow before responding. "You saw the nightmare outside. The injured and dying now outnumber the living. The French troops exceed ours at more than thirty to one. Since they broached the barbicans and moved into the fortress itself, well…" His stare spoke volumes.

The sound of a loud horn blast, relentless and unceasing, caused a complete hush to settle over the room. Even the groans from the dying ceased. The continued blasts could only mean one thing, Clotilde thought, that which all Cathars feared—a decision to negotiate for surrender. All hope was abandoned

Bernard's exhaustion seemed to lift at the horn's blast. A new look, one of intense determination, appeared. Without a word, he stumbled across the crowds in his haste to leave. Blanche looked numbly at her sister. "Don't go."

Clotilde felt stunned as she took Blanche's hand. It was clear that she did not, would not, have her capable, older sister back. "Do not fear. I am here."

A light came over Blanche's features. "We can go home now."

Clotilde responded as gently as she could. "The Catholic Church does not want heretics in their society, dear sister. It is either recant our faith or burn."

Blanche's face looked calm as she squeezed Clotilde's hand. "Do not fear the flames, Clotilde. We will be together."

Clotilde understood Blanche's demented gleam to be an attempt to escape unbearable anxiety. As for her own fears, she longed for the sight of Jean. "Dear Blanche, we shall address that time when it comes. For now, we must help the injured." Clotilde resumed her task, moving carefully among the half-dead forms.

Blanche surprised her by her willingness to hold flagons of water and wipe feverish brows—as long as she remained beside Clotilde.

Clotilde worked without pause, as much to keep her fear at bay as to attend to those who needed her. As she knelt to draw up an old man's bit of blanket, she felt so exhausted that she feared she'd not be able to get up. Suddenly a shadow moved.

"Jean!" As he drew her up, rag-doll like, she sank into his arms as into a sanctuary that could shield the two of them. "I've heard the rumors."

A look of white, hot fury penetrated his grime, lifting his exhaustion as he spoke. Although he managed to keep his tone low, his words were iced in pain. "Yes, and all are true. Pierre-Roger and Raymond de Pereille have already begun negotiations for surrender. Even the Crusaders' army seems eager to end their ten months of relentless siege. It's expected they shall come to an agreement on the conditions of the surrender this very day." Jean lowered his voice to a whisper. "There is other important business which Pierre-Roger must arrange." He guided her to their quarters, drawing her down beside him on the bed. She curled tightly within the cave of his shoulder, feeling his breathing ease toward sleep, his last words etched indelibly in her heart. "Pray God he succeeds."

Clotilde awoke early, unable to sleep in the strange quiet that pervaded the castle. The stillness of the stone-guns filled her with despair as she remembered Jean's words. Careful not to disturb him, she stepped over to the dying fire, placed the kettle over the hottest embers and went to check on her charges.

Most slept, some with eyes open, yet unseeing. A few gave her a wan smile as she moved softly among them. She passed Blanche's cot. She snored deeply as one hand clutched her coverlet. Clotilde's quiet movements were made futile as a cry filled the air.

"Jean!" A shout pierced the silent dawn. Jean jumped up, grabbed Clotilde and held her behind him, until he recognized Bernard.

"Bernard. What has happened?" Jean asked, studying his silent brother. Bernard seemed both at war with excitement at his news and resistant to revealing it. Jean took him by the hand and led him over to the wooden table. "Sit, dear brother, and have something to eat while you tell what you've heard."

Blanche, awakened by Bernard's cry, joined them. All stared as he waved away food, gulped his mead down, and looked up. A ray of light slanted through the narrow window slot, illuminating the agitation that filled his features as he spoke. "I couldn't sleep. So, before dawn, I went to the fortress' entrance, determined to wait until Pierre-Roger and Raymond de Pereille returned from their meeting. Bishop Marty was the only other person there. We were first to hear the terms of the truce." With a smug look, he continued. "The conditions had been swiftly agreed upon."

"What exactly was agreed?" Jean's question held a blend of urgency and encouragement as he waited. Clotilde frowned as a self-satisfied look descended over Bernard's features.

"The conditions seem fair enough." As he hesitated, Clotilde clung to the word "fair." "There were only five specifications." Bernard's look changed to that of a schoolboy anxious at the order of his recitation. "First: Our garrison of soldiers will be allowed to remain for the next fifteen days until all conditions have been met." At no reply, he continued. "Pierre-Roger had been firm about the second condition: Our soldiers and their commanders would receive pardons for past crimes, including those who were involved in the Avignonet affair. The third condition provided for our men-at-arms: They agreed to allow them to withdraw at the end of fifteen days, taking with them their arms and baggage." He watched for a reaction. All remained intent on the remaining conditions. "They did insist, however, that each soldier must appear before the Inquisition and confess his errors. Pierre-Roger fully expects they will receive light sentences only." Bernard paused to draw a deep breath. "As for those remaining..." Bernard's glance took in Jean, Clotilde, and Blanche as well as the crowds of injured. "All other persons in the fortress will be allowed to remain at liberty within Montsegur for the next fifteen days. Every individual could similarly be considered for a light penance, if..."

"If..." Jean's interruption confused Bernard.

"If, that is to say, Pierre-Roger believes that—provided a Cathar renounce their faith and make their confession before the inquisitors—they will be allowed to live." Clotilde gasped as she turned to Jean. Bernard looked solemn as he continued. "Those who do not choose to recant will be burned at the stake." He rushed on, his voice stuttery in the heavy silence. "The fifth, and last, condition, is that the castle of Montsegur shall pass into the hands of the Church and the French crown." Bernard's audience remained silent, frozen in stunned absorption. "That is all. On the sixteenth of March everyone in the fortress will be permitted to leave, their fate determined according to these conditions." He cast a challenging look at Jean.

Jean pursed his lips, his brow furrowed as he spoke. "I find it interesting that Pierre-Roger managed to buy us two weeks of time." Jean's pensive look eased as he patted his brother on the shoulder. "Your report is appreciated, my brother." He drew Clotilde to his side, his compassionate words addressed to all. "We now know the time remaining to us."

* * *

The first week of March passed in a flurry as all adjusted to the sudden cessation of battle. Clotilde marveled at the attitude of joy in the air, stunned that so little conversation dealt with the few days of life remaining.

Although the enemy kept a close watch, their conquerors didn't interfere with the special preparations going on. To assure the full cooperation of those conquered, the French army had taken hostages of some of the most respected and important persons—a relative of Pierre-Roger de Mirepoix, Lord Pereille's son, Jordan, and Bishop Marty's brother, among others.

Clotilde felt a surge of energy as she entered the quarters of the Parfaites, where daily religious observations were being held. Esclarmonde's voice filled the room, radiating the mood of those gathered. "Let us pray together the Lord's Prayer in seeking the support of Spirit for each one of us." Many repetitions of the prayer were done, as well as long readings from the gospel of St. John.

The ceremonies held an expanded measure of gratitude and worship, Clotilde thought, as she observed the group. Those who had shared so much opened even wider in supporting one another with outpourings of love.

Clotilde scanned the crowd, thinking that Jean was one of only a handful that had missed today's gathering. He had gone to meet with Bishop Marty. She wrinkled her forehead in perplexity at the bishop's absence at such an important gathering. During a break in the prayers, Clotilde shared her puzzlement with Fabrisse.

Fabrisse leaned in and explained that many of the Cathars— from deacons and bishops to Parfaits and Parfaites—were arranging to give away their remaining worldly goods in gratitude for the heroic support of Pierre-Roger de Mirepoix and others. She whispered, "It is likely, my dear, that Bishop Marty met with Jean to arrange the distribution of any stores of oil, salt, pepper, and wax."

Doubt remained, but Clotilde nodded, aware of just how much the past week had been a demonstration of love and sharing. Fabrisse smiled as she turned her attention to Esclarmonde, who was giving the concluding blessing. Fabrisse seemed to radiate an Inner Light these days, Clotilde thought, one that effused her frail form. Although weakened by illness, she reflected a child's pure faith and invincible joy.

Esclarmonde joined Clotilde, Fabrisse and Blanche. "My dears, it is such a blessing to have spent this time with you. What a wonderful expression of Spirit you are." Esclarmonde looked around. "I don't see Jean with you."

"Jean is with Bishop Marty, aiding in distributing the bishop's belongings." Clotilde frowned. "Although the bishop has so little to give."

"Sometimes the gift shared, though intangible, is of great value, my dear." Fabrisse spoke softly, turning as Blanche tugged at her skirt.

"Fabrisse, look. The wife of the lord of Montsegur is motioning to you." Fabrisse turned and caught the eye of the Corba de Pereile, her fellow Parfaite.

"Please excuse me," Fabrisse said as she joined the Lady of Montsegur.

As soon as she had gone, Blanche turned to Clotilde. "I hear tell that many soldiers have asked to receive the consolamentum."

"Quite true, Blanche. It is a miracle," Clotilde said. "They have so united with us in God's love that many are choosing to join our faith and remain with us."

Blanche made no comment as they strode out into the crisp breezes of early spring. The air was cool, Clotilde thought, but with a greater brightness now that the shelling had stopped. She drew a deep breath, conscious of the gift of life and not wanting to spend another minute apart from Jean. "Blanche dear, please go back to our quarters and begin preparations for our meal. I must join Jean." To stem Blanche's anxiety, Clotilde spoke sharply. "Do not worry. I shall join you shortly. Go now and prepare enough for all." Blanche departed, staring back as she went.

Clotilde hurried off, her head filled with the puzzling rumors that circulated. They no longer had to do with any rescue from Raymond VII, but instead involved pardon, exile and even missing treasure. She questioned the real purpose behind Jean's meeting with Bishop Marty. During the siege, such meetings were always followed by Jean's secret departure on an errand of importance to the Cathar Church. But that was unthinkable. No one could leave now, except to meet death on March sixteenth. Attributing her anxiety to Jean's absence, she rounded the far curve of the keep and collided with Jean, who swept her into his arms.

"You look perplexed."

"I was thinking about your meeting with Bishop Marty. It seemed unlikely that it would have to do with exchanging goods," Clotilde confessed. "Perhaps more to do with Fabrisse's remark about his having more important things to impart."

"Fabrisse is very wise. The Bishop did have important things to impart." Jean drew her close as he led her in the direction of their quarters. "Was Bernard at this morning's gathering?"

"No, but I trust he will honor tomorrow's special fast. At its conclusion all will prepare one last feast using all remaining food. It shall stand as an early observance of Easter." Clotilde frowned. "Blanche hasn't seen Bernard all day."

Jean smiled. "And Blanche would know. She has taken a sudden interest in keeping close to more than just you, my love," Jean said as they reached their quarters. "I've noticed her watching Bernard, awake and asleep. It is as if she fears anyone departing without her."

"Poor Blanche. And yet she does seem resigned to death approaching. Lighter, but with a frightening edge of, of..." Clotilde lowered her voice as they neared the kitchen. "Shush, Blanche is in the kitchen. Whatever it is that gives her ease, I give thanks for."

"Your cooking smells wonderful." Continuing to stir the cauldron on the fire, Blanche turned at Clotilde's comment.

"I've put every vegetable I can find into this stew. One of the Parfaites gave me a little pepper and garlic." Pleasure filled Blanche's remark as she reached for a bottle. "And, a special treat. Lady Corba gave us a flagon of wine."

Jean accepted the proffered bottle and put it aside as he asked Blanche, "Have you any idea of where Bernard could be?"

"No. But he has been worried lately." Blanche's voice held reproach. "He's long abandoned the Cathar faith as his support. As to brotherly support..."

"What does that mean?" Jean snapped.

"Exactly what she says, dear brother," Bernard replied as he walked up with a swagger, his broad sneer directed at Jean. "I know you've been up to your old tricks—those disappearing acts that leave your brother in the dark."

"Explain what you mean," Jean asked as Bernard sat down and gave a solid thump against the tabletop.

"Just what I've said. I know when you are sneaking in to see Bishop Marty. The two of you are as thick as thieves." He grabbed the tankard of ale Blanche poured and finished it before he continued. "Not just the two of you," he said as he wiped his chin. "I watched Amiel Aicart, his socio, Hugo, and the other chap, the Parfait Poitevin, I think it was, go in with you. What's going on— are you taking private lessons to become a Parfait before you depart this world?" Bernard gave a bitter laugh. "Not that you'd tell me if you were set to become Jesus Christ himself."

"Bernard, I'm sorry I haven't discussed it with you." Jean gave Clotilde a cautionary glance as he turned back to Bernard, his tone light as he tipped the bottle to refill his brother's tankard. "It is as you say. I knew you'd scoff at my desire to seek the highest wisdom teachings of the Cathar religion during my last days on earth." He patted his brother on the shoulder, looking him straight in the eyes. "Out with it now, would you have wanted to be part of our prayer meetings?"

"None of that stuff for me. You couldn't get me to the Believer stage, let alone to Parfait." He gave a dismissive snort before his voice turned serious. "I just wanted to be part of..." He nodded toward Blanche and Clotilde as he raised his glass and turned back to Jean. "To us. Together to the end!"

* * *

Clotilde had cause to remember his words as the end drew near. Not one Cathar even considered recanting their religion. All were meditating on "My kingdom is not of this earth" as they prepared for death at the stake. It was the night of March fourteenth, the conclusion of their fasting and the prelude to their last meal, the feast planned for tomorrow. Every Parfait and Parfaite had been kept busy administering the consolamentum to each Cathar. But what wasn't expected was the numbers of non-Cathars who chose to convert and receive it.

Clotilde was surprised at the number of men-at-arms of the garrison, their valiant soldiers, who chose to take the consolamentum and accompany them into the fire. "These people could have saved their lives instead of going to such an excruciating death," Clotilde whispered softly to Jean as they clung together throughout their last night.

"They've lived alongside the *bonshommes* for so long now that they have come to love them and honor their faith," Jean replied.

272

"This speaks highly not only of the Cathar faith, but of the goodness of our protectors." He rose from their bed and walked to their entryway, stopping to listen.

"Bernard and Blanche are now sound asleep. Even among the sick, no one stirs." Jean lowered his voice as he returned to their bed. "We must speak, my love." He drew the coverlet over them and whispered. "Make no outburst at anything I say."

"I understand." Clotilde drew a long breath and listened.

He began. "The day after tomorrow, on the sixteenth, all will be led out of Montsegur according to the conditions of the surrender." He held his finger to her lips before continuing. "The Cathars to meet their death, the lords and garrison soldiers to fulfill their agreement, and the Parfaits and Parfaites to join their Believers on the pyre." He hesitated, his words barely audible. "But I, my love, must join three others and hide until just after darkness, when we shall be lowered down the west face of the mountain."

After a muffled gasp, Clotilde buried her head in Jean's neck and whispered, "I can't bear to go to my death without you."

Jean touched her lips. "Quiet, my love. Pierre-Roger will let us down with ropes that I am to pull away at the last. Instead, I shall leave them in place for you to follow later. The danger is so great that I have asked Bernard to aid you. Mind what I tell you now. As the last group of Cathars leaves Montsegur, you must slip into the keep and hide. Bernard will join you and, when all is clear, will help you to escape. You will rendezvous with me at a special cave outside Coustaussa Castle."

"But what of Blanche?" Clotilde's voice, although low, held volumes of pain. "I gave my vow to our mother that I would never leave her."

"I know your feelings, my love, but it is leave her or leave me. Whatever your decision, we cannot involve Blanche. I have already risked much in making my request of Bernard." Jean stroked Clotilde's forehead. "I understand your fear for Blanche. But Fabrisse and Esclarmonde will be with her." Jean used his sleeve to brush her tears away. "I too feel great sorrow at leaving the others, but it is for a higher purpose." His voice dropped even lower. "The most important act we will ever do is to safeguard the Cathar legacy."

"For whom? The inquisitors will not stop until they exterminate all Cathars. None will be left to honor our teachings."

"True. But, there is a time to come known as 'world's end.'" He waited for her nod. "At that time our teachings shall reappear. Until then they must be hidden."

Clotilde felt conflicted. "I don't understand." Jean repeated, with greater emphasis, the critical importance of their purpose—now and in years to come. Understanding dawned. Clotilde agreed, until, remembering the schism between the brothers, she whispered, "How did Bernard react to your being entrusted with such an important mission?"

"I told Bernard nothing of the real purpose behind my mission, only that I need his help in retrieving the last bit of gold that we hid in a cave a few months ago."

"I am more concerned that he feel reassured at your including him. But this rope descent..." Clotilde shivered at the image.

"There is much risk for us all, my love. Danger in escaping the castle, and an equally perilous journey once down." Jean drew her close. "Our goal is all."

Clotilde spoke softly, her emotion raw. "I fear being parted from you. Can we not submit together to the flames?"

"We *must* honor our vow to safeguard this treasure. It is our soul's task." Jean's words held a solemnity that imbedded each word indelibly. "Our commitment will not end until many centuries from now. Say you understand."

"I understand one thing only—my fear at parting from you."

"You will never lose me, my love. When death comes, it is only our bodies that will be lost. Our souls shall always be together—*always*."

* * *

The fifteenth of March dawned with a hint of warmth in the air. Clotilde felt too distracted to absorb the day's activities. Her thoughts were far from the planned ceremony, even as greetings were called out to them as they entered the Parfaites' quarters. Today's religious ceremonies would include the giving of the consolamentum to those few yet to receive it.

Murmurs of surprise and support moved through the room as Corba de Perella stepped forward. Abandoning all—her life as Lady Perella, her husband, her two married daughters, her grandchildren and her son—she upheld her faith, ready to accompany her invalid daughter, a fellow Parfaite, into the flames. Jean turned to Clotilde as a steady stream, nearly a quarter of the soldiers of the garrison, entered. "In their conversion lies their victory."

Clotilde studied the two knights who next approached, marveling that although they could march out of the fortress with full military honors, their heads held high, they instead chose to be burned alive beside their Cathar friends. Her heart swelled with love and pride as she met the gaze of those with whom she'd shared so much. The heaviness of guilt added to her sorrow at the knowledge that she was to abandon them at the last moment. Jean, sensing her emotions, pressed her hand as together they embraced many, knowing it would be the last time.

Blanche stayed alongside as they walked back to their quarters. Bernard appeared, stopping squarely in front of Jean. "So much for your God's intervention."

"Dear Bernard, come. We must speak privately, my brother." Jean said as he motioned toward a secluded corner.

"If you think you can fill me with your higher spiritual views at the last moment, think again, little brother." Bernard gave a loud guffaw. "On the other hand, perhaps I may yet convince you of my disbelief." The two walked off, leaving a vague sense of alarm in Clotilde as she wondered whether Bernard may not have so easily accepted Jean's explanation.

* * *

Later that evening, as they sat over the remains of their last meal, Blanche smiled, Bernard fell deep into thought and Clotilde stared into her wine. Jean's voice rent the silence. "I ask your understanding in allowing Clotilde and me a little time alone during these last hours."

"Sure, little brother. Whatever you say." Bernard winked as he held out his arm to Blanche. "We shall make use of our time together as well." Their hasty departure left Clotilde blinking in confusion as she turned to Jean.

"'Tis well they go, my darling Clotilde. We must use this time to review our plan." Jean outlined his departure and Clotilde's need to fall behind and hide within the keep and wait for Bernard. "Bernard will wait until it is safe before helping lead you down the mountain to Coustaussa." He studied Clotilde's anxious look. "My dear brother, having no intent to die by fire, willingly agreed to aid us."

Confident that all was understood, they blessed their dwelling, all the souls that shared it, and the fate awaiting each. Giving honor to God, they made love with a deep, slow, lasting merging that illumined their inseparable destiny.

* * *

The solemn procession began the next day, each man and woman waiting with dignity for their turn to exit the forecourt of Montsegur. Clotilde marveled at the number of children preparing to walk down the hillside with their parents. Not yet of an age to either adopt or renounce the Cathar faith, surely they would be spared from the flames, Clotilde prayed.

The procedure was long, the nearly two hundred and forty Cathar heretics having been instructed to remain until last, allowing the garrison's men, soldiers, knights and lords, to depart first. The crowds began to thin. Clotilde's efforts to linger behind were made more difficult by Blanche's rigid clasp of her arm.

"Do let me go, Blanche. I must find Jean." Clotilde separated Blanche's tight grip. "He's gone to fetch our gospel. Join Fabrisse and wait for my return."

Blanche let out a deep cackle. "Wait? Oh yes, I'll wait." Clotilde noticed Blanche's strange expression was still intact as Fabrisse walked up to take her hand.

Mad—Blanche has truly gone mad, Clotilde thought as she hurried away. Cautious about being observed, she called on the same stealth she had developed as an abandoned child, becoming nearly invisible as she reached the agreed upon meeting place, the far side of the keep. She slipped within the gloom, listening for the slightest sound as she waited for Bernard to appear. Her heartbeat was all that moved as the minutes ticked by. It seemed forever before a shadow appeared. "Bernard?" She whispered as he neared, a smile freeing her tense features. "Can we go?"

"Yes, it is time." He held her arm tightly as he led her out into the sunlight.

Clotilde stared in disbelief as Bernard turned toward the main entrance to Montsegur. "We are to take the path along the west wall, dear brother."

"No. You are taking the most direct route to your God, dear sister." Bernard's face took on a diabolical gleam. "My little brother shall live to regret his disdain of me, but not for long." He tightened his grip on her arm.

"No—say you have not betrayed your brother!" Clotilde shook with disbelief, rage and horror.

"Not in the manner you think, my not-so-dear-sister. To expose his plot would implicate me as well as Pierre-Roger de Mirepoix." He yanked her forward. "And I intend to remain in his lordship's good graces."

"So you have abandoned your brother as easily as your faith."

"My fate is not that of a Believer. It is solely in my hands, as is yours in theirs. As for my brother—he has lied to me one last time." He spat as he dragged Clotilde toward a small group of the French army. One held the arm of a struggling Blanche.

"I refused to leave without you, dear sister." Blanche's expression retained its maniacal glee as, with superhuman energy, she broke free from the soldier's grasp. She pressed her face close to Clotilde's and whispered, "Bernard and I have foiled your perfidy." She let out a cackle. "And now we shall all die together."

"Not I, foolish Blanche. Having officially recanted any allegiance to the Cathar heresy, I shall walk away a free man." Bernard's look of contempt as the French soldiers took her, was unimaginable, Clotilde thought. Blanche seemed equally shocked at Bernard's last words as the officers dragged the two women away. "Hurry! You must not miss the party prepared for you."

Stunned, Clotilde moved down the steep hillside with Blanche clinging tightly to one of her arms and the soldier to the other. She felt numbed by the tableau below, a clearing with many figures moving about like ants scurrying to and fro. Long confined to the interior of the castle, Clotilde let her gaze range the full breadth of the hillsides. The meadows were already greening and dotted with blue and yellow blooms of new life.

Their escort spoke out. "Our men-at-arms have been working day and night to erect a pyre large enough for so many heretics." The soldier's voice was proud as he pointed ahead. "Look! The palisades of stakes and firewood are ready."

Gripping Blanche's hand, Clotilde began to pray a ceaseless prayer for Jean's safety. Soon they were pushed toward a group being lashed to the pyres of straw, pitch and dried faggots. Blanche gave no resistance, walking silently and blindly, as if her soul had already escaped through the crazed gleam in her eyes.

As a soldier shoved her onto a nearby pyre, Clotilde reached out to touch her sister. Her hand was wrenched away and secured to the post behind her. She felt like an animal prepared for slaughter as the soldier avoided her eyes. Mercy, goodness and light had vanished, leaving no trace of humanity as rough hands lashed her feet together. No blinders were provided to shield the hellish sight of soldiers racing wildly about as they touched their torches to the piles of tinder. Clotilde blocked out the pain of the ropes biting into her. All she could move were her eyes, as they sought those of the others.

Clotilde recognized many of the sick and wounded, their expression composed as they were secured by restraints. Many looked heavenward as the flames grew, some casting assuring glances of love to those nearby. Among those, she made out Corba de Pereille, bound alongside Fabrisse, Esclarmonde and Bishop Marty. Too soon the smoke began to rise, filtering out visibility.

Frenzy grew with the shouts of the executioners as they set fire to the palisade, throwing pitch feverishly about so as to quickly spread the flames. Clotilde blinked as a spring breeze stirred the smoke from her eyes and she caught sight of Bishop Marty. His lips moved in prayer. Blanche, bound alongside her, was the last person Clotilde could see. Blanche's lips remained unmoved, her stare as blank as one from whom life has long since departed.

Clotilde closed her eyes at the horrible pain of flames searing her eyelashes. She began her own chant. "Jean, Jean, Jean—return to me." The roaring flames turned the Bonshommes into hundreds of human torches of blackened, bleeding flesh—and extinguished her words. Clotilde's last sensation was one of icy coldness, its mercy erasing the pain of the fire as she felt her soul ascend to God.

TWENTY-FOUR

Montsegur, France-Present

"Three kilometers to Rennes le-Chateau, the sign says." I looked over at Eric, uncertain as to whether he noticed the sign or heard my comment. "It looks as though we'll have to resist Rennes, for this trip at least." I waited.

"Right." He looked at me as though startled to find me there. "Sorry, I can't stop thinking about Montsegur. Rennes' magnetism can't compete." Eric pressed down on the accelerator in emphasis. "And anyway—its mystery isn't ours."

"Are you sure?"

He stared fixedly ahead. "Not entirely. It does lie on a route the Cathar treasure may have taken, and the Priest, Sauniere, did create riches out of nowhere." He pursed his lips in reflection. "Even so, I agree with Veronique. Visigoth or Templar gold is more likely to have been the source of his treasure."

"Fortunately his treasure looks to have been more tangible than ours," I said.

"Right. Even if and when we discover four manuscripts, they won't gleam as they fall into our hands." Eric frowned. "What they will mean is exactly what has kept me locked in a labyrinth of thought." He glanced over at me. "Sauniere may have known. The book quoted him as having knowledge of documents so important as to change the world.

"That's the phrase the inquisitors used. So maybe one of the manuscripts was discovered and hidden by Sauniere."

279

"Might *have* been, more likely." Eric reached over to tilt my down-turned face upwards. "But no longer, my love. All signs point to our being led to each manuscript." He turned back to his driving.

"I agree. There is a powerful energy as we near Montsegur."

"Trust our guidance," Eric replied as we paralleled the Aude River, heading for Montsegur, fifty-two kilometers away. We slipped back into the hypnosis of auto travel until we passed a sign that indicated Usson Castle a few kilometers ahead.

I looked over at Eric. "We should stop. It's the last place the four Cathars, who escaped with treasure, were seen." His hesitation had me add, "Just a peek."

"Usson Castle it is." Eric smiled. "That's it, up ahead." He shook his head. "It's impressive now. I can imagine how imposing it would have been in those days." As we pulled into its parking area, I grabbed our guidebook and got out.

"It says here that it dates before 1035 and was originally called 'Le Son' Castle... The Light." I stared up at the castle as I read on. "Arnaud d'Usson," the lord of the castle, opened his doors to the Parfaits in 1242 and 1243. He even sent reinforcements from the castle to help Montsegur in its last days. The four Cathars who escaped Montsegur were known to have gone to Usson."

The remains of its five-sided keep suggested its power, as did its surrounding walls, I thought, as I stashed the guidebook and grabbed my camera. I added a 28 X 80 zoom lens and a couple of filters to highlight the vivid green of the dense shrubbery enshrouding the castle. As promised, I worked fast, shooting nearly two rolls of film before I finished in the far corner of the keep. As I stored my camera gear, Eric motioned wildly, pointing up at the curve in the lower walls. "That is where we entered."

"What do you mean, you came in up there?" I asked before he turned and headed for the car. Mute, he walked over to the car, ignition keys in hand, staring at the lower walls for a long stretch of silence before he said, "Let's go."

I kept silent until we were well under way. "Ready to talk?"

"For one brief second, I *knew* that place." He looked over at me. "*Really* knew it. But, as quickly as it came, it was gone."

"The castle seemed to resonate with the energy of those last days. I felt it too," I said as we passed a sign saying, "Montaillou Castle." My heart beat like a Geiger counter, giving off more urgent ticks the closer we came to Montsegur.

"Montaillou." Eric rolled the name around on his tongue. "That's the title of one of the books we bought at the English Bookstore in Montolieu." Eric smiled as he struggled with the correct pronunciation of the similar names. "I flipped through it last night, along with the other books." He fell silent as a cascading outpour of water, gushing from a hillside cave, drew his attention. "The 'Gorges de Lafrau.'"

"Gorge de Lafrau." I glanced at the guidebook, deciding we wouldn't get out. As I read I reached over and grabbed Eric's hand. "Oh my God, Eric. Listen to this."

Eric tore his gaze away from the rushing water, slowing the car nearly to a stop. "Out with it."

"The 'Gorges of Fear' is the English translation. It was a place of vital importance in Cathar history, known as the 'sacred way.' The Cathars who left Montsegur with the treasure traveled along these gorges." A chill came over me, not the cooling chill of the water's mist, but one that prompted me to say, "Seems we are retracing their path, only in reverse."

"I feel the whole area, so strongly at times, especially at Usson. Just now I had another flash when I turned and looked into the mouth of the cave. I saw four of us going down the gorges, sleeping in caves, following the water until we reached Usson." He hesitated. "Our journey would take us next to Coustaussa on our way to Queribus Castle. But then..." He shook his head. "Then it vanishes as though someone has thrown a black cloak over it."

"I think we should drive by Montaillou," I said. "Maybe each spot on our route will jog your memory more." He stared back at the rushing waters.

Finally he looked up. "Agreed—a drive by anyway." Within seconds of arriving at Montaillou, Eric waved the guidebook away as he gave a running commentary. "Montaillou was made famous by Emmanuel LeRoy Ladurie. His book, by the same name, was published in 1975 and became a big success. It drew from the records of the Inquisitor, Jacques Fournier, in reviving that Cathar village."

"Not much remains," I said, looking up ahead. "Seems only the characters were brought to life, not the village."

The ruins were even more starkly minimal, I thought, as Eric slowed the car. Tears began to flow as I gazed at the rubble. Little remained of a village and only one corner and the remains of a wall were left of the castle.

"I feel sad for them, even without having read the book."

"I know." Eric replied. "The book and these ruins hold a powerful message that walls are destructible but humanity endures."

"So strongly that I can almost see them." I looked around, glimpsing golden gorse waving in the wind, a bright blue sky silhouetting the stark remains. "They point straight up... as if..." I fell silent.

Eric followed my stare. "As if in defiance. Their constancy is a rebuttal to any who would attempt to destroy the soul of a people."

I jumped as a car behind us honked its horn. Eric motioned the car to go around us, then put the car in high gear and we moved away. He gave a sigh as he glanced in the rear view mirror. "If Montsegur is anything like this, we'll have a hard time keeping it light."

I looked at my watch. "It's only a little past four, still time enough to hike up the pog before dinner if you speed it up a bit."

"The pog, you say?" Eric gave me a quizzical grin as we drove away.

"Montsegur's mount. It's tall and conical, soaring straight up into the air several hundred feet, separated from any mountain range. A castle, a fortress or a temple—whatever it was, it was designed to reach for the heavens."

Eric nodded and fell silent, intent at navigating the winding roads at a higher speed. Such focus lulled us back into silence until we reached the little village of Montsegur. Nestled in a valley at the foot of the phantasmagoric sentinel of Montsegur Castle, its houses radiated a warm rose pink as the sun began to lower.

I felt my throat clench shut as Eric parked in an area designated "Montsegur Museum-Parking." We sat for a moment, our eyes fixed on the castle's sacrosanct profile etched by the sunset. Eric broke the silence. "How do you feel?"

"Very strange." I responded. "Like magnets turned one way, strongly repelled one moment, and turned the other way, strongly attracted the next."

He took my hand. "I understand. As for me, I'm feeling overcome by shame and riddled with guilt at having failed. Overlaying that is anger that borders on rage." His clenched mouth relaxed as he stared up at the castle.

"Exactly! I feel anger too. But mine seems to be mixed with sorrow and overlaid with shock at being betrayed. And, beyond all that, an acute anxiety to get someplace, find someone and stop something." I broke away, consumed with a restless urgency that propelled me out the door. I hadn't noticed how far I'd gone until Eric ran up to me and took my hand. I gave a nervous laugh. "Sorry, Eric. It's sounds crazy, I know, but I feel compelled to run up the mountain to the castle."

Eric took my hand. "Try to restrain yourself. A man is walking toward us." I turned to meet the quizzical look on the man's face.

"Eric Taylor and Dana Palmer?" His English was excellent but lightly accented with what I now recognized as Occitan. It added a certain lyrical counterpoint to his broad, bull shaped solidity.

Eric smiled and extended his hand. "And you must be Giraud Aicart."

"I am." He turned to me. "Welcome to Montsegur. Monsieur Lahille said you are writing about our temple." He stared at Montsegur, shielding the sun's rays.

Eric followed his look. "Yes, our series covers who the Cathars were, what they taught and why the Pope so zealously destroyed them."

"Fear, undoubtedly. I was in World War Two, but not even the inhumanity of the Gestapo could match the Inquisition. For hundreds of years they kept the Inquisition going, exterminating not just every Cathar but anyone labeled as 'heretic.'" He spat on the ground, seeming to clear himself for more practical concerns. "You can leave your car parked here if you like," he said as he began walking toward the museum. "Come see the museum. It has many archaeological exhibits from Montsegur."

"Courtesy of Benjamin Carter, no doubt." Eric's irony sparked an explosion.

"Benjamin Carter, be damned!" Monsieur Aicart turned, his features reddening as he escorted us through the entrance. "Excuse me, Mademoiselle, but that man is an imposter if I've ever seen one. And I've seen them all—new-agers, the German esoteric group camped near Rennes, witches, covens and such. But none as reprehensible as Professor Carter." He pointed to the exhibits. "Have a look around. Excuse my directness, but I was told you are not fans of Monsieur Carter."

Eric laughed. "True. But I trust your informant stressed that it behooves us to disguise that fact for now."

"I understand." Monsieur Aicart replied as he turned to me. "May I get you some tea or coffee?"

"Whatever would best fuel us to climb the mountain." I gazed out at the lengthening shadows. "If we have time to make it."

Monsieur Aicart glanced at his watch. "Yes and no. It officially closes at five, so you've missed any last tours. But I can give you a private one, if we get started soon. The days are getting longer and dusk will descend soon." He gestured toward the exhibits. "That gives you only a few minutes to examine what is in here." He walked away. "But do have some coffee. The caffeine helps with the altitude."

I finished a cup of coffee as we examined the relics, most similar to those in Deodat Roche's museum. But Eric and I marveled at the volume of the display. Monsieur Aicart smiled, glanced at his watch and motioned us to the door. I grabbed my camera bag and followed. As we headed up the hillside, I was aware of a silent message in the waiting stillness.

"I'll continue our talk as we climb. The real treasures are in there," Monsieur Aicart said as he pointed up at the castle. "Your bags will be safe in the car. I'll help with them when we return." He quickened his stride as he said, "Pierre will arrive by seven. Let's hurry."

Undaunted by the steep climb, he kept up a running stream of conversation, "You realize, of course, that there are few Cathar relics in any museum, no matter what Mr. Carter might claim. Since ours came from around Montsegur, any candlestick, buckle or cup is called a Cathar relic. Candlesticks they used, buckles as well, and cups, assuredly—but uniquely Cathar, no. But some interesting items belonging to the soldiers have turned up." He slowed as we approached the monument commemorating the burning of Montsegur's Cathars.

Standing about four feet high, the cross-shaped marker was surrounded by several bouquets. I touched the monument's rounded top, which encircled recessed engravings of a star and three crosses. An opened book was incised below.

"They claim the pyres were lit near here." Monsieur Aicart pointed off to the left. "It was March sixteenth, 1244. For me it is still as fresh as yesterday in the air." He stared at me. "Speaking of fresh air, are you all right, Mademoiselle Palmer?"

"It was there, a bit higher up." I pointed. Feeling dizzy, I leaned against the cool surface of the monument. Looking up, I met the solemn stare of Monsieur Aicart and felt Eric's touch.

"I'm not sure you are up for this." Eric looked worried.

"I'm sure," I said as I turned to Monsieur Aicart. "I'm sorry, sir. This story must be getting to me." My attempt at lightness fell flat.

"*Your* story is getting to you, Mademoiselle." His piercing look added emphasis. "You must, however, follow it through to the end." He moved and we followed—the incline increasingly steeper. "Let me know when you need to rest." He accepted our nods and quickened the pace.

Those were the last words exchanged until we reached the mid-point, a level area where a small building for tickets, books and restrooms, stood. Monsieur Aicart unlocked the chained access and we pressed on. We paused briefly to catch our breath at the twelve hundred-meter mark. I kept my attention on the path, filled with an urge to get somewhere and do something—with energy and purpose not my own.

Eric appeared beside me. "You're moving like someone possessed." I blinked at him through the sweat pouring down my face and continued forward.

I turned away from the castle as it came closer into view. "I can't bear it. I feel a suffocating pain."

"Try to focus only on the here and now. It works for me." He took a deep breath and looked around. "Let the present lay the ghosts of the past."

I let my gaze take in the hillsides. That helped, as did the awareness that Monsieur Aicart was studying my every move. We reached the castle entrance and headed over to the keep in the north corner. As we neared, I ran to seek the circular staircase that led to an overlook facing west.

"You can't go up there." Monsieur Aicart had followed and halted my attempt to climb. "It is unsafe."

"But I have to see someone." I coughed. "I mean something."

"Come with me." Monsieur Aicart said as he restrained me. "I'll take you to a safer place. There you can see where the ropes were put down and the four escaped." My eagerness grew as we reached a section where I could peer over. And watch for…"

After what seemed an interminable time, I heard him say. "This place is powerful with memories, Mademoiselle." Monsieur Aicart carefully drew me away. "And peace. Try to feel that. If anyplace conveys forgiveness, Montsegur does."

Eric hadn't followed us, but instead had headed for the far end of the courtyard, near the buildings that had lined the lower section. "The defensive wall still holds its own, in spite of all the blasts it took." He said as we neared. His smile turned to puzzlement as he took my hand. "You're sweaty."

"She tried to climb up to an small opening high in the keep." Monsieur Aicart explained as I shed my sweater and used it to wipe my brow.

"Where did you get that?" Monsieur Aicart asked, staring.

I silently cursed myself for my thoughtless wearing of my medallion but felt grateful that Giraud had noticed it and not Benjamin. I unclasped it and shoved it in the pocket of my jeans.

"Please—may I see it?" He asked, staring at me. I held it out tentatively.

"Dear child, you shall be meeting with Professor Carter tomorrow." Monsieur Aicart looked alarmed. "Do not question what I am about to say. But you must not show him this!" His eyes flashed as he looked up. "How did you come by it?"

Flustered, I aimed, if not for nonchalance, at least for directness. "I inherited it from my great-grandmother."

"My dear, we must speak of this." He stared into the deepening dusk, the sun gone behind the mountain range. "But for now we must head back. We don't want to leave Pierre waiting. We shall talk later."

Leaving the castle was as fraught with anguish as going up. Emotional anguish, not physical, I thought, as we neared the mountain's base.

Monsieur Aicart was well ahead of us, moving swiftly over a path he'd obviously traversed many times. I finished the journey drained of energy and emotion. Eric remained silent, scarcely lessening his pace until we had reached the bottom, when he said, "I think that's Pierre's car in the parking lot."

It was indeed. Pierre stood alongside it, a look of concern as he neared and asked, "How did it go?" I hesitated as a knowing smile spread over his features with one look at Eric. "You remembered."

"Did, have, and will even more, my friend." Eric's response widened Pierre's grin as he turned to Monsieur Aicart. "Giraud, my friend, we may need to call on you for more than your guide skills." He pointed toward the little lane leading to the *gite*. "Let's discuss it over an aperitif."

"*Certainement!*" Monsieur Aicart said. He seemed less like a museum- innkeeper with every passing moment, I thought, as we reached the entry to his home. It was surrounded with relics, flowers and fountains—and a cat, curled atop a little café table on the patio. As I reached down to pet its soft orange fur, one yellow eye opened sleepily. Monsieur Aicart guided us along a side walkway, through the garden area and over to a separate building with two doorways, side by side. "Your home for as long as required," he said, looking from Pierre to Eric. "Take a moment to catch your breath and join me in the dining room in thirty minutes."

"Thank you, Monsieur Aicart..." I hesitated.

"You are most welcome, Mademoiselle. But please call me Giraud." His graciousness prompted me to ask whether I could receive email.

"Certainly. Your room has all the modern conveniences."

As he departed, Pierre, Eric and I hurried inside. The minute the door closed, Eric took me in his arms, nuzzled my cheek, and whispered, "Thanks be to Pierre for having booked us one room."

"Yes, but..." I sighed as reluctantly we broke away, knowing that, if not, we wouldn't make dinner, let alone an aperitif.

Eric unloaded our bags from the car, looking serious as he returned. "Our conversation tonight is sure to be loaded, given Giraud's reaction when he spotted your necklace."

I rushed to explain. "I'm sorry. I can't explain why, when I've been so careful to conceal it, I wore it today."

He attempted to lessen my fears. "It's as much my fault as yours. I should have spotted it. But it can't be remedied. For now, we need to..." He stared across the room, his focus caught by something. "There's your outlet for email, and a printer alongside. Go to it and trust the necklace incident will prove harmless."

I set up my computer while Eric checked out the room. As the 'You've got mail' icon appeared, I let out a squeal at a long message from my brother. "Eric, come have a look!"

Eric read silently. When he finished, he grabbed me. "My God, what conversational dynamite this will be! Let's print it out."

We entered the dining area, the copy in my hands. Pierre motioned for us to join him in the study. "Giraud is preparing our drinks," he said, his look puzzled as he stared at me. "We've much to discuss. It seems you..." His eyes fixed on my neck. "...displayed your talisman."

I touched my bare throat. "I'm sorry, Pierre. It is well hidden now." I tried to cover my discomfort by handing him the copy of my brother's email. "Here. Read this. Perhaps it wasn't my foolishness, but divine guidance."

Pierre began to read, murmuring as he reread parts. He continued to stare at it, shaking his head. "There truly are 'stranger things 'neath heaven and earth'—and all coalescing in this time and place."

Our conversation halted, heads raised as Giraud appeared with a tray of drinks and placed them on a table in front of the fireplace. "Ah good, the fire is catching. Madame Aicart is seeing to our dinner. She begs you to excuse her absence. She neither speaks nor understands any English," Giraud explained, handing drinks all around. Except for Pierre, whose attention remained on the email. "It seems you have received something of greater interest than this aperitif."

"Better pour yourself a big one, my friend." Pierre said, waiting until we could all raise our glasses in a toast. "To our 'something of great interest,'" he said, as he touched each glass in turn, took a long swallow, and cleared his throat.

"Indulge me, Giraud. I cannot simply quote from the email. It requires a bit of a lead-in, my friend." Pierre took his hand. "My very dear friend—now, as then." Releasing it, Pierre smiled and looked up. "It seems our little family has truly reconvened." As Pierre studied each of us in turn, Giraud's attention went to my naked throat, prompting Pierre to say, "Dana's necklace must have been a shock."

"Very, I..." Giraud shook his head in bafflement.

Pierre walked to the fireplace and, hands still clutching the email, turned to his host. His voice held reassurance. "I know, dear friend. You have a similar medallion—or, should I say, should have had it—correct?"

The anguish on Giraud's face deepened. "Yes. But it was lost long ago."

"What is lost is found," Pierre said as he held out the email and began to read. "Dear Dana, About time you showed some interest in the family. As its oldest representative, I'll try to put you in the picture. Yes, I did inherit something. It is a talisman that shows musicians playing strange instruments. It came with a letter from our great, great, great, great, etc., ancestor. The yellowing parchment confirms we came, not only from lords and ladies, but also from thieves. Our ancestor apologized, saying she had hoped to pass down a much more valuable treasure—a manuscript." He paused. "The letter went on to explain that, when it was discovered that she had taken a necklace belonging to the Aicart side of our family, she had to flee to Canada. She took the necklace, ultimately bequeathing me a mysterious talisman and you the stolen necklace. As to the manuscript, I can't say where it ended up. Hope this answers your questions. If you need further clarification, I have attached a genealogy that our great-aunt prepared. She has traced our family as far back as 1240." Pierre finished reading, muttering a few phrases in Occitan as he stared at Giraud, whose rapt attention remained on me. Pierre took Giraud's hand. "It would seem that you two are cousins, generations removed."

Giraud looked dazed as he grabbed the email. Glasses hastily perched on his nose he began to read. As his fingers moved down the genealogy, his look of amazement deepened. I heard him murmur the name "Aicart" as he paged down the fifteenth century and on to the thirteenth. Reaching the end, tears glistened as he turned to me. "Dear *cousine.*" He enveloped me in a firm embrace.

"I have family here at Montsegur," I said, tears threatening, as I looked from Giraud to Pierre. "And my missing manuscript..."

"It is here, reunited, as am I, with its missing part," Giraud replied as he walked over to the fireplace. He knelt down in front of the large box that held firewood, shoved it aside, removed a loose flagstone in the floor, and withdrew a sealed box. Opening it, he held out the third manuscript. "Surprised?"

Pierre answered. "No, dear friend. Relieved, but not surprised." Pierre began to examine the manuscript, excitement in his voice as he looked up. "That leaves just one remaining." Giraud shook his head as the room fell silent and Pierre accounted for the other manuscripts. He stopped to allow Giraud an expletive or two as he mentioned his suspicion that Benjamin Carter had the remaining manuscript.

Giraud's look revealed more than the strongest French curse could express. As I watched his whole body seethe with anger and rise to fury, I decided that I wouldn't want to be the one to cross him. Giraud fought to bring his emotions under control as he turned from Eric and me to address Pierre. "Ah! Benjamin Carter will arrive tomorrow bringing great danger. The manuscript is surely his focus."

"Pardon." A timid voice halted any response. The room fell silent as Giraud rushed to the woman in the doorway. Her reddened face flushed with moisture, she said, "*Diner, si'l vous plaît.*"

* * *

From the looks on the faces, I could see that no one had slept last night. Our long discussions throughout the evening had ended in concern for what lay ahead. Giraud looked nervously around the breakfast table. "You should be waiting at the base of the mountain by ten. Professor Taylor is certain to arrive on time." His voice rose as he looked at Eric. "You did not mention staying here?"

Eric shook his head. "On the contrary, he thinks we stayed at our *gite* near Durban and drove in this morning."

"Good. Then please move your car to the public parking at the base of Montsegur where they will pull in." Giraud's nervousness lessened as Pierre spoke.

"I, my friend, as a stranger to Professor Carter, should go unnoticed." As we turned to go, Pierre asked, "I expect you are clear as to your approach."

"I trust we are," Eric replied. "Our major role is to conceal our real motives."

"No!" Giraud burst in. "Your major role is to safeguard the manuscripts."

"Very true my friend," Pierre said. "Our role is equally difficult. We must remain behind while Dana and Eric join Benjamin and his lady friend. Their goal is more challenging." Suddenly the atmosphere lightened. "It calls for total attentiveness to long-winded lectures."

Giraud added, "And bowing at his cleverness in finding the Cathar's 'Holy Grail.'" His gargling prelude to a resounding spit faded as his wife arrived.

She glared, gathered the coffee and tea, and departed. Pierre turned to Eric and me. "Go now and succeed at throwing him off the track. In any event, Giraud and I shall be ready…" He looked at Giraud. "If fate decrees."

Giraud shook his head in agreement as he smiled at me. "I want time to get acquainted with my new cousin."

We returned to our room, gathered our gear and headed for the car. A hasty *au revoir* to Pierre and Giraud left us one minute to spare as we drove into Montsegur's parking lot. Eric looked solemn as we waited.

"You look like someone who's rehearsing for the lead role in Hamlet."

"You would pick Hamlet," Eric said. "They all died."

My response was deflected by a squeal of brakes. "That's Evie's car they drove up in." I frowned as I turned to Eric. He laughed.

"Your Ophelia-like look matches my Hamlet." He got out, opened my door and whispered, "Remember—lighten up."

"I'll do it in honor of our four Cathar musketeers," I whispered. My soft smile remained as Benjamin approached. Evie, out of character I thought, hung well behind as Benjamin walked up to us.

"Welcome to my world." Benjamin made a sweeping gesture that encompassed the landscape and the mountain fortress of Montsegur. I was impressed at the enthusiasm in Eric's response. Benjamin seemed pleased as well, as he turned to me with a smug smile. "I see you've brought all of your paraphernalia, ready to take history-making photos."

My eyes widened. "You mean you've..." I leaned in to him and whispered, "brought the Holy Grail here?"

He drew back, his sly expression cautioning me to be wary. "No, my dear Dana. That was yesterday's news." Benjamin turned as Evie walked up.

"Something better than the Holy Grail?" Eric asked, the awe in his voice a bit over-much I thought as he stared upwards. "Something you discovered up there?"

Benjamin turned as Evie took his arm. "Found there or not, Evie would attest to the fact that it is much too important to leave lying in place."

"Absolutely, Benjamin." Evie gave him a look I recognized as 'great sex.' "I doubt any place is secure enough for it."

"Perhaps. Although, as to security, it and its precursor, the Grail, are well-nigh impregnable." His hubris was naked as he lowered his voice. "But it can't remain there long before the Vatican gets wind of it. You two must hurry back to Toulouse if you want an explosive ending to your series."

Eric patted him on the shoulder. "That's a given, old chap. Congratulations."

"How fortunate you are to have met Benjamin," Evie said.

I murmured 'yes,' as I struggled for geniality, feeling grateful as Benjamin intervened by offering me his hand. "Come. I shall conduct a tour of Montsegur."

Benjamin's long strides soon had him well out in front with Eric close behind. I followed at a little distance, trying to outpace Evie—with no luck. She drew near and whispered, "How incredible that we should find ourselves in this place." My response to her double entendre was cut short by a shout from Eric.

"Wait, Benjamin." At Eric's cry, Benjamin halted, looking like a bull at a red flag as Eric asked, "Is there a phone up there?"

Benjamin reached in his backpack and pulled out a cell phone. "No, but my cell phone can pick up Tokyo if necessary."

Eric flashed him an appreciative look. "Great thinking, Benjamin. That just leaves water. We left so quickly that I didn't stop for it."

Benjamin pointed back down our path. "They carry it in the museum shop. We'll wait at the monument." Benjamin motioned up ahead. "But make it quick. We need to reach Montsegur ahead of the tourists." Benjamin glanced at his watch, as Eric darted off. I walked up to Benjamin, both to deflect his frustration and to forestall conversation with Evie.

"I haven't had a chance to thank you for Albi, Benjamin. Being invited to your announcement was a real coup for Eric and me."

Benjamin frowned. "It caused a bit of a brouhaha, what with the press and all. The Vatican has been clamoring for me to send it to them ever since."

"How incredible to discover what everyone has searched for— and then to follow it with the discovery of an even more valuable treasure." I looked back at Evie. "I think the best solution, in terms of guarding such treasures, would be to let the Vatican provide safekeeping within their vaults."

"Their vaults?" Benjamin's look matched his eyes, dark and angry, his fury squelching any response from Evie. "I can bloody well give the Grail more protection than the Pope. The Pope has come undone by my earlier discovery. As to my latest, I can put him off the scent if I can keep him groveling for the Grail."

His gloating worried me. Either he was rash—and I knew he wasn't—or he was so confident he held all the high cards as to be insouciant in playing his desperate game. As we neared the monument, he smirked at those gathered around to honor the dead. "A monument to those whose deaths have given me so much to live for."

I looked away at Benjamin's galling words. Evie caught my expression. "I'm feeling a bit queasy, Evie—too much espresso on an empty stomach. Did you bring any food?"

"No. You should have asked Eric to buy some." Real queasiness set in as she moved close and said, "I know how you feel, Dana—and where it is coming from. I'm sorry, but Alex wasn't right for you. I knew he had other women." It was all I could do not to respond as she added, "After all, anyone who would seduce your best friend." Benjamin walked up, his abrupt tone saving her.

"I can't imagine what is keeping Eric." He shaded his eyes and stared at a figure approaching. "That better be him."

Eric walked up, breathing heavily. "Sorry to keep you." He handed me a couple of bottles of water. "After I bought these I remembered to call our *gite* and let them know we won't be returning tonight." He smiled at Benjamin. "You've got us chomping at the bit to go to Toulouse and photograph your latest find."

"You won't appreciate it until you've seen the dig." Benjamin's act was fading, I thought, as he turned. "Let's double-step it. I've got the dig cordoned off, but I don't trust those stupid tourists." His stride evidenced his climbing skills. Eric and I managed with effort to keep up. But Evie kept falling behind, stopping to rest at every turn. I slowed my rate of climb as she began to wheeze.

She gasped, "Go ahead. As to seeing his bloody dig, I..." She stared down the hill, looking dismayed at how little a distance she'd come. "This is ridiculous. He bet me I wouldn't make it. And he's setting this pace just to collect on his bet." Drawing a labored breath, Evie said, "I'd ask you to go back down with me, but..."

I looked up, spotting Eric waving at me from a section of the hill that I knew was much more challenging. "I'm going on ahead."

"Forget it, then. I'll stop here and have a little sit-down." Blinking sweat away from her eyes, she asked me to tell Benjamin that she'd wait in the car.

Relieved, I redoubled my efforts to catch up to Eric. As I did, I noticed that Benjamin was well out in front. Eric seemed relieved at my news that Evie had opted out. "Good. I doubted you could pull the 'best buddies' act off."

We continued the climb, grateful for so few people this early. As we rounded a curve, Eric drew me under an overhanging rock. "Quick, listen closely. I called Pierre. He's going to call Veronique and see if she found Benjamin's manuscript. And if so, ask her to bring it to Arques."

"And not bring it here."

293

"For Veronique to show up here dangling two manuscripts in Benjamin's shadow would be dangerous. Taking them to Arques is chancey enough."

"She'll have put her neck on the line the minute she lays hands on his manuscript." The enormity of what we were doing suddenly sank in. "We all have."

"We have indeed. It's dangerous to think of Benjamin as being blinded by his ego. He is—but his larger purpose is to find all four manuscripts." Eric hesitated. "No, correction, his current goal is to prevent us from doing so."

"We'd better get on up there before he returns for us," I said as Eric pulled me to a stand and we set off for the last third of the climb. Having done it so recently we made good time, arriving as Benjamin peered at his watch and paced in front of the castle. He frowned as we neared, his stare searching beyond us.

"I knew Evie wouldn't make it." He sounded gleeful. "I never lose a bet."

I managed a neutral reply. "She said to tell you she would wait at the car. We'll have to fill her in on what she missed by not seeing your dig." Walking through the entry, my heart reprised its sinking feelings as I entered the castle's walls. I tried to camouflage my wild emotions with a question. "Benjamin, what is your opinion as to Montsegur having been originally designed as a temple to the sun?"

Benjamin snorted. "Nonsense! The Cathars knew nothing of sun-worshiping. They did claim to be filled with Light, but strictly the light of God's spirit bestowed during the consolomentum." He kicked at the rubble of the courtyard and hurried on, glancing over his shoulder to make sure we followed. "What a circus has been made of the Cathars," Benjamin said as we joined him. "But it is nothing compared to what will happen now that I have found their real treasure." His gloating lightness had been subsumed by something that chilled me to the core. Before we could respond he set off for the northeast corner, stopping at the lower courtyard.

As we caught up, Eric said, "By *real* treasure, I take it the Grail is one part."

"Yes and no. The Grail is separate unto itself, and guaranteed to present me an uphill battle defending its provenance." Benjamin's impatience grew. "Enough discussion. Come and I'll show you what I mean by the real treasure."

He strode away, continuing his non-stop soliloquy. "As to the Grail, the so called experts will discount it as being the Grail, let alone the Cathar treasure. Let them. They'll be laughing out of the other side of their mouth. My latest find is indisputably *the* Cathar treasure." He frowned. "That is..." He halted, his irritation escalating. "Step lively! You will understand soon."

Benjamin looked around before he led us over the wall, down a steep bank of rocks into the lower courtyard and down one more level leading to a narrow ledge below. "The *bonshommes* had a collection of huts clinging to the outside. We mined whatever we could from there—nothing of real value." He inched over the ledge, beckoning us to join him on a precarious sliver of ground that fronted a sheer drop.

Eric went first, holding his arms out to catch me. Worried that I might lose my camera bag, I was relieved to find that I had landed perfectly on the narrow strip. I was surprised to notice the mouth of a cave. It was scarcely discernable as such due to masses of rubble obscuring its entryway. Benjamin beamed as he leaned against its rock face. "The Inquisition recorded testimony from the Lord of the castle, Raymond de Pereille, who used the term *'infra castrum,'* or underground dwellings. His testimony was confirmed by others claiming that Parfaits lived beneath the castle." Benjamin knelt to peer into the cave. "I was convinced that a series of caves riddled the area and were used by the Cathars—not only as dwellings—but as links to other caves." He began to squeeze inside, motioning us to follow.

Placing my camera bag between us, I followed Eric into complete darkness. Benjamin was prepared, however. He shone his flashlight upwards, surprising us by the height of the cavern and the reverberating echoes of his voice. "I found some interesting artifacts in this section. But none so fascinating as the manuscript." Finally he has defined the treasure, I thought, followed by the awareness that he'd dropped the word too casually. Eric's look seemed to agree, I thought, catching a glimpse of it before the torchlight swung away and Benjamin moved on. "Soon we shall reach the source of my discovery." He said as he entered a connecting tunnel.

Bent over double, we moved behind him, scraping the sides and top of the narrow confines as we crouched in single file. Like a mother with a child, I safeguarded my camera gear with as much zeal as Benjamin his treasure.

"A manuscript—however could they write in this space?" I asked as we exited the narrow passageway into a larger cave. As his flashlight aimed at the ceiling, I looked for evidence of soot. "It seems an unlikely place for a scriptorium."

Benjamin snapped back, "They didn't write it here, but they did hide the Cathar treasure here. Until it was too dangerous to leave it all in one place. One was retrieved, but the others..."

Eric interrupted. "Others—you mean to say there are several treasures?" Eric waited what seemed an eternity, with only the sound of heavy breathing in the dank air. The flashlight snapped off, leaving us in total darkness. I strained to remember the direction of our passageway as I reached for Eric.

"Four manuscripts, you fool. And you *know* that I didn't retrieve all of them. More importantly, *I know* that you are aware of their location." Benjamin's anger reverberated from all directions, making it impossible to determine where he stood.

"What on earth gave you that idea?" Eric's amazement sounded genuine.

"Don't play dumb. I saw Dana's necklace. Do you think I would have spoken so lightly about manuscripts if I didn't think you'd react? The fact that you didn't, told me you were on to the others." His next words, so insidious as to filter like poison gas throughout the cavern, erased any doubt as to his capacity for evil. "Your lives depend on my knowing their locations."

Eric clasped his hand lightly across my mouth. The silence was oppressive.

"Mark my words. I locate the manuscripts and you locate your way out of here. Otherwise..." It was Benjamin's turn for silence.

It lasted long enough for me to feel a scream building. Eric spoke. "How do we know you won't let us rot in here anyway?"

"You don't." Benjamin's words rang finality in the pitch-dark void.

"So what's the deal again?" Eric sounded obliging, but my intuition told me he was trying to measure where Benjamin stood.

"You tell me where each manuscript is. I get them and I release you."

"Elementary, but implausible, old chap." Eric said, drawing an audible breath as he moderated his contempt with reason. "In either case, if you don't get us out of here, others—like Evie, for example—will be suspicious and pressure you. I doubt you want the gendarmes nosing around your digs, or interrogating Evie."

"Evie!" He laughed. "I have Evie right where I want her. She'll make the perfect witness." His voice moved into an eerily mean mimicry of Evie's. "Oh dear, my friends wandered off to take photos and never returned. They must have got caught in a landslide, or…" Benjamin gave a contemptuous snigger. "Count on it. Your disappearance will make the news for one issue of the local paper. The gendarmes will attribute it to amateur adventurers taking one risk too many."

Eric held one hand across my mouth as he responded. "From the sound of it, we don't have any real options. So, no deal."

"You may feel differently tomorrow—or the day after—or the day after that." Benjamin's words faded, broken only by a slight rustling noise impossible to pinpoint as it evaporated into the darkness. I froze, listening intently for any clue to Benjamin's movements. Our own breathing was the only sound.

"Benjamin." Eric's call met with total silence. Benjamin had vanished, with scarcely a sound, let alone light. We were alone, deep within a labyrinth of caverns impossible to retrace our way out. Certainly not in complete darkness.

Eric began to pat the wall alongside us. "Dana, stay close beside me and move slowly. We'll try to follow the wall of the cave, moving in a circle until we come upon an opening." He didn't voice a thought that must have come to both our minds, that even if we found an entrance it might lead us deeper into the abyss.

"In case we become separated, I have some extra water. I want you to take it." Eric released his tight grip on my hand. Before I could panic, he rustled in his carrying case and placed two plastic bottles in my hand. "Put them in your camera bag." His said, his hands feeling for it.

"My camera—It has a flash!" And not just any run of the mill flash, I thought as I stopped to slide my camera bag off my shoulder and open it. My fingers, shaking but trained, went directly to the pocket that held the brightest, most expensive and reliable flash on the market. I slid it out as deftly as a magician.

"Wait before you shoot," Eric cautioned. "I think I've kept my back to where we entered, so here's the plan. We'll turn slowly one half-circle. I'll count to three. You shoot. During the flash we'll try to pinpoint any passageway." I felt him touch my arm. "How many flashes will this thing take?"

"I can't be certain. It has a powerful battery, but I've used it regularly," I said, making certain that I'd locked the flash solidly in place. "Our real problem will be moving blindly through the rocky terrain and narrow passages without dropping it. "I swallowed hard as a bigger fear came into my mind. "Or during moments of blindness from the flash. One trip and…"

"The camera are I are in your hands," Eric said, his voice lending confidence. Touching me as gingerly as though I held a landmine, he slowly turned me in the direction I prayed would point us to our exit. "Remember, try to see all around in the brief second of flash." Eric drew a loud breath and began his count. At the count of "three" I pressed the flash button. Its bright light illumined a brief glimpse of a beautiful, if ragged and small, opening. Stepping out into the stygian dark, we moved forward. My outstretched hand hit a wall, my fingers moving gingerly until they felt the edges of the opening. "We did it!"

Eric let out a sign of relief as we tentatively entered. I went in first, holding my camera and flash protectively. After a few crouching steps, head brushing the rough ceiling, we were compelled to resort to hands and knees. I inched along on my elbows, head down, my hands gripping the camera with its critical flash.

"If I remember right, this tunnel wasn't very long." Eric's words penetrated my growing claustrophobia. I tried to stifle a growing doubt about its being the right tunnel. "If memory serves, we should come to a little drop leading into a small cave that will connect us to a larger one," he added. "Go slow."

I slowed my crawl until I felt my elbows come to an edge. "It feels like a drop," I said, hesitating as I tried to sense a fresh current of air. "I'm going to hold onto my camera with one hand as I use the other one to measure the drop." As carefully as a surgeon, I reached down about four inches to what felt like solid rock flooring. "Yes, about four inches drop. Easy does it," I said, moving like an infant at the top of a slide as I slipped over. "I'm going though. Okay, I'm over. I'm going to stand." In slow motion, I inched upwards. "I did it—I'm standing!"

"Wait until I'm beside you," he said, his words followed by a scuffling sound as he entered the space. I knew he was standing when he touched me and said, "Let's try to remember our way in. As I recall, this part of the cave didn't have its entrances directly opposite." Eric removed his hand from me. "I turned full circle and I think I felt a slight draft from over here." He took my hand and held it up. "What do you think—shall we gamble on this direction?" Uncertain, I replied, "I guess, but before we use the flash, let's go over it. We went through three different tunnels, I think." I hesitated. "It's the confined places that I remember.

There were three up to the last narrow entrance that leads into the big cave."

Eric released a loud sigh. "Good! So, that would leave two more to go. Let's stand side by side. When you're ready, let me know and I'll count."

I positioned my camera and flash in the direction we now faced. "Ready." He counted to three and I shot. A brilliant burst of light propelled us toward the dark shadow of what looked like an opening. Eric's "Damn" and a crashing sound told me we'd overshot. I stopped as he said, "I think we're off a little to the right." We inched along the rock wall, my free hand gripping my camera in a red-knuckle choke.

"I've found it!" He said. He waited until I was near enough for our breaths to touch before he took my empty hand and swept it across an opening. "I'll go first this time. We can't risk having you drop the camera." He ducked inside and I followed. "Watch your head. This tunnel seems high enough to allow for a crouch instead of a crawl—but take it slow."

After a few moments of cautious creeping, Eric warned me he was halting. "We should be coming out soon. If I'm right, we will be back at the cave that connects to the original entrance chamber." Eric made a rustling noise. "I'm going to try to stand." A soft expletive and a shower of pebbles gave me the results. "Not yet. But it can't be much further." We resumed our claustrophobic creeping. Only seconds before panic ambushed me, Eric stopped. "I'm going to try standing up again. If I remember right, there shouldn't be any drop off at the end." His try was followed by, "Yes! We've made it. If you inch forward a couple more feet, you should be able to stand."

I moved the requisite paces, stood erect and, using my free hand, reached for Eric. He clasped it, saying, "Very good. Now to remember what direction we headed to reach this section."

"I think left, but I'm so turned around, I..."

Eric hesitated. "I think so too. Let's turn to our left and trust we end up facing the opening. With any luck when we exit we will return to the original cave. Maybe even see a glimmer of natural light." We moved in our prayed for right direction. Releasing an in-drawn breath, Eric said, "Countdown time."

After a nervous "one, two, three" and a flash of piercing light, we made a straight but cautious sprint, trying to memorize the distance to the enticing passage to our larger tunnel. A loud sound—and silence—accompanied Eric's shout, "Careful!" Too late. I tripped, my camera flying out of my outstretched hand as I landed on top of him.

"Are you all right?" I asked, panicked at his silence. I felt for his hand, anxiety growing until I felt a feeble pulse. Moving up to his head, I shuddered as warm, sticky moisture coated my hand. "No! Eric, don't die. You must wake up!"

TWENTY-FIVE

Montsegur, France-Present

The words reverberated back to me, shocking me at their power. I refuse to go quietly to my death, I thought—and I'm definitely not letting Eric go to his. My mind raced beyond our horrible situation as it began to examine alternatives.

First I'll try to find my camera, I thought, praying the flash still worked. God willing, it lives up to its claim to withstand shock. I began to move my hands in a circle. As I reached out in larger circles, I carefully memorized exactly how far I had moved from Eric. Frantic after long moments of touching nothing but rock, I let out a muffled expletive to counter the waves of despair that threatened. I must return to Eric, I decided. Maybe he has regained consciousness. The silence told me what to expect as I touched his body. It was still warm, the pulse still faint. Fear filtered through the blackness. "None of that. Right, Eric." I spoke aloud, taking comfort as my firmness echoed. "We've made it this far. We're almost there. I'll think this through."

I knelt beside him, trying to determine if there had been any fresh flow of blood. I closed my eyes and prayed that when I opened them, he would be speaking, urging us to press on. Forcing a calm my heart didn't feel, I opened my eyes to a dark made deeper by the bleakness of his stillness and the scantiness of my options.

I returned to those options: I could try to move him in what might be the right direction to the opening. I discarded such an action due to the slim odds of making it and the strong likelihood of injuring him even further. Or, I could leave him, take carefully measured steps in one direction and hope to reach the tunnel entry. But what then, I thought. To continue on seemed fruitless without the light of the flash. I closed my eyes and began a wordless prayer for divine inspiration.

* * *

I must have slept, I thought, returning from a place much deeper than any I had ever experienced in meditation. I wondered how long I had been out as I took Eric's wrist and felt for his pulse. "Eric, dear Eric. I love you so. Please don't leave me." I repeated each phrase as a mantra that could hold him to life. How long I repeated it I could only gauge by the hoarseness of my throat as my lips moved in sync with my strokes of his forehead.

"Dana?" An even hoarser voice sounded, but much more feeble. Eric's voice wavered and stopped. I was consumed with gratitude as he tried to sit up.

"Eric, I think maybe you shouldn't try to move," I said as I felt his hand touch mine, his voice filled more with bafflement than pain.

"Everything feels in one piece," he said as he tried to stand and slumped back down. "A bit dizzy." He said, his voice strangely different, not the strangeness of pain, but somehow a familiar difference. "When I was unconscious, I seemed to have gone to another time—a time when I was moving through these very caves. I knew them well, having practiced their routes in the dark." He tried to rise. "We have to continue on. I know we are close to being at the entrance and I don't want to forget."

"Don't move," I said. "You rest while I feel around for the camera again." I began a tentative outreach. "It might not be…"

"Hold it, Dana. Don't move." Eric grabbed my arm. "Any change of direction, our instinct to feel around for the camera, could have us headed directly opposite the opening. I know we are very near. I say we try to resume our original direction, being careful to avoid that outcrop of rock I ran into." He took my hand. "Stay close. We can make it."

"Not without the flash—we need light." I fought to push away as desperation consumed me. Eric pulled me toward him, whispering, "Follow me this time." It was a voice I didn't recognize, and yet it stirred a semblance of memory as he spoke. "*All* need the light. Together we shall find it."

"Together," I replied, lifting my head, curious at whomever it was that took my hand. We began a slow movement to the left, hands tracing the rough wall. After what seemed an interminable passage of time, it was Eric who spoke. "We did it!" His grip tightened. "Step carefully now. If this opening is the original tunnel that leads to the entry-chamber, we shouldn't need a flash at the other end."

I followed him into a tunnel that seemed less claustrophobic. Even so, I kept my head down as I crouched forward. With each step, I murmured, "Dear God, let there be light when we exit this tunnel." Our crawl seemed interminable as fear returned with its message of enduring darkness.

"Go slow for another two feet and then try to stand upright," Eric said as his hand grasped mine. I tentatively rose to my full height and, incredibly, saw a faint, but miraculous, hint of illumination. A soft prayer of gratitude escaped until Eric covered my mouth. "Quiet. Listen."

I heard the sound of heated conversation, as we stood frozen within the shadows of the cave's entrance. "How dare you doubt me? Yes, there were two people with me. But as I told you, they wandered off to take photographs." Benjamin's indignation was nothing compared to the venom in Giraud's voice. I could picture my heroic cousin taking aim with a more potent projectile than spit. A heavy fall of rock and dirt curtained the entry to the cave.

"And I tell you that I watched the three of you climb over the ledge to your dig. You came back up and they didn't. Out of my way! I'm going down."

"Giraud, get back. It's university property. Keep away!" A heavier slide of rocks accompanied the appearance of legs dangling over the ledge. A solid thud was followed by a frantic scuffle as Benjamin fought to restrain Giraud. Eric kept his finger to his lips, moving us back into the shadows.

"I say they're in those caves—and I know why." A loud cry went up followed by, "Turn loose of me. I'm going down."

"You go and you'll never come back, old man," Benjamin said. We knew that Giraud ignored him, recognizing the legs that dangled over the drop down to the shallow edge that fronted the cave's entrance.

"Stand back. I know those caves better than you know your backside."

"How unfortunate then that you lost your footing and fell." Benjamin's retort was followed by a yell as Eric rushed to the cave's entrance. I followed, crouching just within the cave's entrance as I peered up at the overhanging cliff. I gasped at the sight of Giraud clinging to the precipice, a look of fear on his face. Benjamin was slamming his foot against Giraud's precarious handhold. I shuddered as Benjamin lifted a large boulder, poised to hurl it at Giraud's head. Such a blow would plunge Giraud into a precipitous free-fall. As Giraud stared wildly about, he shouted.

"Eric!" At Giraud's cry, Benjamin spun around, thrown off balance by the heavy weight of the rock. He struggled for balance as his body contorted and, his eyes wild with desperation, he plunged over the cliff.

* * *

"I think we all deserve the French Medal of Honor for thwarting Benjamin's diabolical scheme," Eric said as, in the comfort of Pierre's hideaway, he held his glass out. "But in lieu of that, I'll settle for another brandy. Not that the entire bottle could erase the look on Benjamin's face as he fell."

Giraud poured, his lips pursed as he added, "The gendarmes sought my help with their search for his body. I declined, of course, trusting my mountain will have made porridge of his remains."

"Here, here." Pierre joined his glass to those of Professor Marty, Veronique, Giraud's and mine. He turned back to Giraud for a second clink of his glass. "An extra award to you, my friend, for keeping your binoculars aimed on the dig."

Giraud returned the salutation and turned to Pierre. "Your reputation lent weight to my story of the professor's tragic and untimely fall. Not that the gendarmes of this area would doubt it, but..." Giraud winked as he looked at Eric and me. "I owe my life to you two. Why if you hadn't caught me..."

I took my cousin's hand. "None of us could have done it without the other." I smiled at each in turn. "Somehow our cooperation seems to have been established throughout time—and will continue into an indefinite future."

Veronique, who had been strangely silent, sounded deadly serious as she spoke. "It isn't we who are important, but the manuscripts. I was nervous enough retrieving one set. Do you really think, now that we have possession of all four, that either we or they are in any less danger?"

A hush went through the room, broken by Professor Marty's solemn words. "We are, by all means, in greater danger. Even with Benjamin out of the picture, there are others equally determined to have them. They must be kept safe until we know what they reveal."

Pierre broke in. "But how? Benjamin thought his hiding place inviolable and yet Veronique went straight to it. By the way, how *did* you figure it out?" Pierre waited as all eyes turned to Veronique.

"I knew where he had hidden his so-called Grail and thought the manuscript could be in the same place." She gave a puzzled laugh. "But without Evie's parting words, I would have come up empty-handed when I opened the vault."

Evie never could keep a secret, I thought. "What did she say?"

Veronique pursed her lips before continuing. "She and Benjamin stopped by the office early Monday to give me my To Do list for the day. Benjamin had a lot of instructions about what to say and not say to the reporters calling about the Grail. As he finished, Evie added, 'Be sure not to mention Benjamin's vault.' And then—*incroyable*—she turned to Benjamin and said, 'They might find the secret compartment.' Benjamin's look was beyond diabolical." Irony coated her next words. "She must have pledged to fund his next dig. He said nothing. I maintained my oblivious assistant act until they were well under way, when I proceeded to remove the Grail and search for the secret compartment." Her shy satisfaction bloomed as everyone cheered. "Here, Here!"

My stomach did a flip-flop. "Oh my God, with Benjamin dead, maybe Evie will head straight for the vault."

"Quite possibly. But, knowing that Benjamin would check the vault the instant he returned, I inserted another ancient manuscript and a chalice, sixteenth century—it was all I could find at the time. It wouldn't fool Benjamin but it will fool Evie. One thing is certain, knowing how Benjamin's mind works, I'm certain he used their drive up to Montsegur to convince her it is only valuable in the academic sense."

Eric grinned. "Brilliant—I can see it now—Evie revealing a fake manuscript, what a hoot!" He turned to me. "She didn't seem grief stricken at Benjamin's accident. The second the *gendarmes* got her story, she hightailed it out of there."

Pierre looked over at Professor Marty. "It remains to be seen what Evie does. Regardless of any action on her part or of Benjamin's heirs, we must pray that the Vatican's Mafia will be thrown off the trail for awhile." He gave a deep sigh as he patted the Professor on the shoulder. "Seems you and I, dear friend, with our Occitan language skills, will center-post the translations." His look moved from Veronique to Giraud and stopped at Eric and me. "But, as challenging as that shall be, it is only the beginning. From what I can decipher in the short time I examined the manuscripts, their message is imbedded in more than the script. Without a doubt, it will require a lengthy scrutiny to properly decipher them."

The room fell silent until I spoke. "However long and difficult the challenges, it is an ancient contract that each one of us must fulfill. Whatever measures we must take, until their message is revealed, safeguarding each manuscript is vital."

Pierre stared grimly at Eric and me as he replied. "Very true." He looked around the room. "We are so elated by our success that it has blinded us to the fact that *They* will be even more relentless when they suspect someone has located all four manuscripts." He shuddered, voicing that which had hung in the room the entire time. "Having all four manuscripts come together can only make their job easier—and our lives worthless."

Eric spoke solemnly. "Right you are. Their response will make the Inquisition look like a walk in the park. We can't make it that easy for them."

"We could begin by using our series to deflate any belief in Benjamin, or anyone, having found such a treasure." I took a deep breath and waited.

"Misdirection is an excellent interim strategy, dear Dana." Professor Marty took my hand as he spoke. "But we must never discount the skill of our enemies. Whatever strategies we may adopt must assure the safety of the four manuscripts." He gave my hand a squeeze. "Agreed?"

"Yes," I said as I looked at the others. "For now we must arrive at actions to counter the risk of bringing the manuscripts together to decode them." I must have sounded dismayed.

"Right you are, Dana. That challenge seems insurmountable, but the fact that we have all come together and reached the success we have should give us confidence that we are meant to prevail." Pierre took my hand. "As to a safe rendezvous spot, I'll take that one on. I know of cave systems more extensive and unexplored than the Lombrive caverns." He looked around. "Agreed?" After everyone's resounding 'yes' faded, Pierre gripped my hands and asked, "How do you see your role?"

"Nothing less than to begin to prime the world for a new direction." I took a deep breath as each smiled and waited. "I think Eric and I, as part of our skills, should incorporate within our series something that helps trigger a remembrance of the opportunity for transformation available to each one of us. Our Soul's internal treasure." I looked at Eric.

Eric gave me a quick kiss. "So right, my love. I'd write it in such a way that, not only would it dismiss any tangible treasure but would place emphasis on the Cathar's ancient wisdom teachings of Love and Compassion. If I'm successful, it should help prepare many for the revelation of the full secret." Eric looked around the room as he asked, "I'd like to know your thinking."

"It's time." Professor Marty responded. "Surely we are all here to unfold the same purpose—to remember Love."

The room was so filled with the hubbub of enthusiasm that Pierre had to speak louder as he repeated, "Silence. Someone is knocking at the door. Wait while I go attend to it."

Anxiety stirred during the long span of time it took Pierre to return. When Pierre walked into the room, his face ashen and his steps unsteady, his words underscored the enormity of our mission. "That was the Arques police superintendent. The Montsegur search failed to locate Benjamin's body. They are tracing an unlicensed vehicle that the searchers reported as having sped away from the search area." He paused before adding. "The fellow said he couldn't believe they would waste their time chasing a limousine from the Vatican."

ABOUT THE AUTHOR

Nita Hughes was for many years a vice president for Security Pacific Bank/Bank of America. As a global executive in the international private banking division, she served as a financial advisor for high net worth clients in Asia, South America and Europe. She draws on diverse passions, including her love for the south of France, yoga, singing and traveling. Her writing includes contributions to books on autism, corporate training and marketing text. She lives on Maui with her husband, Douglas.

Made in the USA
Lexington, KY
02 December 2009